The Korean Economy

SUNY Series in Korean Studies
Sung Bae Park, editor

The Korean Economy

Perspectives for the Twenty-First Century

Hyung-Koo Lee

State University of New York Press

Published by
State University of New York Press, Albany

For information, address State University of New York Press,
State University Plaza, Albany, NY 12246

Production by Dana Foote
Marketing by Theresa Abad Swierzowski

Library of Congress Cataloging-in-Publication Data

Yi, Hyŏng-gu, 1940–
　　The Korean economy : perspectives for the twenty-first century /
Hyung-Koo Lee.
　　　　p.　cm. — (SUNY series in Korean studies)
　　Includes bibliographical references and index.
　　ISBN 0–7914–2887–7 (alk. paper). — ISBN 0–7914–2888–5 (pbk. :
　　alk. paper)
　　　　1. Korea (South)—Economic conditions.　2. Korea (South)—Economic
policy.　I. Title.　II. Series.
HC467.Y51395　1996
330.95195—dc20　　　　　　　　　　　　　　　　　　　　　95-39691
　　　　　　　　　　　　　　　　　　　　　　　　　　　　　　CIP

10 9 8 7 6 5 4 3 2 1

CONTENTS

FOREWORD

by Patrick Yeoh

The Korean Economy is an ambitious and original attempt to provide a comprehensive diagnosis and a provocative prognosis of the unique path of South Korea's economic development. Hyung-Koo Lee is exceptionally qualified to address this complex and exciting subject. He has brought to bear his extensive public-service experience and strong intellect to the topic. Before his previous appointment as Minister of Labor, Lee served as governor of the Korea Development Bank, and Vice Minister at the Ministry of Construction, the Ministry of Finance, and the Economic Planning Board. As such, he has been deeply engaged in South Korea's economic miracle in recent decades.

After chronicaling South Korea's economic development process and those public policies that have shaped this process, Lee proceeds to argue for a fundamental paradigm shift in economic policy if South Korea wants to fulfill its aspirations of joining the ranks of the world's major economic powers at the turn of this century. The government, instead of playing a commanding role as in the past, will, from now on, have to withdraw from the economic frontline. Its new task will be to encourage greater private-sector initiative by dismantling hitherto protectionist policies that no longer serve the long-term interests of the South Korea economy. Lowering import barriers, deregulating foreign exchange and interest-rate regimes, opening up the service sector (including banking) to foreign competition, and removing structural impediments to the internationalization of South Korean enterprises are some of Lee's prescriptions.

The author also gives a succinct analysis of the vast economic potential of a reunified Korea, a unification that must be proceeded with carefully and gradually as it will be a tortuous process fraught with problems.

In the final chapter, Lee outlines two alternative scenarios for the South Korean economy: one opts for temporary high growth at the expense of fundamental reforms, thus allowing many unresolved structural problems to plague the economy in the long run; the other chooses, as a high priority, to address the structural problems in the economy by implementing fundamental reforms even at the risk of temporarily lower growth, thereby putting the economy on a more efficient and balanced footing for it to advance to the next stage of development. Lee's preference for the second scenario is stated in no uncertain terms.

Indeed, throughout the book, Lee blends strong convictions and insighful observations with objective analysis, articulating them not only passionately, but also cogently.

Readers of this book will find themselves enriched and indebted to Lee for his generosity in sharing his insights and vision with them.

Patrick Yeoh
President, DBS Bank, Singapore

FOREWORD

by Charles S. Sanford, Jr.

Torn apart by the Cold War and devastated by a civil war, the Korean economy was in disarray and its prospects for recovery were bleak indeed. Now, only forty years later, the world observes in wonder how this small nation has transformed itself into a potential global economic power and done so without a history of technology or plentiful natural resources.

South Korea's achievements make it a paradigm for other developing nations struggling to achieve economic viability in a global environment of increasing competition. Hyung-Koo Lee's book reviews the industrialization of Korea and analyzes in detail economic environments facing Korea today. It goes on to propose a strategy for further progress, based firmly on the nation's current porblems and opportunities.

Previously Minister of Labor in the Korean government, Lee has spent the last thrity years helping to shape the economic strategies of Korea while serving in institutions such as the Economic Planning Board, the Ministry of Finance, and the Ministry of Construction. His observations of Korea's changing domestic and international environments are firsthand, making all the more compelling his call for implementation of economic reforms and the rethinking of the roles of government.

The Korean economy is in a transition. The adjustment is from a low-wage, assembly-type production to that of an industrialized nation with technologies and software as the basis for international competitive advantage. The pains of transition are amplified by the pace at which global economic leaders are developing new technologies, as well as by competition from emerging nations pursuing the strategies Korea once employed successfully.

As globalization of economic activity continues to accelerate, the strategic focus of the Korean economy should be, as Lee describes, to anticipate and benefit from change. At the dawn of the twenty-first century, we can expect an era of prosperity for individuals, corporations, and nations that welcome change and respond to it in constructive ways. Those who resist change will have difficulty finding protective shelters and will fall behind. Lee suggests a broad economic strategy for the new century that is rich in insight and detail. He views as likely the reunification of the Korean peninsula, and his vision of the nation takes this into account.

Importantly, Lee's book is a prescription for changing the Korean government bureaucracy, which has been characterized by the hands-on management of economic development. Lee calls for the bureaucracy to allow market forces to influence specific economic activities, with the government's role being to provide a consistent and level playing ground for all potential economic agents. The government should no longer be the sole arbitrator on matters such as who gets preferred access to subsidized financing, which domestic markets are protected from international competition, and which businesses that have failed on their own merits are rescued.

Lee advocates competition among various types of financial institutions as well as internationalization of the financial markets, interest rate control, credit allocation, foreign exchange restrictions, entry barriers, and separation of roles among different types of financial institutions—all of these served Korea well in an earlier era, but continuation of such potentially market-distorting mechanisms will stifle further growth. The gradual erosion of the walls separating securities and banking businesses would be an especially productive change, not only for Korea but in many markets elsewhere, including the United States.

In addition to changing the role of the government, Lee calls for implementation of programs to strengthen the economic vitality of the nation. For example, participation by women in the labor market should increase. Investments that develop human resources, such as education, should be stepped up, as should investment to accelerate the development of new technologies. Entrepreneurial spirit should be fostered. Taxes should be levied in ways to encourage bold, new investments and in particular stimulate development of the technology sectors.

Finally, Lee recommends expedient implementation of reforms. As became clear with the adoption of laws on the use of "real" identifications for financial transactions, certain sectors of the society—those adversely affected by even the most enlightened policies—will resist changes vehemently, threathening the success of the constructive reforms. Nevertheless, moments of opportunity must be seized and policies implemented.

As the world continues to watch Korea, I expect Hyung-Koo Lee's work to provide inspiration and impetus that will help the nation advance toward the ranks of global economic leadership.

Charles S. Sanford, Jr.
Chairman, Bankers Trust Company

INTRODUCTION

Today we are being inundated by the changes taking place in the world. Each period in the history of humankind has had its own share of changes, but today's world is experiencing changes on a scale unprecedented since the dawn of civilization. These changes are not only the natural by-products of the advent of the mass information age, but also testify to the fact that we are living in a period of epic historical transition.

As the Cold War receded with the collapse of communism, it has been replaced by the emergence of a "new world order." Politically, the United States has emerged as the sole superpower. Economically, leadership has been evenly divided between the United States, Japan, and the European Union. In the past, national strength was determined largely by military prowess. However, in today's world, national strength depends on a country's level of technological development, based on its economic power. This new trend is encouraging a realignment among the nations of the world that are bent on pursuing their own national interests. The structure of multinational negotiation based on the Brettonwoods Accord is giving way to regional economic integration such as APEC and NAFTA. With these changes, the legal concept of the state is becoming meaningless, and the economic activity of nations is being oriented toward the interests of each individual, enterprise, and nation. Merchandise trade, which previously involved the site of production and the site of demand, is now increasingly taking place at the site of demand, where products are directly produced and distributed.

These global changes clearly reflect a shift in the existing order—the globalization of economic activity is rapidly taking place and the distinction between domestic and external markets is blurred. Hence, it is becoming ever more difficult to protect domestic industries or markets. The era of unlimited competition has arrived and is here to stay! Now, everyone in this country, from households and workers to the enterprises and the government, is called upon to do his or her utmost amid these global changes, united under the same goal to enhance competitiveness.

Huge changes have also been taking place on the domestic front. First, a glance at the present stage of Korea's economic development would bring home to us the magnitude of structural changes. Since the per capita GNP reached $ 7,000, there has been a noticeable shift in both the trends and structure of consumption: in parallel with rapid technological development, industries are undergoing structural adjustment. The standards of comparative advantage among industries are changing. A new social justice policy should incorporate equitable distribution of wealth, relaxation of the concentration of economic power. Fair trade should be further encouraged. Maintaining consistency between macro level and sectoral level policies is not easy any more. Nor is it easy to strike a balance between economic development and policy implementation.

We are troubled in the face of the vast gulf between our goals and the reality. We are witnessing the explosion of pent-up demand that has accompanied democratization, while at the same time disorder, self-indulgence, and irresponsibility have become rampant in our society, where "authoritarianism" is mistaken for "authority." Amid the changes of today, we develop a longing for reestablishing a social order based on a changed, bona fide social authority, replacing the artificial one imposed during the authoritarian era.

Changes are also spilling into North-South relations, enhancing the prospects for the reunification of the two Koreas. We, the Korean people, all hope for reunification, but at the same time, we cannot lose sight of its potentially huge cost. The more fervent our wishes become toward reunification, the more resolute we have to become to work hard for it. We have to realize that reunification is significant not only as a union of the Korean people, but also as a symbol marking Korea's joining the ranks among advanced countries.

This period of change demands its acceptance and adaptation. We simply cannot disregard the tide of change. If we do so, it would be like the ostrich burying its head in the sand. What price have we paid for refusing to open our doors to the outside world and ignoring the tide of change in the late nineteenth century? Like it or not, we must not be blind to this new era of change and global competition. Acceptance of change should occur with the full knowledge of going into global competition. In this era of economic war, we have to pool our wisdom to make the best of the situation. This calls for the complete overhaul of our economic policy. Structural problems that have been postponed under the guise of gradual solution have to be tackled from the perspective of reform. This has to be approached and implemented with a new way of thinking. We have no time for further procrastination.

This book is intended to explore and discuss ways to triumph in the economic war in this era of change from the strategic point of view—how are we going to tackle the structural challenges confronting us within the scope of economic policy? At this important juncture, when we have to make radical changes in existing policies to ensure the development of more mature capitalism, how are we going to approach it?

This book consists of eight chapters. Chapter 1 is devoted to presenting the changing trends currently sweeping the world along with an outlook on future changes. Chapters 2 through 4 discuss how the Korean economy has evolved from a policy perspective. Particular focus is given to a discussion of the bright and dark sides of the Korean economy. Chapters 5 through 7 examine how Korea is going to transform its society amid this deluge of change. Today, the Korean economy faces the daunting task of removing backwardness to advance the nation's economy in preparation for the twenty-first century. In that respect, Chapter 8 deals with what we will have to do to make that goal come true. The appendices are reserved for the principal economic indicators of Korea over the past forty years.

I feel that writing this book has been an enormous burden for me, considering my lack of learning and time. However, I dared to write this book because I felt that not enough effort was being made to cope with the tide of change sweeping the world today, and therefore, I humbly offer my suggestions on the best way to prepare ourselves for the century ahead.

Changing Society

The twenty-first century will be marked by sweeping changes affecting every aspect of our lives "political, economical, and sociological." The changes will be more radical and abrupt than those we are currently experiencing, and to adapt to them, it is important that we discard the fixed notions we have carried thus far. In another words, a flexibility of thinking is necessary for access to change. I recall a few years ago hearing that the Boston Symphony Orchestra played jazz music for the first time ever in the history of classical music. This would be comparable to the KBS (Korea Broadcasting System) Symphony Orchestra playing popular tunes or a famous opera singer singing popular songs. Trivial as this incident may look, it is an example of sweeping changes without delay.

CHANGING VALUES AND THE EMERGENCE OF A NEW ETHICS

To ensure sustained development of the Korean economy into the twenty-first century, we have to examine how the changes in the values and ethics of our people will affect our society at large. In general, the development of society means qualitative changes to better the social structure, and economic development that acts as a catalyst for such changes. Although economic development, the driving force behind the development of society, is admittedly driven by material factors such as natural resources and capital, it is driven to an even larger extent by the mental factor, that is, "entrepreneurship."

The importance of an enterprising spirit in economic development has long been emphasized by scholars. Max Weber pointed out in his famous work, *Protestantism and Capitalism*, that Western capitalist civilization bloomed from the seeds of Puritanism, which stressed thrift and industry along with realistic vocational views. Alfred Marshall, a modern economist, asserted the importance of the mental sphere in economic development by drawing a comparison between Ancient Greece and Rome. Ancient Greece easily attained economic affluence on the basis of its abundant natural resources, but it sunk into decline for lack of discipline and an earnest mental attitude. In contrast, despite its relative disadvantages in natural resources, Rome established the Roman Empire, ruling for a millennium, because its people had firm goals and a strong will. In *The Theory of Economic Growth*, Arthur Louis also gives top priority to " the enterprising spirit " among the many factors behind economic development.

In fact, studies show that the rapid and dramatic development of the Korean economy would not have been possible without the strong enterprising spirit of the Korean people. Everyone who lived through those times fondly recalls the 1960s and 1970s, when most citizens were happy working long hours on assembly lines to make products for export. The government also had a firm will toward economic development: government officials crisscrossed international financial markets to obtain financing for development projects and worked extensively, formulating economic policies. In contrast, other countries that were also on the threshold of joining the ranks of developed countries failed to do so for lack of entrepreneurship.

In view of these historical precedents, it becomes abundantly clear that economic development and the development of society are predicated on the establishment of solid ethical values and sound social mechanisms.

A Society for the Welfare of the Individual

Although industrial society is marked by a constant pursuit of advancement, the twenty-first century is expected to undergo a second cultural revolution, characterized largely by the quest for individual happiness. In this kind of society, the pursuit of individual interests will be given higher priority than the formation of wealth on a national level, since all people aspire to lead wealthy and affluent lives.

In this type of society, every kind of economic activity will be affected by the tide of change. Take broadcasting, for example. Today's industrial society is based on mass production, mass media, and mass communication. Under these circumstances, therefore, the concept "I" has relatively little significance, drowning in a wave of "mass." This situation does not enrich an individual's life or help bring about personal happiness.

The twenty-first century promises a radical reversal in this trend. The individual will be put on a pedestal. Broadcasting will be on the cutting edge of this change. This would mark the advent of an era of a "narrowcasting system," which is attuned to individual choice, replacing the current broadcasting system. While technological development has so far been geared toward industrial technology, it will in the future be oriented toward the development of technologies that will boost individual welfare. This idea of putting the individual before the mass was given eloquent backing by E. F. Schumacher who wrote *Small Is Beautiful* as a protest against the mass-oriented society.

Changes in Lifestyle and the Second Renaissance

As the interest in individual welfare and the tendency to seek individual identity in the midst of the masses becomes more prominent, the people's lifestyle will change. As technological and economic development accelerates, people will reevaluate the meaning of their existence, leading to greater interest in the arts and the spiritual realm.

With the resolution of the problem of providing basic necessities—clothing, food, and shelter—people's activities will transcend the level of mere subsistence to reach that of enjoying their lives to the fullest. As the human life span rises dramatically because of epoch-making progress in medical technology and nutrition, the "gray society" will appear. In the twenty-first century, women will expand their activities in broader areas—politics, economy, and culture—enabling them to maximize their potential. With people's lives increasingly focused on making qualitative improvements, per capita consumption of energy, food, and various natural resources will dramatically increase.

People will have a greater need for religion and spiritual fulfillment. Accordingly, the number of religious organizations and cultural activities such as symphony concerts and art exhibitions will proliferate. Recreational activities like professional sporting events will expand. The "material civilization" will demand greater access to such leisure activities. The government will have to support more cultural facilities in an effort to meet the increasing demands of people. Therefore, the next century will see the blooming of the Second Renaissance, overflowing with various cultural activities as John Naisbitt foresaw.

Change in People's Ways of Thinking

The worldwide changes just noted and the cumulative effects of Korea's accelerated economic growth have recently had a considerable impact on Korean attitudes. In carrying out the countless development projects that established Korea's economic foundations, such as building the Seoul-Pusan expressway and Pohang Iron & Steel Co., Ltd., Koreans were satisfied with thinking this would enhance their own welfare. However, when it turned out that a continued economic growth over thirty to forty years did not bring the expected level of individual well-being, Koreans started to think, "I couldn't care less about the construction of the Seoul-Pusan expressway when the roads in our town still remain dirty and my village doesn't have an adequate elementary school. I don't give a hoot about huge investment somewhere else."

Koreans have become increasingly reluctant to work for economic development at the expense of their individual well-being. They are no longer willing to work on Sundays as in the past, and companies have a hard time putting workers on Sunday shifts. Company machinery in the so-called three-D sector—dirty, difficult, and dangerous—is often left idle for lack of workers.

Frugal consumer behavior is also becoming a thing of the past. It seems that Koreans are obsessed with spending for today rather than investing their increased income for a better tomorrow: the purchase of large fridges and TVs is increasing. Koreans show a growing penchant for oil-guzzling luxury cars.

Unsound consumption patterns have been fanning social corruption and opportunism. Although real estate speculation has greatly abated since the late 1980s, it had been rampant, sending housing and land prices sky high. Workers, for their part, seem to care more about spending their rising incomes than focusing on enhancing their productivity.

The greed of caring only about grabbing one's own piece of the pie is becoming too widespread in Korea. All kinds of people—workers, civil servants, doctors—in our society seems to care only about pursuing their own interests. Particularly, this fierce pie-grabbing contest that started in the ranks of blue collar workers is now spreading to white collar workers. Even many people who are engaged in specialized work are displaying near-sightedness by running after tangible profits, a trend that severely erodes the credibility and role of the leaders of our society, who are miserably failing to guide public opinion in the direction of developing the society.

Change in the Desires of Consumers

The changes in most Koreans' social behavior is having a tremendous impact on the values of consumers. Consumers now show a tendency to seek qualitative improvement in their lives, whereas up to now they had put more emphasis on quantitative and material affluence. Moreover, thanks to an enhanced awareness and a continuing consumer protection campaign, consumers have become more actively involved in fighting for their rights; they have become more assertive in demanding higher quality and service, let alone lower prices. Thus, refusing to follow in the footsteps of yesterday's consumers, who were passively dominated by the suppliers or companies, today's consumers are becoming more active and individual in their choices, designing their own lifestyles.

Consumer demands are therefore changing in step with their new needs and attitudes. First, consumers' demands are becoming more diversified, with many people developing more sophisticated tastes. They now prefer products of good quality with an added emphasis on fashion and individuality.

Second, as Koreans have come to pursue time-efficient lifestyles, with a heightened awareness about the value of more leisure time, their demand for convenience is increasing significantly. Consumers are not merely stopping at just purchasing products, but are demanding "follow-up" services. To respond more actively to these changes in consumption patterns, companies are gathering information as to what kind of products the consumers want by establishing special sections such as service centers.

Third, Korean consumption patterns are moving upscale. In the past, Koreans were simply content to buy essential items. However, as income levels rise, Koreans come to appreciate a more affluent lifestyle; consumption patterns are becoming increasingly similar to those of advanced countries, where many consumer demands are geared toward the fulfillment of leisure and cultural needs. Moreover, current consumption patterns in Korea are now oriented more toward individual needs, a clear break from the past, when Koreans simply bought goods similar to those of their neighbors. These consumption patterns are common in advanced countries and are now spreading in Korea due to the growth of a middle class with purchasing power.

Fourth, consumer demands for user-friendly products are increasing. Countless micro-electronics products had been developed based on semiconductor technology that did not always consider user comfort. The more elaborate and high-tech contrivances became, the harder they were to use. In a sense, it seemed that people existed for the sake of machines, not the other way around. Therefore, the recent dramatic increase in demand for products with artificial intelligence based on "fuzzy" technology is a natural reflection of such consumer needs.

Change in Private Enterprise's Social Role

The role of private enterprise that led economic development on the basis of innovation and entrepreneurship constantly changes with economic and social development. As Milton Friedman indicated in *Capitalism and Freedom*, in the initial stages of capitalism, producing products by legitimate methods, providing jobs, and maximizing company profits were the sole social responsibilities of private enterprise. In this situation, contributing to public institutions such as universities and supporting charitable organizations, activities that have little to do with maximizing profits, would be considered an inappropriate use of funds.

Today private enterprise is no longer a passive entity with little influence in the marketplace, but has become a powerful social institution that can wield a lot of influence through its monopolistic power. In Korea, conglomerates exert a great influence on the formation of the nation's economic policies through the collective power of the Federation of Korean Industries. The influence of the large transnational corporations in the United States and Japan is powerful enough to alter the course of the world economy. Their influence on the market is such that, in certain cases, they dominate consumers. In this fashion, the roles of the huge organization are now markedly different from those played at the initial stage of capitalism.

As Peter F. Drucker said, there has been an increasing demand for enterprises to bear larger social responsibilities. The reasoning is as follows. First, as the institutions responsible for the production of goods, private enterprises naturally have economic responsibilities toward investors who have stakes in them, their employees, and their consumers.

Second, private enterprises have to take on cultural responsibilities. The need for corporate support for the cultural fields is increasing in order to ease the social impact that corporate activities entail, such as changing consumer patterns and environmental pollution.

Third, private enterprises have the responsibility to make positive contributions to society as corporate citizens through such means as establishing public funds for charitable donations, contributions, and emergency relief for refugees.

Korean private enterprises will also have to redefine their roles in step with this global trend. Thus far, the role of our enterprises has not gone much beyond basic economic activities such as producing goods, expanding exports, and creating jobs. However, from now on, Korea's enterprises will have to make greater efforts to meet their increasing social responsibilities, while faithfully carrying out their basic activities. Moreover, they will have to work hard to help ease the concentration of wealth so as to change the negative public attitude toward the conglomerates, and in running their businesses, they will have to compete fairly and justly with one another.

TECHNOLOGICAL INNOVATION AND THE INDUSTRIAL STRUCTURE

Acceleration of Technological Progress

For society and the economy to change course, conditions need to be created to enable that change to occur. Despite endless debates among scholars from various sectors of society as to what these conditions are, there is unanimity on the point that one of the most critical elements for change is "technology" that allows for the possibility of change. It was previously thought that it took a long time to replace an old technology with a new one, and there is some truth to that. Actually, many classical economists base their theories on the premise that technology remains a fixed factor for a considerable period of time. Today, however, that premise is no longer tenable.

In a report that he submitted to the U.S. Congress, Thomas F. Malone dramatically captured the acceleration of technological development. He condensed the epoch-making events of the earth's supposed 5 billion years of history into a span of 80 days. Those events he summed up as follows:

1. Sixty days ago, single-cell life forms first appeared.

2. An hour ago, primitive humans appeared.

3. Six minutes ago, the skills to make and use stone implements were obtained.

4. Barely a minute ago (actually 40,000 years ago), the Cromagnon men appeared.

5. Fifteen seconds ago, agricultural technology was developed.

6. One tenth of a second ago, the flames of the industrial revolution rose in the wilderness of Yorkshire, England.

7. Within the remaining one millionth of a second, modern-day technologies and post-industrialization technologies made dazzling progress.

Since this is an oversimplified summary of earth's life, some readers might not fully grasp the rapidity of technological progress. As a recent example, let us consider the trend in patent applications in the major advanced countries. In the United States, which is at the leading edge of technological development, approximately 100,000 new patent applications are made each year; in Japan, roughly triple that number of applications; and in other major advanced countries, tens of thousands of applications annually. The effect of technological development accumulated through such patent applications is beyond measure. Innovative technologies that would have been considered revolutionary are now commonplace. Particularly in the areas of electronics, computer, and communications, a year seldom passes without the appearance of new revolutionary technologies. Accordingly, if the first technological revolution was brought about by the invention of steam engine and spinning machine in the nineteenth century, the second one was made possible by petroleum and the invention of automobiles, telephones, and airplanes up to the mid-twentieth century. With rapid progress since the late 1970s in such areas as computers, telecommunications, biotechnology, new materials, and most notably in semiconductors, the third technological revolution is now in the making.

Another noteworthy phenomenon is the shortening length of time between when a technology is first developed and when it spreads and is applied socially. For instance, it took sixty-five years for the electric motor to be fully commercialized in 1866 after it was first developed in 1821. However, the transistor required only three years for commercialization after it was developed in 1948. Although in the early days it took generally three years to develop an integrated circuit, the core of modern microelectronic technology, entering the 1980s, the development period was shortened to the extent that within a four to five year period, three generations of integrated circuits—1M DRAM, 4M DRAM, and 16M DRAM—were developed.

A New Conception of Time and Space

In today's world, wherever events occur, they make an almost immediate impact on individual decision making all over the world. Moreover, there is very little delay between something happening and news of it reaching individuals all over the world, influencing their decisions and actions. Let us look at some recent examples.

The clash that occurred between Moslem pilgrims in Mecca, Saudi Arabia, on Thursday, July 31, 1987, instantly affected international oil prices, pushing up the price of oil, across the board, in the international markets on August 3, the next Monday, the first day of trading after the bloody incident. Similar actions at the New York Stock Exchange have an immediate and powerful impact on stock markets throughout the world. The "Black Monday" crash that hit Wall Street on October 19, 1987, is a perfect example.

The global economy is showing a simultaneous improvement and deterioration. Before the mid-1970s, the economy of each country moved according to its own unique circumstances. However, after the first oil shock, the whole world economy went into recession except for the OPEC countries. Even after the second oil shock, during 1979–1980, the global economy showed simultaneous improvement and deterioration.

The barriers of time and space that have acted as the greatest obstacle to the development of human society are becoming less and less formidable.

The Shortening Life Cycle of Products

Technological innovations are enabling the development of more convenient, higher quality, and more diversified products in response to consumers' demands, greatly shortening a product's life cycle. In the case of home appliances, after color TV was invented in 1957, it took as long as eighteen years for the next major product, the home VCR, to be introduced. Compact disc players, bilingual TV, hi-fi VCR, and high definition TV were developed respectively in 1977, 1978, and 1983. Starting from the mid-1970s, however, the life cycle of new products has shrunk to two to three years. Another notable characteristic in technological development, along with an increasing number of technological innovations, is the combination or fusion of technologies. Individual state-of-the-art technologies for semiconductors, computers, new materials, and biotechnology are being put together to maximize the effects of new technological developments, and the industrial application of these technologies is effecting profound changes in industry.

With the rapid technological development of semiconductor technology, most electronic goods are increasingly becoming lighter and smaller. Revolutionary improvements in function are enabling a single chip to perform the work that used to be done by a large computer. Moreover, the price of these chips continues to drop and gain wider application with technological innovations, promising significant future.

Technological Development on a National Scale

Due to increasingly fierce technological competition, the hierarchy among the nations is changing. Let me relate a funny story. In the late 1970s, a Japanese scholar visited Princeton University and talked about technology development in Japan. He threw a bombshell by saying, "Although the United States is still perceived as a technological superpower, Japan's industrial technology has overtaken that of the U.S."

His reasoning was that, although the United States was focusing on the technology for space exploration that could land them on the moon, it had neglected investment in industrial technology. The explosive remark by the Japanese scholar has since become vivid reality. Somebody says that now in the United States, when mothers buy a U.S.-made refrigerator, their kids would protest why she did not buy a better valued Japanese product. In the past, the expression "Made in USA" symbolized the highest quality. However, today, "Made in Japan" has become the label guaranteeing the highest quality. Moreover, the core components in the Patriot and Cruise missiles, which drew the attention of the world as the symbol of the U.S. technological prowess during the Gulf War, are said to be mostly Japanese products. Even the camera the U.S. astronauts took to the moon was a Japanese-made product.

Moreover, U.S.-made products have not been selling well in the world market and have been losing out to Japanese-made products in their home market. Awakened by the seriousness of this situation, the United States is stepping up its efforts to enhance industrial competitiveness through active technological development. Advanced countries, including the United States, are erecting higher barriers of technology protectionism. This is making it extremely difficult for Korean domestic industries to introduce core technologies essential for product development or the technologies related to the development of products at the introduction in their life cycle. Even when these advanced countries agree to transfer their technologies, they demand the payment of enormous royalties or add more conditions to the contract. European countries, for their part, are pursuing joint projects for the development of high technologies.

Another notable trend is the increasing cost of new product development. At the same time, due to much shorter product life cycles, when a company fails in a technology development project into which it has just poured a huge amount of funds or when its competitors develop technology ahead of it, its very existence may be in peril. To minimize such danger, the world's leading companies and countries are increasingly tying up with one another for technology development.

More countries are allocating portions of their national budget for technology development or actively supporting private companies in their technology development efforts through financial assistance or tax benefits. In those projects that private companies alone cannot tackle or that entail huge investment risks, governments make them national development projects and pursue joint development with private companies.

The Necessity for Independent Technology Development

Technology development in Korea has thus far concentrated on developing applied technologies that have adjusted introduced technologies to local needs rather than the independent development of unique, new technologies. As the developed countries strengthened their protective measures, this kind of technology development policy is reaching its limit. As a matter of fact, the statistics show that, after our technology introduction, items peaked at 763 cases in 1989 but plummeted to 582 cases in 1991.

Therefore, Korea has established a goal of upgrading its level of technology to that of the OECD by the end of 1990s. To realize this goal, our government continues implementation of the five-year production technology development plan and the G-7 project. Moreover, it is planning to boost the rate of investment in technology development to 3.5 percent of the GNP by 1996 and to 5.0 percent of the GNP by 2001.

Advanced Technology and the Leading Industries

As technological innovation is accelerating and the competition to develop technology is getting more fierce, technological progress is being made at a dazzling pace. The industrial structure has been directed toward knowledge and technology-intensive industries based on highly advanced technologies. Thus, the role of the industries producing tangible goods, such as agriculture and manufacturing and the so-called real sector directly related to these industries, will diminish in significance, while the so-called symbolic sector, such as the service industry that deals with currency and credit, will play a dominant role in the future world economy.

Korean industries are also expected to undergo tremendous changes. In the twenty-first century, they are expected to have done the following. First, they will make further progress in advanced technologies. On the strength of technological innovation, development of our advanced technology will far exceed that of world market growth, thus emerging as the mainstay of our exports by the year 2000. Second, great progress will be made in our information and software technology.

In the twenty-first century, the information and communications industries, industries related to the production and processing of data and the manufacturing of equipment for these industries will emerge as the new growth industries. On the other hand, industries will put more emphasis on software areas such as information, technology, and service rather than on hardware such as raw materials and energy. Also, as home shopping and home banking become widespread, every aspect of our lives will be affected by the wave of information.

Moreover, the information industry itself will experience a structural transformation as the importance of the hardware businesses, such as machinery production, declines and that of software businesses, such as information services, rises. As for the information communications service sector, value added networks (VAN) will show dramatic growth in such fields as financing, distribution, and tourism; database, ISDN, and LAN are also expected to grow dramatically.

Third, as the service sector becomes more diversified and further boosts the quality of its services, its importance in the economy will greatly increase. With each industrial sector becoming more information and knowledge intensive, thanks to rapid advances in technology, networking industries such as finance, communications, and distribution will grow markedly. In the manufacturing sector, as well, the importance of services such as R&D, management, and after-sales service will increase. Moreover, financing, insurance, and community or individual service industries will overtake the traditional service sectors such as wholesale or retail sales, transportation, and warehousing. High-tech services such as database, new media, and C&S (computers and service) will show remarkable growth.

Fourth, labor-intensive industry will continue its decline in Korea. Typical labor-intensive industries such as apparel, footwear, and toys have been continuously losing their market share since their cost competitiveness eroded due to steep wage increases and the intense competition from the developing countries. To better cope with these challenges, the labor-intensive industries will have to focus on high-quality and high-value-added products aided by the development of new products and enhancements in fashion and design.

CHANGES IN THE INPUT-OUTPUT STRUCTURE

The Fall in the Proportion of Raw Material Input

Progress in technology has brought about two notable changes in the industrial sector: the appearance of new products and changes in the input/output ratio.

Let us look at the impact of technological progress, with particular focus on the changes in the traditional factors of production such as raw materials, labor, and land, which are expected to effect revolutionary change in production activities.

In the late 1970s, the Rome Club of indutrialized nations predicted that the global economy would face a sharp rise in the cost of raw materials as well as a severe fuel shortage, based on the development experience and the pace of technological development of the advanced countries. It was thought that a sharp rise in raw material costs would pose a serious stumbling block to the economic development of the developing countries, which had started industrialization late. However, they missed the target by a wide margin. Currently, the cost of various raw materials such as nonferrous metals, iron ore, and oil is relatively stable. However, raw material exporting countries are experiencing economic hardship.

Such a failure in prediction by the Rome Club is quite understandable considering the dramatic changes that occurred in products and input/output ratios since the late 1970s. As a global tendency, products are becoming increasingly lighter and smaller, and this trend will continue to accelerate thanks to recent epochal progress in a microelectronics technology, which includes semiconductors.

In parallel with this trend, the raw materials content in most of today's products is decreasing. An IMF study found that the amount of raw materials consumed per unit of product in the mid-1980s was two fifths of that from the early twentieth century. In Japan, the level of raw materials consumption in the mid-1980s declined to 60 percent of that in the early 1970s. Another telltale example of such change is cables. Formerly made of copper, they are now increasingly being made of glass fiber, which costs only 2 percent as much as copper. Raw materials used in production will decrease sharply as industries make the transition from manufacturing to knowledge-intensive sectors and from sectors consuming large amounts of raw materials to those consuming knowledge.

This trend provides us with a couple of pointers. First, an economy cannot sustain its growth through fuel production alone. The drop in fuel cost brought about by falling demand will result in the collapse of raw material prices. The huge budget deficit of the United States and the crisis in most debtor nations, especially the Latin American countries, are cases in point. Second, Korean industries have to continuously lower the raw materials' input ratio through continued technological development. If it lags behind in the current competition to reduce raw materials consumption per product, then Korea will lose its competitive edge. When that happens, the Korean economy will start to lose its momentum and start to decline.

Decrease in Labor Input

It is already becoming common among major advanced countries that, despite the increase in industrial production, the number of factory workers is decreasing as is their proportion of total employment. The emergence of robotics and advances in factory automation have greatly reduced the labor force needed for production activities. In the United States, for example, in the 1920s, workers' input accounted for at least 30 percent of effort that went into production of an item. This meant that the work of factory workers accounted for a third of the work involved in manufacturing. However, in the 1960s, the ratio of workers' input declined to one sixth the total input.

In Korea as well, the employment in manufacturing industries has declined. This trend is attributed to automation, which has replaced physical labor with machines. To the industrial readjustment, this involves the transition from labor-intensive industries to knowledge-intensive industries. British industry over the past half century has declined, largely because the reduction in labor input per product occurred at a much slower pace than in other advanced countries. Therefore, any industry or any society that insists on employing physical laborers while neglecting technological development will have to face the consequences. The diminishing importance of workers in production has caused a radical change in the concept of employment itself.

The change in the concept of employment has the following economic significance. In the past, developing countries had no alternative but to achieve economic development by making products with cheap labor and exporting them. Their comparative advantage in labor-intensive industries was based on cheap labor. However, today, when the importance of labor is declining, those countries that focus on introducing new technology in production, exporting, and enhancing competitiveness will grow steadily, while countries relying on labor-intensive industries decline.

The Shrinking Proportion of Youth and the Rise in Female Workers

Wage increases and the changing labor supply structure are among the most prominent changes Korean society is currently facing. While wages in all industrial sectors grew at an average annual rate of 11.9 percent from 1981 to 1987, wages grew even further in 1987. From 1989 to 1991, the wage increase ratio hit yearly averages of 20 percent. By sector, wage hikes were the most remarkable in large companies and, by occupation, in the ranks of blue collar workers. Due to these rapid wage increases, the wage level of Korea, in terms of hourly pay, exceeded those of our closest competitors like Taiwan, Hong Kong, and Singapore. Thereafter, Korean companies have come to accept high wages as an inevitable cost of doing business.

The growth of the elderly population and the increase in the number of women in the labor force rank high among the significant changes currently occurring in the Korean labor market. The growth in the number of elderly people and the shrinking proportion of the young and active population, coupled with the increasing participation of women in the job market, will make a huge change in the employment structure in Korea.

First, a decline in the number of young people will result in a shortage of active, productive workers. The graying of the population and the growing ranks of women workers will encourage companies to hire more people as hourly or daily workers. Therefore, the traditional seniority-based life-time employment in our country will change into a Western employment system valuing individual ability.

A change in the thinking of workers is also one of the important changes sweeping the Korean labor market. Korean workers, whose willingness to work has been legendary, are now placing more importance on leisure and rest time.

Change in Production Systems and Factory Automation

In the early twentieth century industrial society, the speed of technology development was slow and the average life cycle of a product was five to eight years. Therefore, most companies used mass production systems, relying heavily on technologies standardized among producers. However, in the twenty-first century, when society will come under the full influence of information technology, mass production will be replaced by lean production. Moreover, with the conventional mass production method, it will become next to impossible to meet the increasing needs of workers and rising wages. To effectively cope with this changing industrial environment, companies will have to produce more diverse, higher quality, and higher value-added products. They will inevitably have to adopt the lean production system utilizing machinery such as industrial robots, automated warehouses, and transportation equipment.

Korea has been automating production processes since the 1980s in an effort to tackle the labor shortage, deal with wage hikes, and enhance productivity. However, the level of automation here is low compared with our competitors. In particular, overall wage levels in Korea are increasing and more investment needs to be made in automation, since automation will enable almost all areas of business from production to the placing of an order, planning, selling, and monitoring consumer warranties to be handled through computers. Automation has become a norm—an integral element in production.

Factors Determining the Hierarchy of Nations

With the major changes in production and industry, the factors determining the hierarchy of nations are changing. First, thanks to technology development, there is reduced consumption of the natural resources necessary for the production of goods, and the trade in natural resources is becoming more liberalized. Since competitiveness will be determined increasingly by the ability to develop new products using advanced technology, the countries with an advanced technology base will dominate the world economy.

Influenced by such various changes in the industrial environment and with much reduced chances of military conflict occurring among nations after the end of the Cold War, the factors determining the hierarchy of nations are also changing. After the Second World War, countries had to build up military strength and develop nuclear weapons to join the ranks of superpowers. However, in the twenty-first century, national strength will be measured by the level of individual welfare. Therefore, all nations in the world will have to develop powerful economies to survive in the twenty-first century, the age of economic war.

2

The Development Process

National Leaders often make simple comparisons between the past and the present when discussing the economic conditions in their countries. They want to emphasize that they were desperately poor in the past, but have become rich now—all because of their leadership. I do not intend to spin tales like "Korea was dirt poor during the Japanese colonial period, but is now affluent" or "Let's compare the 1960s with the present. Then, we could barely afford a bowl of steamed barley on our tables." Rather, I want to review the process of our economy's development to help formulate development stategies that will be necessary for our economy to emerge as a leader in the world economy in the twenty-first century.

THE DAWN OF ECONOMIC DEVELOPMENT (1961)

A National Economy Heavily Dependent on Foreign Aid

In 1945 when Korea gained independence from Japanese colonial rule, there was little industrial infrastructure. Korea was not able to even fully operate the few industrial facilities it had because of a lack of skill and fuel. Adding insult to injury, the Korean War almost completely wiped out Korea's production facilities and infant infrastructure. Massive relocation of people and a rapid increase in the population drove up unemployment and made normal operation of the economy virtually impossible.

Korea had to rely heavily on aid from its allies to survive and forge ahead. The nation's budget was supported by a fund created by selling the flour, barley, and cotton sent by allies. However, the average Korean, in the midst of such turmoil, poured everything he or she had into the education of the children, determined that they would not hand down poverty to the next generation. For example, the number of students above junior high school level rose from 710,000 in 1954 to 830,000 in 1959. Because of this intensive investment in education in the 1950s, Korea was able to produce a high-quality labor force that became the driving force behind the remarkable economic growth of the 1960s.

FULL-FLEDGED ECONOMIC DEVELOPMENT (1962–1971)

Establishment of a Development Strategy

In the process of launching comprehensive economic development plans in the 1960s, a tremendous amount of energy was devoted to selecting the best, most appropriate development strategies. At that time, the focal points of the discussions were

1. Should the country pursue domestic or export-oriented development?

2. On which types of industry should the primary attention be—agriculture or manufacturing?

3. How could these projects be financed? How could domestic savings be expanded? Should foreign capital be brought in?

4. How could balanced development be achieved?

The highlights of the economic development strategy was decided upon after lengthy discussions: externally oriented development; development of light industry and infrastructure; domestic savings expansion and foreign capital attraction. The adoption of such a development strategy was based on several factors. First, to escape the confines of a narrow domestic market and scarce natural resources, Korea had to adopt a bold outward-looking development strategy. Second, in view of expected export growth and the state of available domestic production facilities, and in line with an export-oriented industrialization strategy, it was concluded that the development of labor-intensive light industry was the best course of action. In the initial development stage, when domestic technology was at a low level and financial resources were scarce, the focus had to be on the development of the textile, plywood, and footwear sectors. It was felt that those industrial sectors would maximize employment and use technology that was easy to learn. Third, as the country embarked full-force on the economic development plan, foreign capital was needed to meet the enormous investment needs.

Accomplishments in the 1960s

The economic growth rate, which had been between 4 and 5 percent, doubled to an average annual growth of 8.8 percent during 1962 to 1971. The per capita GNP soared from $82 in 1961 to $289 in 1971. As the industrial structure changed dramatically, the proportion of the economy accounted for by agriculture and fishing diminished from 39.1 percent in 1961 to 27.2 percent in 1971. However, the mining and manufacturing sector grew from 15.5 to 22.5 percent during the same period. Exports increased rapidly. Exports, which were US$41 million in 1961, grew 26 times to US$1,068 million in 1971. Construction of the Seoul-Pusan Expressway and modernization of ports and power plants necessitated massive investment in infrastructure but laid the foundation for future economic growth. The rise in the nation's GNP pushed up the domestic savings ratio. Thus, domestic savings, which had accounted for 21.6 percent of total investment in 1961, account for 60.9 percent in 1971. This boosted Korea's internal investment resources.

All in all, the greatest accomplishment of the economic development in the 1960s was the successful completion of a solid economic development foundation that allowed Korea to wean itself from foreign aid and grow on its own.

ACHIEVING SELF-RELIANCE (1972–1979)

Establishment of a Self-Reliant Industrial Structure

The third and fourth economic development plans were launched during this period. A major objective was to achieve continued economic growth in the face of domestic and foreign changes, such as the worldwide economic slump and the Middle East oil crisis. To establish a firm basis for economic growth, emphasis was placed on financing all investment needs with domestic resources. Concurrently, to supplement insufficient domestic capital and secure the foreign exchange necessary to purchase raw materials and capital goods, an export-oriented policy that focused on light industries continued to be followed.

Meanwhile, in the early 1970s, light industry exports began to sag, thus highlighting the need to develop new exportable products. At the same time, export-oriented economic policies resulted in an imbalanced industrial structure. Therefore, to overcome these obstacles to further growth, import-substitution policies dependent on the construction of the heavy and chemical industries were instituted (see Table 2.1).

Table 2.1.
Strategic Industries in the 1970s

Industry	Large Factories and Industrial Estates
Steel	Pohang Iron and Steel Company established (1973)
Machinery	Changwon Machinery Industrial Complex groundbreaking (1974)
Shipbuilding	Hyundai Shipbuilding Company established (1973)
Petrochemicals	Ulsan Petrochemical Industrial Complex completed (1972)
Electronics	Kumi Electronic Industrial estates (1971)
Automobiles	Hyundai Automobile Company established (1972–1976)

Another basic objective to achieve self-reliance was to enlarge the domestic market by boosting the agricultural and fishing sector.

As a result, in the late 1970s, when the third development plan was completed, Korea was self-sufficient in growing rice, the current account showed a surplus, and domestic investment resources had been replenished.

Moreover, during this period, technology development began to be recognized as an important development strategy. To facilitate the introduction of advanced technologies, the government simplified approval procedures for technology introduction and provided tax incentives for technology development.

Imbalanced Growth and Balanced Development

Korea's economy achieved remarkable growth thanks to the 1960s economic development plan. However, a rapid export-driven growth created considerable side effects. Aggravated sectoral imbalances generated societal problems. Domestic industry suffered because of the imbalance between light and heavy industry. The export-oriented industrialization program widened the gap between those engaged in export businesses and those in domestic businesses and the society was being separated into two layers.

To resolve this structural problem, the government developed strategies to rectify imbalances between various economic sectors: manufacturing and agriculture, urban and rural areas, small and large enterprises. First, the government focused on strengthening the basis of agriculture with low-interest loans. Further, it implemented a two-tiered rice pricing system, whereby the government set one price for purchasing rice from farmers and another for selling the rice to city dwellers or distributors to narrow the income gap between urban and rural citizens.

At the same time, the government instituted a policy to develop the heavy and chemical industries to correct the imbalance in the manufacturing sector caused by a growth policy that favored light industry. Six industrial sectors—steel, machinery, automobiles, electronics, shipbuilding, and petrochemicals—benefited greatly from generous government assistance. Because of this policy, the heavy and chemical industries grew tremendously, which brought about advances in the industrial structure.

However, the push to advance the heavy and chemical industries went too far, resulting in excess capacity and a weakened corporate financial structure. The adoption of the plan to develop the heavy and chemical industries was good in terms of development strategy, but problems arose for which solutions had not been prepared. The method and timing of the strategy and the maintenance of a good balance between different sectors were just such problems.

Economic Development in the 1970s

In the 1970s, the Korean economy continued its economic growth, despite external changes such as the oil crisis and weakening of free trade. The economy gained momentum again in 1976 when Korea moved into participating in the development projects of Middle Eastern countries such as Saudi Arabia. The base of industrialization was further strengthened by increased facility investment, export expansion, and infrastructure modernization. Thus, between 1972 and 1978, the economy grew at a rate of more than 10 percent and per capita GNP exceeded US$1,000.

There was also steady progress in industrial restructuring. Between 1972 and 1978, commodity exports increased 39.1 percent, reaching US$10 billion in 1977. Heavy and chemical industry exports began to dominate. The increase in domestic savings boosted growth in total investments between 1972 and 1978 to 15.2 percent annually. Investment in agriculture and fishing declined, while that in mining and manufacturing grew.

Thus, vigorous implementation of the economic development policy—the ambitious development of heavy and chemical industries being the most notable example—made a tremendous contribution to the acceleration of economic growth and the advancement of the industrial structure. However, such a policy did have some drawbacks and created pressing problems. First, the two-tiered rice pricing regime that the government implemented to boost farmers' incomes became a serious stumbling block to balancing the national budget. As time went on, the government had to increase the price it paid farmers, but it could not raise the price it charged consumers. This widened the gap between the government's buying and selling prices of rice, aggravating the budget deficits.

Second, a problem inherent in the process of developing the heavy and chemical industries could easily be seen. The various policy loans and tax incentives generously provided to promote the heavy and chemical industries resulted in currency expansion and further aggravation of the budget deficits. Also, some of the investments were made without careful study of their effect on the national economy. This resulted in overlapping investments. Because the government chose strategic industries, economic inefficiency was enormous. Moreover, enterprises naturally expected the government to bail them out because the heavy and chemical industry projects that they had undertaken were at the government's prodding.

Third, inflation was a problem. The Middle Eastern construction boom and the ensuing domestic prosperity brought about an average annual wage increase of 30 percent. Moreover, the construction companies that amassed huge fortunes in the Middle East came home and invested money in land. This sent prices sky high. This succession of events caused one of the worst bouts of inflation in modern history. As inflation continued, it hurt export competitiveness and eventually endangered growth prospects for the economy.

IMPLEMENTATION OF AN ECONOMIC STABILIZATION POLICY
(1980–1987)

A Powerful Economic Stablilization Policy

Inflationary pressure, which gradually abated in the early 1970s, rose again in 1978. In 1979, consumer prices rose 18.3 percent, while wholesale prices rose 18.8 percent. For the two to three years around 1980, Korea had transitional difficulties as the economy was thrown into stagflation.

It was decided that, to resolve these accumulated problems, growth potential should be restored by stabilizing the economy, instituting adjustments in the heavy and chemical sectors, and enhancing industrial efficiency. Accordingly, the government put first priority on stability, autonomy, and opening the Korean market to foreign goods. Therefore, it implemented an ambitious economic stabilization policy to catch the three hares; that is, the international balance of payment surplus, price stabilization, and high growth.

Economic stabilization became the fundamental policy objective in the economy. The economy, which had experienced negative growth in 1980, urgently needed a new basis for continued growth. Price-destablizing factors, exacerbated by the serious inflation in the late 1970s, continued in the 1980s. Since factors that could aggravate the balance of payments deficit also persisted, it was necessary to pursue economic growth only to the extent that it would not adversely affect price stability and the balance of payments. Accordingly, the government encouraged domestic demand and promoted export. While raising national income and maintaining necessary liquidity by managing the fundamentals of fiscal and financial policy, the government tried to balance the demand and supply of food and stabilize its price.

As the economy grew and the private sector started to play a greater role, the government decided to boost the economic growth potential by making a free market economy policy objective. In an effort to correct the irregularities and inefficiency that stemmed from monopolies and to enhance competitiveness, emphasis was placed on eliminating practices restricting fair competition, as can be seen from the example of the enactment of the Fair Trade Law. Rational restructuring of the industrial support system was begun. The Industrial Policy Coordination Committee was established to strengthen government support of industry. Concurrently, to improve the efficiency of monetary control and facilitate fund distribution in accordance with the market mechanism, the government also tried to transform the monetary management system from direct regulation such as credit controls to indirect regulation such as a currency reserve policy and a rediscount policy.

Moreover, the liberalization policy became the backbone of economic management after the late 1980s. Beginning in mid-1980s, trade protectionism proliferated and advanced countries pressured Korea to open its market. An agressive market opening program was instituted to ease this trade friction and bolster the international competitiveness of Korean industries.

Single-Digit Price Stabilization and the Strengthening of Growth Potential

One result of these economic stabilization measures was that the consumer price increase, which had reached 28.8 percent in 1980, stabilized to the single digits and dropped 7.1 percent in 1982 and 2.3 percent in 1984. Wholesale prices, which had risen to a high growth of 39.0 percent in 1980, rose only 0.2 percent in 1983. In1986, the Consumer Price Index itself declined compared to the previous year. The economy had recovered its competitiveness and productivity. From 1986 to 1989 further boosted by favorable external conditions known to Koreans as the three lows—low oil price, weak dollar, and low global interest rates—the economy achieved a high annual growth rate of 12–13 percent. The balance of payments that had always been in the red moved into the black.

The economic stabilization policy of the early 1980s was effectively implemented because people from all walks of life—the government, private enterprise, households, factories, and farms—understood and worked toward stability.

Nevertheless, the management of the economy was not adequate enough to firmly establish a sound basis for expanded growth potential, although it did contribute to the achievement of economic stability:

First, financial liberalization up to mid-1980s came up short, although it did mark a turning point in the history of Korea's economic development. In particular, the deregulation of interest rates constituted a centerpiece of the financial liberalization policy. However, as consistent application of the financial liberalization policy began to slide in the late 1980s, discussions on the liberalization measures slackened and interest rate deregulation did not even appear on the agenda. Between 1986 and 1987, the money supply was expanding, the economy was strong, and the exchange rate was appreciating. Because of those favorable conditions, I personally believe that Korea missed the most opportune time to deregulate interest rates.

Second, implementation of the real-name financial transaction system was delayed. In 1982, the government had decided to enforce the compulsory system while it restored order to financial market, which was in a state of chaos because of the Youngja Chang fiasco. Her failure to pay notes she floated sent shock waves through financial circles. However, the system was not instituted because of lack of consensus and understanding.

Third, the method of industrial restructuring should have been improved. The government did well by enacting the Industrial Development Act, which shifted its assistance for restructuring from the support of particular industries to support of the functional aspects of exports, technology, and human resources development. However, there were still problems. Although the act greatly improved restructuring the assistance system to become functional, the government was still able to favor specific industries. Although limited assistance had been inevitable for specific sectors, the government should have established criteria for eligibility so that inefficient industries would not get assistance.

Fourth, the government response to people's equity demand assistance was insufficient. Between 1986 and 1987, because of democratization, consumers' pent-up demands were unleashed. The government, pushed into a corner, was inconsistent in its policy enforcement and could not respond quickly to the changing internal and external environment. When enterprises demanded a flexible money supply, workers wanted wage hikes, and farmers sought protection for their livelihood, the government enacted stopgap measures instead of convincing the public all demands could be met. Therefore, it had to expand the money supply, which plunged the nation's financial accounts into the red again and sent wages skyrocketing.

The Three Lows and Government Economic Policy

Going into the late 1980s, the external economic environment was more favorable—a weak dollar, low oil prices, and low global interest rates— and domestic prices had stabilized because of the economic measures. In 1986, for the first time in Korea's modern history, the nation's current account shifted into the black. The economy registered a high annual growth rate of 12 percent. Industrial restructuring also made headway. The share of the manufacturing sector in total GNP rose from 29.9 percent to 31.7 percent during the period.

Additionally, the government redoubled its efforts to streamline regulations to expand private sector autonomy and enhance the power of market forces. It also emphasized equitable distribution of wealth and development balanced among regions and classes. Moreover, because of the improved balance of payments and the resultant lower foreign debt in 1986, it responded to the opening and internationalization trend of the economy by developing appropriate legislation.

To increase private sector autonomy and enhance market forces, the government enacted the Fair Trade Act, which eliminated practices and regulations that had restricted competition. Further, the government tried to improve public enterprise management efficiency by holding companies accountable for their performance and by encouraging them to sell shares to the public. The government also developed policies to improve the general welfare of the people by extending the medical insurance system, by implementing restructuring projects in agriculture and fishing, and by providing assistance to the urban poor. At the same time, by revising labor laws in 1987, the government promoted workers rights and established more rational labor-management practices.

Specifically, the policies stressed reducing rising trade friction by expanding imports, as long as the balance of payments surplus was maintained at the optimum level and managed efficiently. At the same time, by actively pursuing economic cooperation with other developing countries and by promoting overseas investment, the government started to be a more active member of the international community.

KOREAN ECONOMY IN TRANSITION (1988–1994)

All countries need and want economic development. In today's fast-paced rapidly changing global village, any country that fails to actively participate in the world economy will soon be left behind.

In 1988, when the surplus in the balance of payments was US$10 billion and Korea had successfully hosted the Seoul Olympic Games, Korea felt that the country had become an advanced nation overnight. However, in 1993, this euphoria has been replaced by depression. Korea is faced with transitional problems: a sagging economy, weakening international competitiveness, and mounting inflation. What is worse, most of the problems confronting the Korean economy now are, by their nature, symptomatic of structural adjustment and cannot be resolved in a short period of time. Therefore, to successfully overcome today's challenges and emerge as a leader of rapidly industrializing economies, we have to work harder.

Low Growth and Sagging Investment

The Korean economy, which, since 1986, had been humming along at an annual growth rate of 12 to 13 percent and capitalizing on the "three lows," began to slow down. The growth rate plummeted to 8 percent in 1989 and further lowered to 5 percent in 1993. I do not believe that 5–8 percent growth rate is low at all. I feel that the high economic growth rate during the "three lows" period (1986–1988) was rather abnormal and driven by external factors. In fact, a 5–8 percent growth rate was much closer to the optimum level for the Korean economy. However, it seemed disastrous to the Korean people, who had grown accustomed to an economic growth rate of more than 10 percent. Some people even had serious doubts about the future of their economy.

Admittedly, Korea's economic growth rate seems rather low when compared to the rates of 10 percent or more of ASEAN (Association of South East Asian Nations) members that have been industrializing rapidly. Nonetheless, the growth rate is still remarkably high, compared to the 2–4 percent growth of the advanced countries, including Japan and the United States. The problem is, however, that the slowdown of the Korean economy is not attributable to the deterioration of external conditions but to the structural problem of our economy. In this respect, the recent trend in the total investment ratio to GNP of Korea is drawing attention in connection with the prospect of the future economic recovery, because economic growth is, above all, fueled by investment.

Then, what trends can be seen in the nation's total fixed investment rate, that is, total fixed investment rate in proportion to GNP? This, contrary to popular belief, has grown steadily. The fixed investment rate, which was in the 29 percent range in the mid–1980s, grew to 31.8 percent in 1989 and 35.6 percent in 1993 (Table 2.2). However, this high growth rate came mainly from increased housing construction, while facility investment declined in the manufacturing sector, particularly in high-tech heavy industries, which is essential to economic stimulation. Thus, unless facility investment in the manufacturing sector recovers after construction investments go down, there is a possibility that the economic growth rate will decline further. This makes restoring confidence in investing in the manufacturing sector a daunting task.

Mounting Inflationary Pressure

In late 1988, a presidential election, the Olympic Games, and the after-effects of a surplus in the balance of payments all worked together to jolt the stable economy that had existed since the early 1980s. Specifically, the abnormally high incomes during the "three lows" period led to speculative activities, which created the problems of a "bubble econ-

Table 2.2.
Major Economic Indicators

	1981	1987	1990	1991	1992	1993
Economic Growth Rate (%)	5.9	13.0	9.3	8.4	4.7	5.6
Per Capita GNP ($)	1,734	3,100	5,659	6,498	6,749	7,466
Current Account (US $100 million)	–46.5	98.5	–21.8	–87.3	–45.3	4.5
Exports ($100 million)	212.5	472.8	650.2	718.7	766.3	822.4
Imports ($100 million)	261.3	410.2	698.4	815.3	817.8	838.0
Domestic Investment Ratio (%)	29.9	29.6	37.1	39.3	36.1	34.4
Total Fixed Investment Ratio (%)	28.4	28.9	36.6	38.2	35.8	35.6
Total Savings Ratio (%)	22.7	36.2	36.0	36.1	34.9	34.9
Consumer Price (%)	21.6	3.0	8.6	9.7	6.2	4.8

Sources: The Bank of Korea, Major Economic Indicators, National Account; the Korea Statistics Bureau, Korean Economic Indicators.

omy" and caused a steep rise in land prices. Moreover, aggressive democratic wage negotiations jacked up individual incomes, consumption grew, and prices rose rapidly.

Thus, consumer price index, which had been 2–3 percent in the early 1980s, more than tripled to 7–9 percent between 1988 and 1991. CPI showed a moderate level of 5–6 percent between 1992 and 1993, which was still higher compared to that of early 1980s.

Exports and a Balance of Payments Deficit

Korea is now ranked the thirteenth largest trading nation in the world, with a total trade volume hovering above US$160 billion as of late 1993. However, annual export growth plummeted from 30 percent in the "three lows" period to 2.8 percent in 1989 and to 4.2 percent in 1990. Growth rates such as these are comparable to those recorded in 1982 when exports were the lowest in the 1980s. Fortunately, the growth rate has shown a fairly strong resurgence to 10.5 percent in 1991 and more than 11 percent in 1993 and the future for our exports seems to be brighter.

Meanwhile, imports grew a remarkable 17–18 percent during 1989–1991 because of the accelerated opening of the domestic market and continued conspicuous consumption. As facility investment slowed going into 1992, the rate of increase for import has been declining noticeably. Nevertheless, Korea's industrial structure is still conducive to imports because of weaknesses in the capital goods, parts, and materials industries. Accordingly, to resolve the trade deficit problem structurally, Korea needs to come up with fundamental measures to realign the industrial structure.

The trade surplus once exceeded US$10 billion. However, since 1990 it reverted to a trade deficit. One exception was the 1993 trade surplus of US$0.5 billion.

The Manpower Shortage and Reduction in Working Hours

Rate of increase in our economically active population has shown a gradual decline, falling from 4.7 percent in 1987 to less than 3 percent ever since. It is expected that this decline will continue because the population structure resembles a jar bulging in the middle because of the declining birth rate over the medium to long term. In view of these demographic changes, the manpower shortage in Korea will persist in the future. In particular, the number of women workers in the economy is growing; the aging of the work force is accelerating; and the proportion of workers with higher education is increasing. Therefore, women and senior workers are now filling the gap left by the lack of a core male skilled labor force.

Although the overall unemployment rate stabilized at less than 3 percent, that of the college graduates was relatively high, more than 5 percent.

On the other hand, the service sector is drawing more labor than the manufacturing sector (Table 2.3). Since young people tend to avoid "three Ds" (dangerous, dirty, and difficult) sectors, the rate of increase in the number of blue collar workers is declining rapidly.

Meanwhile, with the progress of democratization, labor unions have boosted their activities. The number of labor unions, 2,742 as of late June 1987, almost doubled to 4,103 toward the end of the year. Although the increase in the number of labor unions since 1990 slowed with the normalization of labor relations, the number grew sharply—compared to early 1987—to 7,527 in late 1992. While powerful labor union activities have resulted in a steady reduction of working hours, they have also jacked up wages, thus weakening industrial competitiveness.

Recent Characteristics of the Korean Economy

Transition to an Open Economy. As Korea's position in the international economy moved up, the opening of the domestic market to foreign competition was accelerated. Barriers to the importation of foreign industrial products have almost disappeared and the tariff rate has declined continuously from 21 percent in 1985 to almost 8 percent in 1993. Furthermore, since not only industrial products but also service industries have come under increasing pressure to open, service sectors began to liberalize at full speed. Beginning in 1987, businesses such as the distribution and production of films, import and wholesale trade of tobacco products, marine transport services, and travel guide services

Table 2.3.
Workers Increase, Percent by Sector

	1987	1989	1990	1991	1992	1993
Manufacturing	6.0	–3.7	0.1	1.8	3.4	-3.9
Services	4.4	6.8	7.1	6.6	5.7	5.9
Blue Collar	11.5	4.8	3.2	3.8	–2.4	–3.4
White Collar	4.7	7.3	7.2	5.6	10.2	6.1

Source: Korea Labor Research Institute and Sectoral Analysis of Labor Trends (Second Quarter, 1993)

have been opened to competition. In addition, in accordance with the UR agreement in December 1993,* all service sectors except for those in the areas of health and education will be liberalized.

The opening of the domestic market to foreign competition is unavoidable in today's world where globalization is the name of the game. However, Koreans are worried that service sectors and educational industries will be hard hit by market opening since they are not yet fully developed.

Development of the Service Industries. Although Korea's rapid economic development has so far been driven by brisk export growth, particularly in the manufacturing sector, recent trends indicate that growth in the manufacturing sector has slackened compared to growth in the service sectors. Accordingly, the manufacturing sector was losing its momentum as can be seen in the reduction in its share in GNP. Although production in the manufacturing sector accounted for 30.3 percent of GNP in 1985, it declined to 29.2 percent in 1990 and to 27.1 percent in 1993.

The weakening of the manufacturing sector and the growth of the service sector was an inevitable consequence of the process of industrial restructuring. However, in view of the country's economic conditions and the maturity of its economy, this trend occurred too early. If the manufacturing sector continues to be depressed, it will accelerate the premature aging of the economy, further reducing the growth potential.

One of the greatest causes of the premature aging of the manufacturing industries is the lack of technology development. Korea cannot survive in the era of technology innovation with entry-level, low-grade technology. Furthermore as protectionism of technology in advanced countries is growing, the introduction of technology becomes more difficult. Thus the development of an indigenous technology is imperative. Accordingly, the government should increase its assistance to manufacturing industries as they focus on reinforcing their profitable operations by developing better technology. Another important factor is the alarming rate at which the service sectors that generate high profits are growing.

Economic Growth Led by Domestic Demand. Export growth, which had been the engine of Korea's economic growth, started to decline rapidly after 1988. In 1990, the surplus in the balance of payments switched to a deficit. Such a decline in our export growth was attributable, in large

---

*As a result of the Uruguay Round agreement, service, agricultural products, and intellectual property rights have been included in the scope of the multilateral trade negotiations.

measure, to the loss of competitiveness in labor-intensive industries such as textiles and footwear. The contribution of exports to economic growth was declining fast, while domestic demand, including domestic consumption and construction, was increasingly driving the economic growth (Table 2.4).

The declining reliance of the economy on exports was meaningful in that the ground was being laid for the economy to achieve continued growth unaffected by the external economic conditions. However, the size of the domestic market was not large enough to sustain continued growth of Korea's enterprises. Accordingly, greater effort should have been made to expand exports to ensure the continued high growth of the economy.

Table 2.4.
Percent of Sectoral Contribution to Economic Growth

	1981	1986	1990	1991	1992	1993
Domestic	4.3	9.0	13.3	12.3	2.4	4.7
Exports	4.8	9.0	1.6	3.6	3.7	3.6
Manufacturing	9.9	18.3	9.1	8.5	1.6	1.5
Services	3.7	11.1	12.3	10.0	3.2	3.1

Source: The Bank of Korea, National Account, 1994.

Concentration of Economic Power and the Ensuing Rise in Inefficiency

Due to the lack of accumulated capital and natural resources, Korea has chosen a policy of selecting promising growth industries and promoting them as strategic industries to best use its limited natural resources. In this process, the large companies (conglomerates) have gained enormous economic power. Although the number of enterprises with more than 300 employees accounted for only 1.4 percent of the total manufacturing enterprises in 1992, their share of shipments and value added reached 55.2 percent and 54.2 percent, respectively. These proportions are considerably higher than those for shipments and value added for Japan's large companies, which were 48.2 percent and 43.8 percent, respectively.

Moreover, the large companies have continued to expand the scope of their operations into service industries, such as financing, and into manufacturing industries by diversifying. What is even worse, they have a monopoly on bank loans, which has seriously harmed the small and medium-sized industries, the backbone of the economy.

Such concentration of economic power in large companies has become a stumbling block to restructuring industries by preventing the efficient distribution of resources. Large companies even bail out their inefficient subsidiaries by guaranteeing loans. They even engage in unfair trade practices such as discriminating against companies outside their business group. Admittedly, large companies have made a tremendous contribution to the growth of the economy. Nevertheless, the declining efficiency in competition stemming from the concentration of economic power has become a huge burden on the growth of the economy. Therefore, to achieve continued economic growth while maintaining an efficient industrial structure, we now have to do our utmost to relax the concentration of economic power.

The government should actively nurture small companies engaged in promising growth industries and at the same time ensure the development of mutually complementary relations between large and small companies. To that end, the specialization and cooperation affiliation in industry should be actively encouraged.

Weakening Resolve for Economic Growth

During the period 1986–1988, the Korean household income rose dramatically thanks to a good economy, skyrocketing land prices, and sharp wage increases. Since then, people's strong commitment to work has been wearing thin, as they have been increasingly drawn to leisure. They have become more demanding about their working conditions such as the work environment and hours, and they tend to shun manufacturing jobs where the working environment is inferior to that in other industries.

As a result, the number of hours worked in the manufacturing sector has continued to decline from 235.5 hours per month in 1985 to 211.7 hours in 1993. Additionally, as the rise in unearned income has boosted the growth of the service industry, the flow of personnel to this industry has increased, thus causing a manpower shortage in the manufacturing sector.

In addition to a deteriorating work ethic, the enterprising spirit of our entrepreneurs has also been waning. Since business owners experienced a rash of serious labor disputes that started in 1987, they have become reluctant to build more new production facilities. They prefer to invest in service industries such as the leisure industry or they avoid investment altogether.

Therefore, to ensure the continued growth of Korea's economy, Koreans have to revive one of their greatest characteristics and merits: diligence. Labor and management should work together to foster loyalty and develop the corporate culture of their own companies. Entrepreneurs, for their part, have to work hard to succeed in their businesses, which are the essence of the enterprising spirit, and more resources must be poured into technology development, to reshape the method of doing business.

3

Economic Policy in a Time of Transition

The Korean economy that has unfolded since 1988 looks as if the whole nation were running toward a wall, blindfolded. No one in his or her right mind would do such a thing. In such a situation, it is very important to pool the nation's collective wisdom and change course before hitting the wall. Such wisdom cannot come from the government alone. Only when all the people come to realize the severity of the situation can they all—from the government and politicians to workers and the press—come together, take responsibility for their actions, and make changes to move forward. After all, we are all accountable for the performance of our economy since 1988.

THE ENGINE OF A GROWTH-ORIENTED ECONOMIC POLICY

Optimistic and Pessimistic Views

Coming into 1990s, views on the status of the Korean economy have become increasingly polarized between optimists and pessimists both at home and abroad. Optimists feel that the current difficulties in the economy are symptomatic of a temporary transition after the high-growth period of the economy. If this temporary trend dies down, the Korean economy should show a healthy level of growth, as the Korean economy has done before.

Therefore, some people in the press, foreign and domestic, view the recent problems in the Korean economy, such as the deficit in the balance of payments as transient. They say that the Koreans ought to take pride in their remarkable achievements instead of worrying about "nonexistent problems." In their minds, Korea should soon be able to join the OECD and thus become one of the truly advanced nations by the year 2000.

On the other hand, many pessimists are quick to point out that the recent troubles in the Korean economy are attributable to a fundamental shift in the factors that have been driving the economy. They feel that the current problems are structural in nature; if a new major breakthrough is not made, it will be difficult for the economy to grow.

In particular, what most worries the pessimists is that there is no longer a dominant industry in Korea that can lead economy growth. Textiles, footwear, electronics, automobiles, shipbuilding, and steel—the industries that once powered economic growth—have slowed because of wage hikes, technology development, and the competition from ASEAN nations such as Thailand. They also point out that no new industries have yet emerged to lead the Korean economy into the future.

The Engine of Growth

It would be of interest to see which side is right. However, a much more important point is that both sides agree that the economy is now at a crossroads.

In fact, in 1990–1993, looking at the performance of the economy reveals that it is not functioning as it used to. It is true that a slight slowing of the growth rate is not worrisome, since it is not good for an economy to grow 10 percent annually as before because of the need to maintain stability. However, now that the factors that led the growth of the economy are about to change fundamentally, we need to take a fresh look at the prospects for continued growth.

Generally, the following ingredients are required for economic growth: technological advances, a work force, an enterprising spirit, savings, resources, sound management, and a strong will. Technological advances are very important for economic growth, as R. M. Solow, an American economist, asserted in his analysis of growth factors in the first half of the twentieth century. He said that 87.5 percent of growth factors were attributed to technological advances. The work force is certainly a major growth factor although its importance has decreased somewhat due to automation.

Against this backdrop, what specific factors enabled the rapid growth of the Korean economy? Developmental economists point out four major factors: (1) cheap and abundant, yet highly skilled labor; (2) a strong will for economic growth; (3) the government's sincere commitment to development; and (4) a favorable international environment.

The Korean economy achieved continued growth after the 1960s because the economy that grew on the basis of these factors boosted the people's savings, which enabled the continued accumulation of capital. That capital, in turn, was reinvested and resulted in economies of scale. Most people would also agree that improved technology contributed to the advance in domestic technology, which paved the way for the rapid economic growth. However, the factors that contributed to accelerated economic growth in the early days have recently shown a variety of changes. The labor advantage has disappeared because of high wages and a personnel shortage in the manufacturing sector. The government's commitment to economic policy, as well as the strong work ethic and thrifty lifestyle of the people, have greatly eroded. External conditions have worsened, in part because of increased protectionism in advanced countries. Thus, it has become very difficult to protect the domestic market from rising pressure to open the markets. On top of this, Korea is being squeezed out of its former markets by China, ASEAN nations, and other newly industrialized economies (NIEs). The economies of scale have become harder to achieve because consumer demand has turned to more personal and high-quality goods. This has accelerated a change in the production system to leaner production. Technological development has become more complex because of increased protectionism in advanced countries, low-level domestic technology, and a lack of commitment to technology in the manufacturing sector.

With such changes in the factors that have driven the economic growth thus far, it is crystal clear that without fundamental reform the economy will not be able to continue to grow as rapidly as in the past.

Recent Economic Growth Policy

A growth policy must be geared toward activating investment to stimulate the previously described leading growth factors. In addition to paying attention to the supply side, the government should also focus on resolving difficulties with the domestic demand and exports.

We sometimes see clashes between those who say that priority should be given to the demand side and those who say that more emphasis should be placed on supply side. However, in Korea's case, which still has little impact on the global economy, the growth policy should focus on the supply side.

As the economic growth rate declined along with the disappearance of favorable external conditions after 1988, the government got worried about this trend and started to take active growth-oriented measures.

Among these measures, particular importance is attached to the economic stimulation of April 4, 1990, and the (March 14, 1990) measure to enhance competitiveness in the manufacturing sector. The economic stimulation package of April 1990 entailed postponing the promised real name financial transaction system to stir up the sagging investment climate among corporations and guide the 1 percent drop in interest rates in the second phase of the financial liberalization program. The measure required that the government also add 1 trillion won to the special equipment facility fund and increase assistance for the technology development fund for companies. Moreover, to control the land speculation, it regulated the funds of nonbanks involved in land acquisition and put greater emphasis on building houses for low- and middle-income people.

Meanwhile, the measures implemented in March 1991 to enhance the competitiveness of the manufacturing sector called for providing 1,500 billion won for investment in production technology development through 1995. Moreover, the government decided to improve financial management to revive the stagnating manufacturing sector. To that end, it came up with plans to improve screening for financing to prevent funds from flowing into the nonmanufacturing and consumption-oriented sectors. The government also augmented the fund for assisting small companies with the purchase of domestic machinery (3,800 billion dollars) and made credit control for large companies more flexible. Additionally, to nurture technical personnel, it instructed universities and junior colleges to train more science majors and sought to expand investment in social or overhead capital infrastructure and land for industrial use.

When we look at the preceding two measures taken by the government to boost growth, I notice that the first one (April 1990) focused on achieving tangible, short-term growth of the economy, expanding trade financing, providing the special facility fund, and encouraging the reduction of interest rates. The more basic measure to improve the competitiveness of the manufacturing industries was not introduced until more than a year later. This measure, enacted in March 1991 to enhance the competitiveness of the manufacturing industries, took Korea one step closer to the fundamental resolution of its problems. It was also an indication that the growth policy was back. Moreover, the measure to enhance the government showed a strong commitment to implement this very comprehensive measure. The measure has achieved effective results in reviving exports.

I personally feel that our growth policy failed in its diagnosis of problems and that the prescription did not prove effective. Since the government considered slowing the economy during the 1989–1990 period, a temporary phenomenon following boom years, it implemented short-term, tangible results-oriented stimulation measures.

However, the economy began to undergo fundamental changes in its growth factors before the 1986–1988 economic boom. Overwhelmed by success during this period, Korea delayed infusing fresh blood into the growth factors of the economy.

There is a saying that, if economists fail to distinguish between structural and transitional problems, they cannot prescribe the correct cure for problems. Likewise, it is only natural that if policy makers fail to distinguish the structural change in an economy from its temporary ups and downs, they can make huge mistakes.

STIMULATION OF THE ECONOMY AND INVESTMENT POLICY

The British Disease and the Korean Disease

As the loss of vigor in the economies of advanced countries began to evolve into a structural and long-term trend, the phrase *the disease of advanced countries* gained wide circulation. In particular, Britain, which had shown the most severe symptoms of this disease, began to be referred to as the best representative of the advanced countries with the disease.

Although it is difficult to explain the term, the *British disease* it would be safe to say that it was an apt description of the state of the British economy when people were more interested in pursuing their own interests than working for the public good. The economy was troubled by low growth and high prices, and the trade deficit had become chronic. Before the Second World War, Britain was the greatest economic power. The British boasted that "the sun would never set on their empire." However, it suffered from this chronic disease for the following reasons.

First, frequent labor disputes stirred up by the powerful labor unions had a negative impact on productivity. British labor unions have a long tradition. Since they followed the closed-shop rule, they had a strong influence on their members. On the strength of such powerful organization, they wielded enormous influence on industry and politics. Using such vast power, they incessantly staged disputes and struck. In response to this the British government maintained a noninterventionist policy. The labor disputes, thus, took a toll on production.

Second, as the Labour Party strengthened its quasi-socialistic economic policy, the nonmarket sector, represented by public service such as social security, grew rapidly. After the Labour Party took over, it established a comprehensive social security system based on the famous Beveridge Report. As the nationalization of major industries bloated the nonmarket sector, the economy lost vigor and the people's work ethic was damaged. Third, frequent transfers of power created a lack of consistency in government policy. Change in government between the Labour and the Conservative parties caused a shift in policy lines too often, which made it difficult to implement policies such as industrial restructuring that required long-term attention. In addition, the lack of effort by the bloated administration to reorganize itself, coupled with the erosion of the people's work ethic, sapped the economy of its vitality.

Considering that the main characteristics of the British disease are high prices, a trade deficit, and a fading commitment to work, it seems clear that our economy is showing symptoms similar to those of the British disease. The rising specter of chronic low growth because of the lack of investment, high prices, a trade deficit, and the fading enterprising spirit are sapping economic vitality. Therefore, although it would be difficult to say definitely that these economic phenomena are symptoms of the "Korean disease," it would be hard to dismiss such phenomena. It is true that the difficulties the Korean economy is experiencing are different from those of the British economy in many respects.

A climate of investment lethargy and lack of productivity growth because of severe labor disputes, a fading work ethic, frequent policy changes, instability in the political arena, and a loss of confidence in growth should be enough to convince anyone that these are truly symptoms of an unhealthy economy. In fact, such trends result in low growth, high prices, and a trade deficit.

Thatcherism and the Korean Economy

In this respect, a study of the Thatcherism that healed the British disease would provide insight to revive the vitality of Korea's own economy. Of course, there are many vociferous critics of the economic accomplishments of Thatcherism. Further, those economic accomplishments have not yet been fully appraised. Nevertheless, it is generally recognized that Thatcherism was very successful.

After taking office in May 1979, Thatcher implemented a hands-on economic policy, "Thatcherism," to resolve the British economy's structural problems and restore its sagging industrial competitiveness. The basic principles were the realization of a small, but powerful government, the maintenance of a consistent, uncompromising attitude on the principles, and the inculcation of a "can-do spirit" in the British people.

Now, let us look more closely at the policies implemented during her years. To cut government spending, subsidies to public enterprises and spending related to social welfare and housing were reduced. The number of civil servants was cut. About twenty public enterprises, including British Airways and British Petroleum, were privatized. Various government regulations were either abolished or relaxed; foreign exchange controls and the stock exchange were reformed.

Each year when the budget proposal for the new fiscal year was announced, a medium- to long-range fiscal strategy, which established goals to restrain the rate of increase in the reserve base and in the fiscal budget deficit for the next three years, was also bared and implemented. Open market operations were actively employed as a means to restrain currency expansion. Moreover, corporate and individual income taxes were lowered while indirect taxes were increased to promote investment and encourage people to work hard. In 1982, the British corporate tax rate was 52 percent, the highest in Europe, but it dropped to 35 percent, the lowest level in Europe, after 1985. The income tax rate was also gradually lowered from 33 percent to 25 percent during the same period. In addition, the employment law and the trade union law were revised to set limits on strikes, abolish the closed-shop rule, and reduce immunity for unionists. By so doing, the government could crack down on the trade unions and encourage them to adjust their role in the economy.

A great deal can be learned from these basic principles of Thatcherism and the major policies implemented according to it. In establishing economic policies in the future, Korea needs to evaluate these things carefully. In assessing these policies, special attention should be paid to how Britain approached fiscal spending cuts. Although Korea does not have as enormous a fiscal deficit as Britain did, Korean government spending, which consists mostly of consumption-oriented expenditures, has recently been increasing at an alarming rate. In 1991, the fiscal deficit soared to 2 trillion won. As long as the government shows no firm commitment to restraining its spending and makes no effective use of resources based on clearly established priorities, the soaring fiscal deficit will continue to have a huge negative impact on the private sector economy. Considering that fiscal spending will increase to make good on campaign pledges, the government will need to make a greater effort to become a smaller but more efficient and powerful organization.

Another point involves the management of medium to long-range plans. Thatcher's government presented targets for restraining the growth of the money supply and fiscal spending for the following three years, when it announced budget proposals for each new fiscal year. In so doing, it not only enhanced people's confidence in the government's economic policy, but also ensured that enterprises and people could trust and follow the government's policies because they got feedback on its performance.

In Korea's case, the economic development plan has been established every five years. To implement the plan, an economic management plan is drawn up and carried out annually. Unfortunately, policy makers take over. For that reason, it is difficult to know what the specific goals are and how much progress has been made toward achieving those goals. Therefore, Korea needs to set up concrete long-term policy goals in its economic policy. Furthermore, it would be desirable to consider introducing a two to three year medium-term economic management plan that would facilitate the alignment of vision and reality.

Curing the Korean Disease and Investment Policy

To cure the Korean disease, it is most important to heighten people's awareness of overall government policy, just as Thatcher's government did, and at the same time stimulate the economy by restoring a positive investment attitude.

Investment is often compared to an artery or scale of growth; that is, the amount of investment affects the growth rate. The course and characteristics of investment determine the speed and durability of growth. Investment increases value-added production immediately by stimulating demand for, say, machinery. What is more important, however, is that it has the long-term effect of increasing future income by enlarging supply capacity by facility expansion.

Another important aspect of investment is its multiplying effect; investment results in income, which in turn results in more investment. Through this repetitive process, an initial investment can create income several times greater than the original amount. These characteristics of investment prompt people to invest to reap yields several times greater than the original investment, rather than apportion the small original sum.

The reason that the Korean economy has been able to stage such a model economic performance—nearly 10 percent growth a year—despite various difficulties is that it continued to reinvest nearly 30 percent of its GNP. Its overall economic conditions were not as stable and conducive to investment as in advanced countries. Korea did not have sufficient funds to invest. What drove this continued investment? Korea's entrepreneurs were determined to grow, willing to take risks and make aggressive investments in the future.

Risk is inherent in investment since it involves a decision aimed at achieving unpredictable future profits. Therefore, without determination, you cannot invest. Koreans are all aware that, when they invested in the heavy and chemical industries and when they invested in high-tech industries like semiconductors, there was a deep concern. Many objected to these investments on the grounds that such huge outlays would involve too many risks. Investment in the semiconductor industry drew the strongest objection not only because of the uncertainty of demand and the lack of technological development in the sector but also because of the short life cycle of semiconductor products.

Nevertheless, the government and enterprises pushed ahead with the investment. This reflected their unique enterprising spirit and determination to grow. Thus, the heavy industry and chemical industry sector, having accounted for a mere 40 percent in the early 1970s, has now risen to beyond 60 percent in the beginning of 1990s and to 70 percent as of 1994, as a result of the transition to technology-intensive industries. Moreover, semiconductors have emerged as the hottest export item. They accounted for 30 percent of total exports in the electronics field.

Since uncertainty is inherent in investment, there is always a chance for failure. We had our share of such trial and error in the investment in the heavy industry and chemical industry sector. However, if one does not invest for fear of making mistakes, then the future will not be bright.

In that respect, it is a problem that Korean investment, the engine of our economic growth for the past few decades, is not as vigorous as it was in the past. Research on equipment facility investment in Korean industry, done by the Korea Development Bank, shows that the rate of increase in private sector equipment investment has continued to decline from 25.2 percent in 1990 to 21.0 percent in 1991 and further to 6.8 percent in 1993. Particularly, in the manufacturing sector, the rate of increase has declined from 21.6 percent in 1990 to 15.2 percent in 1991 and further to 2.5 percent in 1993—causing serious concern over the hollowing out of industry.

Quantitative decreases in investment aside, there is much room for improvement in the structural aspects of Korea's investment pattern. Many analysts feel that the difficulties Korea's economy has faced since the Seoul Olympic Games are because not enough investment was made in quality, as opposed to quantity, during the heady period 1986–1988. In fact, investment in R&D and efficiency measures were neglected; focus was on facility expansion. Hence, as external conditions deteriorated that affected our exports, the economy began to face hard times. Korea's problems were aggravated by the fact that, instead of concentrating on building production facilities for new products and investing in rationalization to overcome the external challenges, it responded by simply expanding facilities targeted for domestic demand.

Accordingly, future investment policy should focus, first, on maintaining a reliable policy and implementing consistent investment promotion. Second, it should be directed toward increasing tax benefits to assist long-term structural adjustment of enterprises and help them seize investment opportunities. At the same time, efforts should be made to encourage a change in investment patterns so that they can become more quality oriented. Third, to revive the risk-taking, bold investment pattern of the past, the ambitious, enterprising spirit should be rekindled. It is also important to create an environment in which economic policy will be given precedence over other policies and in which the government, enterprises and the people can cooperate to ensure stable social development. Although it is important to expand investment incentives, it is much more important to restore a healthy investment climate for entrepreneurs. In other words, just as the fear of inflation is a major stumbling block to economic stability, so does the continuation of economic growth rest on the attitude toward investment among business people.

THE PURSUIT OF ECONOMIC STABILITY

The Aftereffects of Accelerated Growth

One of the most notable phenomena in the Korean economy since 1988 has been the decline in the economic growth rate. The economy, which had grown at an average annual rate of 12 percent between 1986 and 1988, slowed drastically to 6.9 percent.

The psychological effect of the economic slowdown was tremendous because it followed such a spectacular growth period. However, from an economic perspective, it was not such a startling fact. The business cycle is a series of peaks and valleys. Therefore, high growth is naturally followed by sluggish business activity. It was asking too much to expect the economy to continue to perform so well. Real household income rose more than 50 percent, registering an annual average growth rate of more than 12 percent, for three consecutive years, 1986–1988.

Therefore, in response to the movement of the economy, Korea implemented a stabilization policy after growing more than 10 percent for three years running. In every era and society, economic stabilization measures such as a tight monetary policy and the strengthening of aggregate demand control are not popular with people. It was particularly difficult for Koreans, who had experienced continued high growth since the 1960s, to endure the pain caused by the sudden implementation of an economic stabilization measure. Therefore, as business circles began to clamor for the release of more money, the government discarded the unpopular stabilization policy and opted for a growth-oriented policy.

As the priority shifted toward growth, an economic stimulus package was launched. What was the result? As is known, the remedy proved worse than the disease. Economic problems are, by nature, divided largely into two groups, structural and temporary, due to the business cycle. Thus, problems in Korea's economy were aggravated because our government paid much more attention to treating visible, outward phenomena than to attacking the deeply rooted fundamental structural problems.

Growth or Stability

Stability and growth are equally important economic policy objectives. Neither can be forsaken nor chosen easily at the expense of the other. However, when stability is emphasized, growth slows. On the contrary, when growth is put before stability, stability becomes hard to maintain. The expression "chasing two hares" aptly describes the situation.

At the same time, the complementary nature of stability and growth cannot be ignored. For example, to sustain continued growth, it is necessary to maintain a high rate of investment, which in turn needs hefty domestic savings. In this case, hefty domestic savings can be accomplished if the real interest rate on savings is guaranteed by economic stability. That is why growth and stability are said to have a complementary relationship. Furthermore, when the economy is unstable, it can hurt domestic savings, which can interfere with the development of investment resources. It can also reduce export competitiveness, thereby eroding the growth base of our economy. Moreover, an unstable economy can lead to land speculation, which can distort the order of the entire economy. These conditions can lead to aggravated gaps in income distribution that can give rise to social discontent, which will, in turn, distort the growth structure of the economy and dampen the zeal for growth.

In this respect, we can say that stability is a necessary condition for economic development. However, since economic stability alone cannot bring economic development, economic stability alone is not sufficient for economic development.

The policy to achieve stability, a necessary condition for growth, can be manifest in various ways depending on the stage and conditions of economic development in the nation. However, the stabilization policy should first and foremost aim at radically removing factors that interfere with stability. At the same time it should maximize the advantages of a market economy. Moreover, comprehensive economic management should be strengthened to eradicate those factors that interfere with stability and make the most of the increasing free market liberalization of the economy.

Factors Interfering with Stability

What causes inflation? Theories of inflation say that it is caused largely by excess demand, excess monetary supply, steep production cost increases, monopoly pricing, and imported inflation. Demand-pull inflation results from demand exceeding supply. Thus, price rises caused by excessive consumption would fall into this category. Cost-push is the result of factor cost increases on the supply side pushing up consumer prices. For example, a rise in product costs caused by an increase in manufacturing costs that are further driven up by wage hikes is a good example of cost-push inflation.

In such a case, if the wage increase is matched by an improvement in productivity, the result would not be higher costs and hence would not lead to inflation. However, if labor unions demand too much of a wage increase and the wage hike outstrips the rise in productivity, there will be higher product prices. This would raise commodity prices, which would again result in wage hikes, perpetuating the vicious cycle. From the macroeconomic perspective, wage hikes and price increases are doomed to rise, trapped in a neverending spiral.

Inflation caused by an excess money supply is explained by monetarists through the formula $PT = MV$. Let us suppose the velocity (V) of currency in circulation is constant over the short term. In this case, if more currency (M) is supplied than is considered to be the optimum level of transaction (T), prices (P) will rise, showing that the price and monetary flow are in direct proportion to each other.

In addition, when an enterprise that has a monopoly arbitrarily raises the price of its products to increase profits, it can cause inflation. Also, such overseas factors as increases in the prices of imported raw materials and foreign exchange inflow can cause inflation.

The unstable prices in the Korean economy in the late 1980s cannot be explained by any one particular alone. Rather, it resulted from a combination of factors. The major factors are described next. First and foremost was excessive spending. When the 1988 Summer Olympic Games hosted by Seoul ended as a great success, Koreans were proud of their achievements. This euphoria translated into greater spending. Also, the rise in disposable income stemming from wage hikes expanded consumption which again aggravated the inflationary pressure. As can be seen in Table 3.1, the rate of increase in consumption, which was less than 10 percent in 1986, rose dramatically to 15 to 20 percent after that.

The second factor was the impact on other sectors of the expansion in construction investment. The rapid increase in construction in newly developed cities, for example, resulted in a shortage of construction materials. This led to higher prices for those items and, combined with

Table 3.1.
Consumption Expenditure Trends

	1987	*1988*	*1989*	*1990*	*1991*	*1992*
Individual Income	21.4	21.0	33.8	19.2	19.4	21.6
Rate of Increase in Consumption	14.5	16.8	26.7	15.7	19.9	15.8
Expenditures (Food)	11.9	14.7	17.6	15.6	17.6	10.5
Consumer Prices	3.0	7.1	5.7	8.6	9.3	6.2

Source: Bank of Korea, *Research Statistics Monthly* (June 1992).

the increase in construction workers' wages, touched off a chain reaction in price hikes.

The third factor was the sharp rise in the price of real estate. Sharp increases in real estate prices not only encouraged excessive spending on the part of landowners, but also lowered the relative value of other properties. Furthermore, this led to higher rents, which increased the cost burden for enterprises. This became one of the major factors behind inflation of the late 1980s.

The fourth factor was the expansion of government fiscal spending and the currency. The government expenditure has recently shown a growth rate of more than 20 percent, much higher than 1985's 8.4 percent. Structurally, although in the past a large fiscal surplus could absorb an excessive money supply, the fiscal surplus started to decline severely since 1989. Finally, the surplus was reversed into a deficit of US$1 billion in 1992. Moreover, although M_2, a broader definition of money supply that includes savings accounts, maintained a relatively stable growth rate, the rate of increase in financial loans, subject to market fluidity, showed a dramatic increase from 18 percent in 1988 to 26 percent after 1989 (Table 3.2). These trends could be interpreted as a sign of the government's slackening resolve for a tight monetary policy. As a result, there was a destabilization of prices.

Stabilization Policy Directions

Despite the Korean government's policy efforts, it failed to stabilize the economy. The major reasons for the failure and points to be emphasized in the future policy directions are described here.

First, the Korean government did not stick to its austerity policies. As I said before in discussing increases in government expenditure and

Table 3.2.
Financial Expenditure and Increase in Financial Loans

	1988	1989	1990	1991	1992
Expenditures (%)	21.9	33.0	19.3	22.9	14.5
Financial Loans (%)	18.3	26.7	26.7	25.5	20.5
M_2 (%)	18.8	18.4	21.2	18.6	18.4
Fiscal Account (10 billion won)	269.8	44.4	75.5	-170.0	-7.0

Source: Bank of Korea, *Monthly Bulletin* (June 1993).

policy loans, the government did not stick to its tight-money policies, which caused an increase in circulating currency. Without forcefully executing policies, "a primary concern in the establishment of any economic stabilization program," the government's diligent efforts set in motion only nonessential policies that had little effect. No economic stabilization policy is received well by the public. That is why it takes courage and perseverance for a government to implement such policies. In Korea, however, the government failed in the management of aggregate demand, the basis of price stabilization. The government could have served its own good if it had held firmly to its austerity policies for government budgets and finance.

A successful tight-money policy requires policy makers' commitment and consistent attention to follow through, as was done in Britain. Hence, the government should provide the general public with guidelines on austerity policies and indicators and encourage the public to follow them. The government should lead by adhering to the guidelines, thus, building the public's confidence in the government's policies.

Second, the government did not evaluate in-depth the impact of other policies on the austerity policy. For example, the government should have considered all the angles when it implemented policies to boost the economy and build 2 million new housing units. It should have implemented those policies in keeping with the foundation of austerity measures. When major projects such as building 2 million housing units in suburban Seoul, developing the West Sea region, and extending the subway were done simultaneously, they destabilized the then-stable economy.

Therefore, in the future, policy considerations should include a thorough review of the impact of any individual policy on other policies. By so doing, policy makers can intensify the efforts to carry out all policies in line with a major policy direction, in this case, stabilization of the economy. In other words, the government should take a close look at any large scale public works projects to set priorities. Each project should be implemented according to its priority. When two or more large-scale construction projects are started at the same time, the government should pool its collective wisdom to control the duration and cost in order to minimize the negative impact of such projects on the overall economy.

Third, the government should curb its tendency to implement policies without foresight. Because prices seldom go down naturally after going up, it is difficult to lower prices artificially. On the other hand, the government can cope with inflationary factors prior to implementing stabilization policies by setting forth policies to regulate price cartels and establish a fair trade system.

Fourth, noting that inflation is often caused by psychological factors, the government should make every effort to put to rest public concerns and win the confidence about stabilization of the people. Once the presidential election was over at the end of 1992, the stabilization of the Korean economy became a major popular concern. Consequently, the government should put economic stabilization at the top of its list and follow-up with consistent policies.

INDUSTRIAL POLICIES AMID STRUCTURAL CHANGES

What Is an Industrial Policy?

Industrial policies are among the most important economic policies a nation has. Growth strategies and stabilization policies center around gross economic indices, industrial policies are categorized as macroeconomic policies. Hence, the private sector feels the direct effects of industrial policies. To what extent government should intervene and on what standards has long been a source of controversy.

In the United States and Britain, where the free-market economy is considered the ultimate, industrial policy itself does not exist in concept because the governments of those nations do not believe in the efficiency of government intervention.

In contrast, Germany, whose industrialization began much later than in other advanced nations, and Japan, whose top priority was reviving its industry after the devastating defeat in the Second World War, have well-organized industrialization strategies and policies. In developing countries like Korea, governments regard industrialization policy as an integral part of the general economic policy.

Academics are split over the content of industrial policy. Some feel that industrial policy should cover the promotion of promising industries, the restructuring of declining industries, and the maximization of efficiency of industrial organizations. When the actual implementation of industrial policies is considered, however, policies can also be broken down into those for strengthening the industrial base, promoting specific industries, making industries more efficient, industrial restructuring, and reorganizing the industrial order. Industrial policy measures include taxation, policy loans, government subsidies, regulation of trade and new market entries, authorization of importable goods, quota systems, and indirect restrictive measures. Other measures are employed as well.

Korea's Industrialization Policy—A Brief History

In the early stages of Korea's industrialization, the Korean government's emphasis was mainly on strengthening the industrial base and on chosen industries. In the late 1960s and early 1970s, those strategies translated into selective promotional regimes, such as the Industries Promotion Law or Industries Support Law, designed to advance the shipbuilding, machinery, electronics, iron and steel, petrochemical, and nonferrous metal industries.

In the 1980s, policy priority was placed on revamping Korea's industrial structure. The government, for example, tried to identify and correct cases of overlapping investment in the heavy and chemical industries (HCIs), to make more efficient the shipping and overseas construction sectors that were suffering from structural maladies, and to bail out insolvent companies.

In 1986, when the Industry Development Act went into effect, the government-led development strategy gave way to a private-sector-led strategy. The government adopted a generalized, functional industry support system in favor of a strategy of promoting specially designated industries. By dividing sectors into two categories, "one for those needing strengthening in international competitiveness and the other for those having totally lost international competitiveness," the Korean government laid the foundation for overall industrialization strategies.

However, from the late 1980s until recently, the government's policies seemed to be set back to the selective industry support strategy. Expanded pecuniary and nonpecuniary support to specific sectors— footwear, textile industries, and so forth—is indicative of the government's return to the earlier strategy. Some even contend that the government should abandon its strategy of private-sector-led economic development and go back to a government-led development strategy.

Such an argument was presented in the form of the new industrialization policy. This raised much controversy.

THE NEW INDUSTRIAL POLICY

The term, new industrial policy (NIP), first attracted public attention in January 1992, when the then deputy prime minister Choi Kak Kyu mentioned it in a speech to the Korea Efficiency Association. In March of the same year, the NIP was widely discussed when a major vernacular daily newspaper carried an article on the NIP. The NIP calls for the government to proceed with industrial policy from a different perspective to invigorate corporate Korea and enhance Korea's international competitiveness. Eight tasks are presented in the NIP:

1. Clear up bad loans and improve the government regulations of banks.

2. Reduce the amount of mutual payment guarantees on loans.

3. Provide long-term industrial loans.

4. Improve the debt-to-equity ratio of domestic industries.

5. Promote technological development.

6. Strengthen cooperation between large firms and components-producing small and medium-sized firms.

7. Reestablish the government's role in setting industrial policy.

8. Upgrade the nation's industrial structure to that of advanced nations.

At the moment, it remains to be seen whether anything new was added by reporters. It also is not known whether the government actually withdrew the policy after running into adamant opposition from business circles. What is important is that such a new policy was discussed.

Industrial Policies During the Transitional Period

Korean industries currently face many challenges: a lack of technological prowess in product design and core technologies; a heavy dependence on imported intermediate goods and components, that is, mainly for simple assembly of finished products; lack of a flexible manufacturing system (FMS) to meet the individual, diversified demands of consumers; an insufficient complementary relationship between big firms and small and medium companies; and lack of an industrial infrastructure. Consequently, future industrial policy should emphasize reviving the manufacturing sector by immediately addressing fundamental challenges. To that end, four suggestions follow.

First, the government's industry backup system needs to underscore the provision of a general incentive system (GIS) that would strengthen overall industrial competitiveness and improve quality. The GIS is needed, because with an expanded domestic economy, an effective economic development policy is unlikely to emerge if the economic planning is done by government officials with limited information and personnel. In other words, the past policy of selective industry promotion will not be effective in a highly industrialized future society because it presupposes that the government, as a decision maker, has adequate information and knowledge on any given field. Second, the government's policy support of industry should be temporary. The degree of government protection of industry, likewise, should be reduced gradually. By so doing, domestic industries will fare better after government protection is removed. Third, declining industries should be removed from the government's promotion list. The government is unwise to channel financial support and policy efforts to comparatively weak industries, because it cannot efficiently redirect its efforts and resources to competitive industries and the reorganization of declining sectors. Fourth, it is better to employ the GIS than a direct support system. This suggests that industrial policy should focus on addressing long-term and structural challenges with inducement measures rather than following after myopic and cosmetic results. The GIS should be at the heart of the government's support policy. Tax incentives are more desirable than direct support measures such as subsidies, price supports, and policy loans. I would like to emphasize that the government should exert greater effort to present the public with a forecast of the future direction and objectives of the Korean economy. Only when the government predicts can the various industries come up with adequate investment plans and thus develop in harmony.

TRADE POLICIES IN THE GLOBAL AGE

Korea's Foreign Trade Structure and Trade Policies

Technology-poor Korean industry, early on, could not adequately develop the components and parts sectors. Therefore, it developed mainly with revenue from the assembly industry, which processes or assembles imported intermediate goods. Furthermore, it was nearly impossible to spur development of technology-intensive capital goods instead of consumer goods. Accordingly, Korea imported intermediate and capital goods and exported consumer and simple assembled goods, which are now losing their international competitiveness because other developing countries are rapidly outpacing them. The production of simple assembled goods does not require high technology and employs low-wage, skilled workers, who are readily available in other developing countries. Furthermore, advanced nations with trade deficits are imposing restrictions on imports of consumer goods, making the promotion of Korean exports more difficult. Korea has no alternative but to import an increasing number of components and raw materials in proportion to its incremental exports because the nation depends heavily on them. Korea is also dependent on imported capital goods because it has yet to develop adequate technology to produce its own capital goods. Against this backdrop, the government is accelerating the opening of the domestic market. Currently, Korea imports capital and intermediate goods and consumer goods.

In such a climate, Korea has faced sluggish exports and a rise in imports. The balance of trade showed a deficit. The government presented various trade policies and strategies to deal with the situation. Between 1988 and 1990, the government tentatively implemented general measures such as simplifying customs clearance procedures. In 1991, as the trade deficit rose, however, it enacted full-fledged policies and strategies to strengthen the international competitiveness of the domestic industry, to promote exports, to reduce imports, and to improve the trade balance. Major policies, then, included tax breaks on market exploration expenses, easing of restrictions on currency transfer, promotion of capital goods industries, and the introduction of promissory notes for trade. The measures implemented may have contributed to promoting exports, but they did not encourage domestic firms to enhance their competitive edge or overhaul the overall industrial structure. Accordingly, future trade policies should be implemented gradually and systematically to invigorate the nation's total trade sector, not simply to concentrate on short-term trade growth. In that respect, the future course of trade policy should address the points described in the following paragraphs.

First, individual trade policies should be implemented in harmony with the macroeconomic management. For, only when a nation's economy is supported by stabilized foreign exchange, interest rates, and sound labor-management relations can the nation's exports be expected to grow. Therefore, the government should push hard for efficient management and implementation of macroeconomic policies.

∿ Second, the government should strive to improve the trade environment by deregulation. The nation's economic planners should work for policies to lower overhead costs for exports and remove barriers to export. To that end, they should accelerate the liberalization of foreign exchange rate, simplify the import-export process, and improve customs clearance procedures.

⸮ Third, policy makers should seek ways to strengthen the nation's export base. Additional effort is needed to determine, in advance, the export restrictions. Export infrastructure, ports and the forwarding system, require regular upgrading. The planners, therefore, should provide exporters with policy guidelines. A good example of a potential problem for exporters is environmental degradation. Environmental problems are sure to have an impact on Korea's exporters. To cope with the global concern for environmental conservation, energy-saving and environment-friendly products deserve attention from exporters and the government. The government should provide indirect incentives to producers of such goods. As the global movement is toward formation of regional trade blocs, the government should formulate trade policies conducive to securing ground for Korea.

⸜ Fourth, the government should provide more incentives for general trading companies. Therefore, the emphasis should be on gathering and using information. However, a manufacturer might be overextended if forced to produce goods and gather information at the same time. Hence, the government should use the extensive networks and integrated information systems that have been built by general trading companies. In particular, prompt use of existing systems is essential because Japanese general trading companies with powerful networks and capital are moving into the Korean market. To successfully deal with these developments, the government ought to strive to promote and strengthen local general trading firms.

Korea's International Trade Imbalance

The nation's trade imbalance has emerged as a grave concern. The government's line, however, has been that a trade surplus for Korea would better its chances of being recognized as an advanced nation, whereas a trade deficit would hamper its efforts. That may explain why many Koreans are apprehensive about the size of the current trade deficit.

It is true that a trade surplus is more beneficial to a nation than a trade deficit. However, trade deficits are not a major concern for an economy. The principal issue here should be ascertaining whether the trade deficit will snowball because of an unpredictable future export environment or whether the deficit is a temporary, "buffering" phenomenon that will be followed by balanced trade.

Accordingly, it is necessary to compare import and export elasticity to the GNP; that is, how much influence imports and exports have on GNP. As Table 3.3. indicates, not much fluctuation is found in the import elasticity to the GNP. The nation was in a boom period of low oil prices, a low dollar, and a low international interest rate. In summary, this means Korea's imports grew as the nation's GNP moved up.

Table 3.3.
Import/Export Elasticity Relative to Korea's GNP

	1986–1988	1989–1993
Export Elasticity	1.01	0.68
Import Elasticity	0.81	0.97

Source: Bank of Korea, monthly economic statistics.

To reverse such a trend, short-term, stopgap policies will not work. For Korea to have a continued trade surplus the elasticity of export to GNP has to be improved to 1 or more even though the current rigid import structure cannot easily be shaken. Thus, Korea's economic structure ought to emulate that of an advanced nation, in which exports grow faster than the GNP.

The first task of the government to ease the trade imbalance should be to curb imports and promote exports. Along with that, the government should provide incentives to export sectors that are leading the GNP growth. In the middle- to long-term perspective, the government should improve Korea's import structure by decreasing imports of capital and industrial goods in the related sectors.

Trade Policies in the Global Village

> "Merchants have no country. The mere spot they stand on does not constitute so strong an attachment as that from which they draw their gains."
>
> (Thomas Jefferson 1814)

Going into the last half of 1980s, the Korean economic planner stepped up market opening and globalization efforts. *Globalization* is no longer a strange word to Koreans. Korea is now well on its way to "globalization." The government has been gradually opening domestic foreign exchange and capital markets. Opening the service sector to foreign competition has been hastened by the successful conclusion of the Uruguay Round (UR) negotiations on financial market opening.

Korean firms are rapidly moving into foreign markets, which has added momentum to the economic globalization of the nation. Naturally, companies that have been heavily dependent on the government support find that they need to upgrade to stay competitive. Further, domestic concerns must become more competitive in both domestic and foreign markets. Consequently, it is time to transform the public's and policy makers' attitudes to cope with these developments.

Internationalization or domestic market opening has the following implications. First, Korean industrialists must realize that Korea's trading partners will want to expand reciprocity. In other words, Korea should open its market wider if it wants its trading partners to open their markets. Korea should respond in proportion to the benefits it has gained through international trade. Just as Korean companies can operate in other nations, so should they let other nations' firms in on equal terms.

Second, the fair trade principle will be applied to Korea. The principle is applied to Korea when advanced nations including the United States put pressure on Korea to open its markets and restrict Korean exports. Trading partners do not take into consideration Korea's flimsy technological base, farmers, sluggish economy, or trade deficit. What they want is transparent trade practices. They even consider a "Buy Korean" drive and anticonsumption campaigns in the domestic markets unfair trade practices.

It is important to realize that, with markets open to competition, foreign companies will enter not only major industrial sectors but also the service sectors, notably, distribution and banking. In addition to exporting goods, Korea's trading partners are setting up business facilities in Korea. Today's definition of international trade includes exchange of goods as well as services. In the past only finished goods were considered. Production and supply systems are included today, whereas in the past only forwarding goods to customers was regarded as international trade. The problem is that the government must apply nondiscriminatory national treatment to foreign companies that run businesses in Korea.

Coping with Opening the Domestic Market

An interesting cartoon in the newspaper dealt with domestic market opening. It said, "YS stands for Kim Yong Sam, DJ for Kim Dae Jung, and JP for Kim Jong Pil. Who in the world is Mr. UR?" The Uruguay Round of the General Agreement on Tariffs and Trade (GATT), one of the most pending trade issues of the nation, was so poorly publicized that some Koreans thought *UR* was someone's name.

How have Koreans approached the question of an open domestic market? Koreans have felt that protecting their market to the best of their ability to gain time and prepare adequately for an open market is best for Korea. The government has tried to do so, accordingly.

Korea's trading partners, asking for further market opening based on the principles of fair trade and reciprocity, are increasingly annoyed by the lukewarm response from the Korean government. They have tried various means to open Korea's market, including threats of discriminatory treatment of Korean exports and retaliatory measures. This demonstrates the difference in points of view of Korea and its trading partners on open markets. The Korean government will find itself in trouble if it simply tries to stall without presenting them with a market opening schedule. Therefore, the government should opt for gradual market opening schemes to gain enough time to ready domestic industries for the expanded market opening.

There is encouraging news from the electronics sectors. Samsung Electronics and Lucky-Goldstar, both electronics giants, have agreed to share technology patent rights. The agreement was reached largely because the two firms were facing extremely tough competition in overseas markets and because foreign electronics products, particularly from Japan, are moving full-scale into the Korean market.

Another problem with government's policies and strategies is that they are kneejerk and nominal. More than any others, trade and commerce policies require thorough preparation and consideration of profits and losses. Once a nation's market is open, it is embarrassing and impossible to close it again.

Trade negotiators should strictly balance the pluses and minuses of an agreement because it deals with the actual economic interests of the nation. I recently read an article written by a Korean reporter who covered the news on the EC conference for a single European market. His article clearly showed Korea's minimal negotiating efforts in respect to the integrated EC market, which will have larger potential than the U.S. market. Furthermore, in view of Korea's heavy dependence on the U.S. market, diversification of overseas markets is of utmost importance. Unfortunately, Korea had only one diplomat participating in that important conference to gather materials on the EC single market. The reporter wrote that when he saw the diplomat walking to one of the Japanese delegates to ask for some materials, the reporter did not know what to make of it.

The dual challenge of openness and globalization will be successfully met if Koreans work together. The government, for its part, should realize the importance of building a consensus before going to the trade negotiation table. The people must be determined to discount the negative effects of opening their markets. Nongovernmental organizations will have to come up with fair testing methods to detect, for instance, hazardous chemicals in pesticides and the performance of imported goods.

One thing Koreans should remind themselves of in the processes of market opening and internationalization is that they should take the initiative. When it is necessary for Koreans to speak up, they should do so in the trade negotiation process. Instead of passively following decisions in trade talks, the government should actively take part in trade negotiations, study the barriers imposed by trading partners, and ask for correction. To do that, specialists should be encouraged. At the same time, methods for gathering and analyzing data need to be beefed up. This can be done by producing more experts in specific fields or on specific nations. As the saying "the best defense is a good offense" suggests, Korean industrialists can do themselves a favor by moving into international markets. They should consider exploring new makets and localizing production in response to the global trends toward bloc formation. The best survival strategy in the global village would be to explore overseas markets even more to aggressively make up for the nation's concession to trading partners.

More Rounds Coming

Developing countries expect new trade pressures following the conclusion of the Uruguay Round of the GATT negotiations. These pressures will most likely be in the areas of the environment, external investment, technology, and labor policies.

First, as environmental concerns grow, certain trade restrictions to help solve this problem are being discussed. In the trade agreement on endangered species, restrictions have been developed indifferently. Trade restrictive measures, to prevent developing countries from pursuing export-oriented trade policies without sharing the cost of environmental protection, will be studied as well.

At present, the Organization for Economic Cooperation and Development (OECD) is reviewing this matter by organizing a joint task force between its Trade Council and Environment Council. In addition to this, at the first ministerial conference of environmental affairs held on March 24, 1994, in Vancouver, Canada, some measures for environmental protection were specifically discussed. They were environmental tax and international standards for determining "environmentally safe" products.

In the process of globalization, the correlation between external investment and trade, which previously were treated separately, is deepening. Subsequently, serious reviews of investment regulations in trade are carried out. Multilateral invesment agreements among nations are being gradually concluded with resultant tougher trade rules. Even in the GATT and the Asia-Pacific Economic Cooperation, the settlement of investment agreements is being reviewed.

In the area of technology, the Techno-Round will question restrictions on governments' efforts and promotional measures to enhance corporate technology development. In other words, under the premise that a government's technology policy can influence trade by supporting corporations' R&D directly and indirectly, some restrictive measures should be prepared. In the Uruguay Round negotiation, this matter was partly reviewed. A movement for related restrictions will get stronger in the near future.

Nevertheless, it is questionable how serious the United States is about cutting R&D subsidies because the U.S. government currently supports a number of government-financed R&D projects and is likely to continue to financially support technology and industrial development of U.S. companies.

Finally, there will be a Blue Round that focuses on the abolition of unfair labor conditions. The United States made strenuous efforts to include labor-related restrictive rules in the current GATT regulations as well as include it in the recent Uruguay Round negotiations. It is noteworthy that the United States is trying to prevent Mexico from exporting low-wage, low-price products supported by unfair domestic labor laws and practices by establishing a Labor and Environment Council as a condition for final settlement of the NAFTA. Meanwhile, developing countries argue that labor policies and problems should be handled by the International Labor Organization, not the GATT.

THE CORPORATE FINANCIAL SITUATION AND FINANCIAL POLICY

Loan Function in a National Economy

Loans have several functions in a nation's economy. One is to mobilize capital to fill shortages when an economy is growing. Another is market control. Loans control markets through credit policy in times of inflation or economic recession. Loans use domestic savings to provide financial resources for investment. In policy terms, loans guarantee real interest on savings packages, encourage savings, and attract various financial resources from diverse financial institutions. The market con-

trol function of loans is maintaining economic stabilization by controlling various monetary indices in response to price fluctuations.

Credit policies are implemented to control markets. To that end,
direct and indirect methods are used. Indirect methods include open
market operation and control of the reserve and rediscount rate by the
central bank. Korea lags behind in the development of its financial
markets. Therefore, though indirect methods are employed, they are
not effective. Accordingly, the more effective way to implement credit
policy in Korea has been the use of direct controls such as direct credit
management measures and control of overseas assets. As a nation's
economy matures, indirect credit policies are more efficient. Therefore,
the government should expand financial liberalization and deregulation efforts to turn direct credit control measures into indirect control
policies.

Corporate Korea's Financial Difficulties and the "Marshallian K" Controversy

Employing the aforementioned credit policies to control prices entails
enormous difficulties. The reason that credit policy enactment is hard to
manage is that, when an austerity policy is implemented for economic
stabilization, it may bring about economic recession, because such a
policy can cause financial difficulties of industries. However, if the government effects an expansion policy, it can result in inflation.

A good example is the argument that went on between the then-
finance minister and the chairman of a major firm. The industrialist
argued that the money supply should be increased because the ratio of
currency volume to the GNP was much lower than in advanced
nations. However, the government took a different position, contend-
ing that the money supply was far from small and that the rate could
not be an absolute criterion for total currency volume. The industrialist's argument later was dubbed, the *Marshallian K* argument because to
argue on the basis of the ratio of money stock to GNP was quite similar
to the Cambridge University economists' equation of the quantity theory of money.

Viewed from the standpoint of an economic principle, *Marshallian
K* is not a constant; rather it can vary from nation to nation, taking on
the properties of variants. Accordingly, it is not quite adequate to argue
on the basis of the absolute value of *Marshallian K* that Korea needs a
greater money supply. In the end, the *Marshallian K* argument fizzled
out. It is interesting not from the academic point of view but because it
was one of many assertions that domestic business people made to the
government concerning the necessity of an increased money supply
under a financial crunch.

Why Do Companies Have Difficulty Securing Enough Funds?

Many reasons and dimensions are to be considered in determining why corporations experienced financial difficulties. The bearish stock market made it difficult for companies to find sufficient funds. In other words, with a sluggish stock market, companies found it difficult to mobilize enough funds from the money market. Companies went to banks for funds. With limited funds, such companies could not meet their funding needs.

Another problem was that, with the rapid growth of the service sector, including construction, increased demands for capital from that sector made it difficult for the manufacturing sector to find adequate funds. Such an obvious factor cannot be ignored.

A graver problem was that Korean industry's financial crunch was structural. In other words, the financial difficulties of Korean industry occurred largely because its competitiveness had weakened. For that reason, sales went down and revolving funds decreased. This meant industry's financial troubles could not be cured by increasing the money supply. Neither could the economy in such a situation be revitalized by a greater money supply.

In 1993, for example, the rate of increase in current account profit was dropped to –1.5 percent from 1992's 10.5 percent. This meant that funds accumulation in Korean industry was quite low, and with sluggish sales growth, companies' inventories increased, resulting in a minimal capital turnover ratio. Furthermore, as the price control function of interest rates did not work properly, lenders and borrowers could hardly be matched. When there is a huge difference between real and institutional interest rates, more loans are transacted outside financial institutions. Consequently, even though there seems to have been a sufficient infusion of capital, sectors that needed funds found them difficult to obtain. Korean companies, furthermore, were heavily reliant on outside funds. Firms in the United States and Japan meet most of their funding requirements with the owner's capital. Therefore, the ratio of owner's capital to external funds is 6 to 4 while in Korea it is 4 to 6. As long as the nation's industry has such a high external fund dependency, it will continue to have capital shortages.

Reshuffling the Nation's Financial Industry

Recently, the worldwide trends in banking have been leaning to across-the-border transactions and the globalization of banking. Innovations as automation and banking securities have been picking up speed.

Advanced nations have lost competitiveness in the manufacturing sector. They are asking developing nations to open service sectors including banking, because advanced nations have a competitive edge in those sectors. Thus, an urgent task for the government is to enhance the Korean banking industry's competitiveness. Accordingly, while supporting the real economy, Korea's banking industry ought to adjust to the new banking environment. To do so, it needs to strengthen its competitiveness to become more competitive as an industry.

In that regard, Korea's banking industry should come up with standards to measure the efficiency and growth of the sector in order to carry out a systematic growth strategy. Proper evaluation criteria could vary. These will concern the stabilization of the domestic financial system to establish credit order, restoration of the price control function of interest rates, consideration of users' convenience, and internationalization to cope with the globalization of the banking industry.

In terms of stabilization, Koreans need to ask themselves if their notion of financial stability is based on a vague expectation that the government will try to maintain a stabilized financial system. Accordingly, the government should try to widen public access to external financial information. At the same time, Korean companies need to increase their debt-to-equity ratios. The government needs to prevent the insolvency caused, in the past, by government-regulated financing. It should establish sound bank management with various policies.

Although the government has, so far, liberalized interest rates and deregulated the financial sector to increase the effectiveness of the nation's financial system, those steps were taken to cope with pressure for open markets. The actions were based on principles but had a flimsy philosophical basis. Hence, policy makers need to change their thinking and give more autonomy to domestic banking institutions to strengthen the sector's competitiveness. To accomplish that, the government needs to implement more policies for autonomy and deregulation.

Along with such liberalization efforts, the government should pay more attention to improved customer service and the enactment of international regulations and laws. That way, the nation can successfully deal with changing financial demands.

The revamping of the nation's banking industry should aim at the establishment of domestic credit order. So far, the nation's banking industry has been developing along the lines of division of labor. It follows that, in such cases, rearranging the domestic banking industry to take on additional roles is in order. Therefore, while encouraging the development of the banking industry in a way to elevate the efficiency of the sector to that of well-arranged financial institutions, centered around the original functions of banks, the government should maximize economies of scale and, at the same time, make individual banks competitive. Peripheral and related services as well as mergers among small banks should be promoted as well.

When banks want to enter other sectors of the financial industry, the government should stick to the current principle, allowing them to enter other sectors through the establishment of subsidiaries. However, the planners need to work on and announce as soon as possible the principles and details of how banks can enter other fields of business. Additionally, the government should be aware of possible problems when reciprocity and national treatment are enforced, when the financial market is open, when proceeding with rearranging Korean banks' services, and when offering inducements for mergers to achieve economies of scale. In the United States and Japan, where traditionally a division of labor has been adopted for banking, the governments are pushing for banking reforms to accommodate a universal banking system. Korea should revamp its financial policy toward extended services for the banking industry as quickly as possible.

4

Democratization of the Korean Economy and Implementation of Nord-Politik

POLICY REFORM FOR DEMOCRATIZATION

"The test of a first-rate intelligence is the ability to hold two opposed ideas in mind at the same time and still retain the ability to function."

(F. Scott Fitzgerald 1936)

During the second half of the 1980s, particularly after former president Roh Tae Woo's June 29 declaration that promised a more democratic Korea, the process of democratization picked up speed. During that process, Korea experienced severe growing pains. Defining *economic democratization*, a broad term, is not easy. Academics define it as democratic management and utilization of the economy. This definition encompasses concepts from the abolition and improvement of nondemocratic elements in an economy to improved income distribution.

Until recently the following goals have been argued and discussed in reference to democratization of the economy.

- an efficient market-economy-related system of fair competition
- decentralization of economic resources as exemplified by restrictions on chaebols, the vertically integrated conglomerates that dominate Korean industry.
- redistribution of income
- securing a social welfare system
- liberalization of the banking system
- equal allotment of profit
- narrowing regional economic differences and other such differences.

These issues were dealt with, more or less haphazardly, during the implementation of growth policies.

During the democratization process, an increasing number of people asked for economic reforms such as the concept of public land ownership and the real-name financial transaction system. A new government often swears to implement ambitious reform measures only to back down when it meets adamant opposition from conservatives and people with vested interests. In many cases, reform measures are watered down or abolished for that reason. Therefore, it follows that for successful implementation the need for reform measures should be agreed upon by the reformers and the conservatives.

In this chapter, I will review public ownership of land, the real-name financial transaction system, and income redistribution—all of which were considered reformist policies or policies for democratization of the economy during Korea's transitional period.

Introduction of the Concept of Public Land Ownership

In the last half of the 1980s, policy makers worked on two major reforms: the introduction of the concept of public ownership of land and the real-name financial transaction system. The former is hard to define. Generally, however, it is defined as a restriction on ownership and use of land to better use it for the common good.

The concept was introduced at the period of high land price speculation, which had a negative impact on the economy. During the rapid process of industrialization and urbanization, there was land speculation because an ever-increasing number of people, with more disposable income, needed land. Only a finite amount of land was available, so prices rose fast. The problem with introducing the concept of public land ownership was that government restrictions on land ownership would encroach directly on a citizen's right to own private property, which is at the heart of a democratic capitalist society. In addition to such opposition in principle, some contended that even though introducing the concept might help quell the surge in land speculation, the concept might act as a stumbling block for businesses that need land for factories, which would thereby increase land costs.

The reason the government did introduce the concept in the face of such strong opposition and possible losses was the pressing need to quash heated land speculation, a major crippler of the nation's economy. Furthermore, because there is so little land and it cannot be reproduced, it should be used in a way to guarantee maximum value to all Korean people. Hence, it was argued that introducing public land ownership was inevitable.

That argument rings true considering that even industrialists, who should work hard at productive activities, owned too much land for nonbusiness purposes. Some were involved in the land speculation.

There is a saying among Korean business people that three months after opening a factory a crisis occurs, but if you can hold out for three years, you will succeed. Three years does not mean a three years of expanded sales and increased production; rather it means that in three years the price of the factory site will go up enough to make up for possible losses. The mentality reflected in that saying is indeed surprising. According to a study conducted by the Office of Tax Administration, the proportion of nonbusiness real estate to the total assets in industry is over 35 percent. This signals distorted entrepreneurship.

However, money will be invested in a profit-generating business. Therefore, even though the government calls for healthy entrepreneurship, it cannot stop business people from investing in lucrative areas, in this case, real estate. Therefore, the only way to stop this trend is by removing the cause. This constitutes a reason to turn the concept into law. Nonetheless, government intervention is aimed at guaranteeing private property in the context of a liberal democracy. It definitely does not indicate that the government could opt for a socialist approach of denying private property entirely.

The idea of public land is present in European nations, Taiwan, and other nations, although the extent may vary. Technically, Korea already has a law reflecting the concept. Section 122 of the Constitution states that the government can, as stipulated in the law, restrict and place obligations, if necessary, on the ownership of land to efficiently use the land mass, the foundation of production and livelihood of the people. More specifically, Korea has the 1972 law on the administration of land use, the 1978 law on permission for land transactions, and the law on notification of land purchases and sales. Those laws reflect a broader application of the concept of public land ownership. In 1988, the public land ownership concept was more concretely translated into a law that put a ceiling on the amount of housing land that could be owned by an individual, a law on the monetary contribution to public land development, and a tax law on excessive profits by landholding. Of all the laws mentioned, the three laws implemented in 1988 are closest to the concept of public land ownership.

Of the three laws, the law limiting the size of a housing plot an individual can own was intended to bring about a more equitable distribution of land and stabilize the housing supply. The ceiling on housing plots varied. In the six largest cities in Korea, including Seoul, it was 200 pyung (1 pyung = 3.954 square yds.); in medium-sized cities such as Chuncheon, it was 300 pyung; and in planned areas in small towns and villages, it was 400 pyung. The law on paying contributions from profits made on the sale of land was to prevent land speculation by making the profit-earner contribute a sum of money for use later in its equitable distribution and to more efficiently use land to foster sound growth of the national economy. In other words, when a land developer gets permission or an authorization from the national or local government to build housing or industrial estates and the development causes the land price to rise more than that of other land in the region, he or she is obligated to pay the government 50 percent of the price difference between the purchase and the sale of the land.

The purpose of a tax on excessive profits by landholding is to return the extra profits from idle land, the value of which has increased because of land development projects and other socioeconomic reasons, to the national treasury through taxes to ensure equitable taxation, stable land prices, and effective use of land. The law calls for a landowner to pay 50 percent of extra profits from the assessed increase in the land price every three years. These laws, which reflect the concept of public land ownership, are thought to be effective in that they may be able to curb land speculation. Nonetheless, there is a problematic side as well.

One way to make the three laws more acceptable is to improve the application of a comprehensive land tax and capital gains tax. Some argue that it is not fair to apply the ownership ceiling only to housing areas when actual land speculation is also occurring in forest land. Most hotly debated is the accuracy of the government's listed land prices, which are the basis for taxation of excessive landholdings. Furthermore, public resistance to the second law is strong because taxation should be on projected profits, not on profits made. Some contend that, to avoid taxation on idle land, construction started all at once across the country and contributed to price instability; it undermined efficient land use and disrupted the balanced development of urban areas. Introduction of public land ownership is still in its infancy. The concept is not firmly institutionalized. Hence, various problems could occur in the implementation of the concept. Accordingly, the government should make every effort to correct problems and thereby help the laws reflecting this concept to take hold. The government also should study the feasibility of expanding application of a comprehensive land tax and capital gains tax. Excessive government intervention could undermine the autonomous growth of the economy.

The Real-Name Financial Transaction System

Economic transactions can be divided into real and financial transactions. Real transactions such as real estate are conducted using a real name. Therefore, it is possible to trace who bought what from whom. Financial transactions, however, can be done under borrowed names or made-up names. Hence, tracking down transactions cannot be institutionally guaranteed.

The reason financial transactions in Korea were possible under borrowed names or made-up names was a law ensuring secrecy of savings and installment deposits. The law was enacted to secure financial resources by increasing savings for investment to spur economic development. To do so, the government had to attract funds from outside banking institutions by providing incentives since real interest rates were below the inflation rate. The law undoubtedly made irrefutable contributions to increasing domestic savings during the initial stage of economic development. Nonetheless, the law also had negative effects.

Efforts to Implement a Real-Name Financial Transaction System

It is not easy to revamp an existing law with only good intentions.There are bound to be side effects to such measures. For that reason, to seize the moment to implement the real-name financial system has never been easy. That may be why the real-name financial account system has not taken root in Japan. However, in April 1982 when the Jang Young Ja scandal disrupted the financial order, the time seemed ripe to implement the system because a new financial order was called for. Due to this financial fraud, approximately 300 billion won pledged for short term loans were dishonored, causing the trade of discounting bills to be ceased for some time in the short-term monetary market, as well as in the private financial market.

When the scandal occurred, there was a desperate need for a real-name system in view of the taxation structure. Income of honest, hard-working people rose, and a hefty tax was levied on that income, while money placed in savings accounts was subject to a 15 percent tax regardless of the interest earned. When one borrows money from a bank, the interest on the loan is considered an operating cost, while a 40 percent corporate tax is imposed on profits from investments made out of the owner's pocket.

Furthermore, a tax rate of up to 76.5 percent could be applied to the dividends from stock investments. Accordingly, even though entrepreneurs had money to invest, they did not invest in corporate activities. They placed their money in a savings account and borrowed money from the bank to run operations. That way, they had to pay a much lower tax. In other words, financial laws and regulations back then forced businesses to run on debt.

Considering such loopholes, the government decided to lower the corporate tax and simultaneously implement the real-name account system. However, the government's efforts met fierce opposition. The main argument of those against the real-name system was that it would constrain corporate activities and undermine firms' capital accumulation. At that time, because of the banking scandal, savings were difficult; corporate activities did not seem to deteriorate because of the implementation of the real-name system. The critics of the real-name system also believed that computerization of all financial transactions should precede enactment of the system. They doubted that it would be possible to complete computerization of transactions on such short notice. Nonetheless, computerization was already underway. Thus, there should have been no problem enacting the real-name system immediately. Although there seemed to be no administrative difficulties in effecting the real-name system, the National Assembly deferred the enactment of the system. At the end of 1982, the National Assembly passed a law stating that a Korean citizen must conduct financial transactions using his or her real name. However, in the addenda of the same law, it was written that considering administrative preparatory progress and economic conditions, the real-name system would go into effect on a date set by presidential decree no earlier than January 1, 1986, which effectively put off the policy implementation indefinitely.

Implementation of the Real-Name System

The government officially announced that it would introduce a real-name system in early 1991 and formed a task force to prepare for the implementation. The effort, however, met strong opposition from business circles and the government, which resulted in the dismissal of the task force, and the implementation date was delayed again.

However, coming into 1992, political parties pledged implementation of the system in the presidential election campaign. Furthermore, the Federation of Korean Industries (FKI), a powerful organization of big business groups, reversed its previous position in opposition to the real-name system and called for gradual implementation of the system. This was followed by FKI's request for unconditional, all-out enactment of the system.

In the meantime, when we put the opponents' views into context, there seemed to be no reason for further delay in enacting the real-name system. For example, decreased long-term domestic savings and the bearish stock market might be temporary phenomena. Both could be improved once legalization of the "underground" economy got underway. In view of the fact that as financial liberalization got underway, the gap between official interest and market clearance rates would narrow, the timing for implementation seemed more favorable than not.

The concern about the negative effects of a possible shift from financial to real assets, might be real; nonetheless, as real estate transactions were expected to be less active, the possibility of negative effects from assets changing hands ought to be minor.

The high debt-to-asset ratio of Korean industry and its investment in real estate to make quick money rather than in equipment facilities, which were cited as primary reasons for not implementing the real-name system in 1982, seemed to be still the case in late 1992. Hence, to correct such practices in the nation's industry, the implementation of the real-name system was inevitable. At last, The real-name financial transaction system (RFTS) was enacted in August 1993 to effect social justice by balanced and fair taxation, normalizing financial transactions and correcting distorted corporate practices. Table 4.1 compares the practice of RFTS in other industrialized countries.

Economic Development versus Redistribution of Income

Rapid industrialization inevitably further differentiates the speed of development between sectors of the economy. The same gap exists in income levels between rapidly and slowly developing sectors. In the long-term, such gaps widen and worsen balanced sectoral distribution of income, leaving the door open to further deterioration. This occurred in Korea's economic development process.

Korean industrial and agricultural sectors have seen everwidening income differences. Naturally, an increasing number of people moved from rural to urban areas. However, the job market could not absorb the increased number of job seekers. Further, they were not appropriately trained to go directly into industries.

For that and other reasons, an urban poor began to evolve in major cities of the nation. That called for speedy social development in terms of improving employment opportunities, education, health, and other services. In the latter half of the 1970s, however, migration from rural areas slowed or came nearly to a halt. Therefore, the aforementioned problems abated to a certain extent. Nonetheless, the problems of the income gap between urban and rural areas and absolute poverty remained to be solved. Also lingering as a grave concern was the excessive concentration of economic resources in the hands of a few rich people and chaebols because of stratospheric land prices. Up until now, Koreans had shared the view that economic development would solve the problems of widening income gaps and poverty. However, even in advanced nations, efforts to improve income distribution over two to three gener-

Table 4.1.
Real-Name Financial Transaction System in Industrialized Nations

	U.S.A.	Germany	England	France
Implementation	The RFTS is firmly established as a financial practice because of strong emphasis on credit ratings	Opening false-name accounts is prohibited by law; the RFTS is implemented based on a regulation calling for identification certification before opening an account	Every financial transaction is done through a bank account; when such a transaction is made, the recipient of the bill is to be identified by his or her real name; therefore, the RFTS is firmly established as a financial practice	The RFTS is firmly established as a financial practice except for opening of an account to issue bank notes; even then, identification precedes the opening of such an account
Guarantee of Privacy	The details of financial transactions can be provided only at the request of the government audit bureaus, when required by a court of law under the Freedom of Information Act, and for statistical data-gathering purposes	The only exceptions are when a client permits it, when the office of bank supervision asks for it, when a court asks for the details of transactions related to a case the court is dealing with	Data are provided through Bank of England and the institutions recognized by the BOE	Data can be provided only in response to a written request from the government or government-related institutions, including banking institutions, a bank's supervisory institution, courts, and attorneys-at-law
Taxation	Comprehensive taxation	Comprehensive taxation	Withholding tax, except for corporate banking, long-term savings deposits, and savings deposits of nonresidents	Comprehensive taxation for enterprises; individuals can choose either comprehensive or withholding tax

ations were not enough to better it. Thus it seems that achieving balanced distribution of wealth is anything but easy. It prompts a government to start acting to narrow the income gap before it is too late. The necessity of employing such measures is evident as it is highly likely that "fast-track" and "slow-track" industries will widen their income gap.

Policy Directions in the Area of Income Redistribution

Policy makers must first believe that policies for the redistribution of income and economic growth are compatible. Many Koreans seem to think that if income distribution policies were implemented, economic growth would be hampered. Capital accumulation would be difficult because much capital would go to the poor, who are bent on spending rather than saving. Some contend that with expanded income redistribution, people with no particular incentive to work harder would no longer make an effort to enhance productivity.

Their arguments have validity. Conversely, however, when income distribution imbalance worsens, it can restrain economic growth. The poor would not strive to increase their living standards. Furthermore, if an absolute majority of the people were discontent about imbalanced income redistribution, social problems, which would certainly endanger economic growth, could occur. Economic development is generated by increased productivity. However, without adequate remuneration for boosting productivity, people cannot afford comfortable housing, health insurance, and leisure or cultural activities. This gives rise to more discontent and is detrimental to growth in productivity. Consequently, policies for economic growth and income redistribution should be pursued at the same time.

The intensity of the redistribution policy should be commensurate with economic development. Sectoral development gaps are likely to worsen; so will sectoral income differences. It follows that the government should steadily pursue policies to bridge such gaps. This, however, does not necessarily mean the rash introduction of a welfare system from an advanced country. Therefore, prudent, selective introduction of welfare policies is in order.

Income redistribution policy should be enforced while stressing the basic capitalist principle of competition. Emphasizng that principle is important because of unbounded introduction of redistribution policies could undermine industrial competition. Therefore, redistribution policies should provide maximum incentives to industries and ameliorate distorted income redistribution and the social welfare system.

Specifically, the first step in a redistribution policy should be to guarantee and develop income opportunities or sources of income. All of these ought to be aimed at general social development for a more humane existence. To that end, the government should step up efforts to expand job opportunities and qualified workers through industrial and job stabilization policies. The government also needs to secure more housing, healthcare coverage, cultural and leisure facilities, and more pleasant surroundings.

The government should develop a better social welfare system. The social welfare system could be split into a social insurance system based on contributions from all those covered and a public relief system for those who cannot earn a living. Social welfare policies should be implemented to complement a capitalist system. Accordingly, social welfare policies should be enforced to the extent they do not impinge fair rewards for personal labor.

In advanced nations, social welfare systems are handled by citizens' pension plans, industrial workers accident compensation insurance, and employment insurance. All except employment insurance are in effect in Korea. As part of the new economic five-year plan, employment insurance system will go into effect in 1995. This indicates that in terms of policies, Korea will shortly have all the needed welfare systems. The problem is that each welfare system is managed separately, thus overlooking their interrelationship. Therefore, the government should view the individual welfare systems as an interlocking system and pay more attention to those who are denied benefits, modify the contributions, and expand public relief. Along with these efforts, the government should reform the taxation system because it takes money to operate social welfare systems.

In particular, the employment insurance system, the heart of the welfare system, could have more negative than positive effects if the system is not regulated properly. Therefore, the system should be run in conjunction with job generation, job training, and conciliation efforts.

THE KOREAN BUBBLE ECONOMY

The Phenomenon of the Bubble Economy

The bubble economy phenomenon first appeared in the United States in 1987 in the aftermath of Black Monday, when the stock market crashed. It was evident in Japan where real estate and stock prices were plummeting. In Korea, the phenomenon was suspected because of tumbling stock prices in 1992. A bubble economy is one in which, because of sudden price hikes, prices of goods are much higher than basic market prices. Consequently, if a nation has a bubble economy, there is a danger of a sudden collapse in the price of goods, endangering the soundness of the economy itself. The bubble phenomenon is caused mainly by speculation. This can happen to goods whose prices are easily affected by limited supply and superfluous demand. Examples are stocks and housing, which vary widely in quality and have unpredictable future price fluctuations.

The Effect of the Bubble Economic Phenomenon

The area where the bubble phenomenon is most obvious in Korea is the real estate sector, which includes housing and land. The problem is the negative effect of the bubble economy. Positively speaking, the bubble economy could increase internal revenue, which is good for the government. Due to increased collateral, companies would be better able to borrow from banks and thus invest more in facilities. Domestic demand can increase because of the additional capital from the increased land prices.

The problem is that the negative side is much heavier than positive side. First, when land prices skyrocket, bad feelings between the haves and the have-nots also go up. Further, a chain reaction of such price hikes can spark inflation. Corporations also engage in unproductive activities.

During the late 1980s and early 1990s, when Korea experienced an extreme bubble economy, the aforementioned symptoms surfaced. Some farmers sold their livestock and farmland to buy stocks. Blue collar workers were averse to the "three D jobs," those that are dirty, difficult, and dangerous.

The bubble phenomenon is problematic when it goes on, but when the bubble bursts it can generate even more gruesome side effects. Overall investment could decline because of a constrained mood toward investment. Companies could have a hard time getting loans because of the sudden drop in the value of their collateral. Even when firms have adequate assets, they go through rough financial difficulties due to a lack of revolving funds. The security of banking institutions is threatened by insolvencies caused by huge drop in collateral values. In some cases, banks even go out of business, as was the case in the United States. Therefore, banks set stricter requirements for loans, further worsening the financial crunch for businesses. At the level of the national economy, the people suffer asset losses and constrained consumption as a result of their involvement in indiscreet investment in assets.

A Cure for the Bubble Phenomenon

The government made policy efforts to minimize the negative impact of the bubble phenomenon, such as low morale at work. The government's policy efforts to cure the bubble economy since the end of 1980s are to increase the supply of objects for speculation and restrict real estate transactions by putting in a permit system and computerizing land transactions.

Both policies worked to a degree to curb land speculation. In the future, speculative buying and selling of land should be curbed. However, the government should not suppress land purchase for actual productive use. To that end, the government should get on with institutional reform.

NORTHERN POLICY AND NORTH-SOUTH KOREAN ECONOMIC COOPERATION

Northern Policy: Did It Achieve What It Intended?

A "Northern policy" was actively pursued since the last half of the 1980s and to a certain extent it was successful. Picking up momentum with the visit of Gorbachev, then-president of the former Soviet Union, a Korean-Russian summit was held. Afterward, diplomatic relations between Korea and Russia were normalized. That was followed by establishment of diplomatic relations between Korea and China. "Nord-politik," therefore, was no longer a dream for Koreans; it was real. I still remember how excited Koreans were when the first Korean-Russian summit was held. Critics have said that Koreans have a tendency to get easily excited and then fizzle out. Nonetheless, such a characteristic, I believe, is not inborn in Koreans. I would rather attribute it to history.

Korea, since the collapse of the last dynasty, Chosun, has learned the hard way that without power and dynamism, it will suffer unfair treatment. What developing nation would not be thrilled to find itself in a position to help out a superpower, the former Soviet Union, on equal footing?

However, with Nord-politik Koreans should not lose sight of actual goals as was claimed by some critics. China and the former Soviet Union have been chasing reform and open-door policies because they need to. Therefore, Koreans should use Nord-politik to their own advantage. National interest should be of prime concern when pursuing South-North Korean economic cooperation, even though it should also be carried out in a way conducive to national reunification.

Accordingly, although Nord-politik and South-North Korean economic cooperation should contribute to confidence building in political and diplomatic terms, they also should be accompanied by measures covering economic interests. In particular, private-sector-led advancement into the markets of the northern nations should precede political and diplomatic agreements. International economic relations normally start on the basis of mutual economic interest. Therefore, only when economic relations expand, can we expect relations to lean more toward Korea's economic interest, which will contribute to the cause of enhanced political and diplomatic confidence building.

Implementation of Nord-Politik and South-North Korean Economic Cooperation

To get achievements more conducive to national interest than professed causes in Nord-Politik and South-North Korean economic cooperation, I would like to make the following suggestions.

First, planned short- and long-term goals are required. Open-door policies and economic planning for North Korea, China, or the former Soviet Union should be thoroughly studied. By comparing them with the Korean industrial structure, Korea should try to establish complementary industrial relations in terms of trade and technology exchanges. In the initial stages, consumer goods' export would attract attention. However, middle- to long-range planning is necessary to develop long-term investment efforts such as technology exchanges and building local plants.

Second, the government, banking industry, and firms should cooperate. If possible, the private sector should lead the way and move into those nations by overcoming political and diplomatic constraints. At the same time, banks and the government should provide assistance by establishing local banks and government offices. Of particular importance is the establishment of local banks, for without them, transfer of funds, settlement of accounts, export insurance, and local investment cannot be done. At the same time, the government, on the basis of diplomatic achievements, should set up specific assistance plans by the elimination of double taxation, investment guarantee pacts, and protection of local firms and nationals operating in those nations.

Third, the government should improve its risk-management capability by information analysis. For a long time, relations between the northern nations and Korea have been somewhat distant. Though recent press reports contain a great deal of information about northern nations, the accuracy of the reports is questionable, and they lack depth. Therefore, the government should fund experts and prestigious government-invested and private economic institutes to conduct in-depth research and analyses of the northern nations. Along with these efforts, the government ought to establish branch offices of banking institutions to collect and analyze banking and industrial information from those nations. People are suggesting that Korean businesses exercise control and not advance blindly on those nations. The risks are there because Koreans have insufficient information about the nations. Therefore, if more complete data were available, Korean entrepreneurs could lower their risks and move ahead more confidently and rapidly.

Fourth, investment in the northern nations should be for the long-term. Considering recent trends, it is very unlikely that Korean interests in the northern nations will fade. However, enthusiasm could soon be replaced by indifference. It is axiomatic that only those who sowed the seed and sweated, deserve the hard-earned fruits of labor. Without taking chances, there is no great reward. Therefore, Koreans should be wary of short-term investment in the northern nations. Reasonable enterprises for investment require an active commitment.

Finally, dog-eat-dog competition must be avoided as much as possible. When the Middle Eastern construction boom was at its peak, Korean construction firms engaged in ruthless competition among themselves, which only weakened Korea's overseas construction sector. Even now, the Korean economy is shouldering a financial burden from the weakened overseas construction sector. Therefore, Korean firms ought to voluntarily cooperate and move into the northern nations. For example, if the government sets up an organization to coordinate over-all investment in the northern nations, banks and companies could pool their knowledge and resources. They could calculate which businesses would most likely succeed. Those enterprises would go first. This would result in a better allocation of limited resources. Such an organization should not become a tool to protect selected companies' interests but rather a neutral consensus-building mechanism.

South-North Korean economic cooperation is something that encompasses Korean expectations and dreams for reunification. It will enable many separated families to reunite and many South Koreans who left the North to visit their hometowns. That is why the government should be judicious and not raise expectations or allow big disappointments. Routine efforts should be avoided. Whether the northern policy could provide momentum for an early unification and prove to be a "new world of opportunity" or be quite the opposite depends heavily on how much effort Koreans put into improving political and economic conditions on the Korean Peninsula.

Korea has been brilliantly successful in its economic development plans. By the same token, if it approaches the northern policy with the same fervor and careful planning, the northern nations will prove to be a new frontier for even higher hope.

5

A Major Turnaround in Economic Policy

As Arnold Joseph Toynbee mentioned in his major work, *A Study of History*, the history of humankind has been challenged and responded, and only the nations and peoples that successfully met the challenges are prosperous.

With that perspective, the transitional challenges Korea met in the late 1980s, a fading spirit of thrift and slackened economic vitality, could have worked to Korea's advantage if they had been met properly. Whether the Korean economy can join the ranks of advanced nations and get a chance for a second takeoff depends heavily on how Koreans respond to challenges.

THE KOREAN APPROACH TO BECOMING AN INDUSTRIALIZED NATION

The Implications of an Advanced Economy

For Korea to choose efficient development strategies, it has to put into proper perspective both its current stage of economic development and the definition of the advanced nation that it wants to be. Academically speaking, the definitions of advanced nation and economic development vary according to nation and point in time. However, generally speaking, economic development is defined as an increase in per capita income over a long period of time with no increase in the number of people in absolute poverty and no worsening in distribution of wealth. From a historical point of view, the economic development process suggests an economic system, not merely an expanding economy. Therefore, some academics view it as the process of economic development from a precapitalistic to a capitalistic economic system.

Koreans firmly grasped the concept of economic development in the early 1960s, when they launched full-fledged economic development plans. The focus of economic development in the 1960s was quantitative development as the slogan "a war against poverty" illustrated. In other words, the emphasis was on expansion of per capita GNP, the growth of trade, and personal consumption. However, as I mentioned already, in determining to what degree a nation has developed, it is desirable to consider both quantitative growth such as per capita GNP and qualitative growth such as the changes in industrial structure.

As there are many views on economic development, so are there many yardsticks with which to measure economic growth. The most frequently used gauge figures out how many people work in agriculture, industry, and services and calculates the added value and gross production of each industry in a nation. One major economist who tried this method to determine the level of development of an economy was Collin Clark. He found that the more a nation develops economically, the more workers moved from primary industry to the manufacturing sector and then to the tertiary sector. He defined a more advanced nation as one in which more workers are in the tertiary sector. W. G. Hoffman also tried to figure out the stages of economic development in relationship to shifts in industrial structure. He defined a developed nation as a nation with more value added from capital goods industries than from consumer goods.

Economists Charles P. Kindleberger and T. H. Boggs tried a different approach to determine the degree of development of a nation. They used the balance of payments. They contended that a nation goes through four stages of development. As a nation develops, it evolves from being an immature debtor nation into a mature debtor nation into an immature creditor nation and finally into a mature creditor nation.

Finally, economist Rostow viewed the economic development of a nation from a historical perspective. He contended that a nation develops from a traditional society to a society preconditioned for takeoff, to the takeoff stage, to the drive to maturity, and then to the age of high mass consumption.

Korea's economic development stage can be viewed from different perspectives. However, when viewed in Rostow's eyes, the nation experienced the takeoff stage in the early 1960s and now is now technologically mature. Shortly, Korea, I think, will move into the high mass consumption stage.

Changes in the Environment of Economic Development

The environment for economic development in Korea has changed significantly. Externally, the conditions that helped Korea attain economic development have been fading. The U.S.-led free trade environment of the 1960s and 1970s based on the IMF and the GATT system is now changing into World Trade Organization system. New exclusive regionalism, aimed at maximizing benefits between geographically close nations, is surging. In the coming years, the advanced economies will not see the high growth rates of past decades. Korean exporters will have trouble finding their niche in the world market, as the newly developing nations, China, and ASEAN nations, model their plans after Korea's economic strategies. With the increased importance of technologies in economic development, advanced nations are curbing core technology transfers as much as possible and keeping an eye on technological development in developing nations.

Internal development conditions in Korea have changed as well. People's attitudes have changed significantly with the switch from an authoritarian regime to a democracy. Korea's economic development conditions in terms of production factors have changed greatly. The major pillars of Korea's economic growth strategy have been export-led industrialization and the fostering of labor-intensive industries that use the idle work force laid off by the weakening agricultural sector. However, the basis for such growth has practically collapsed. That is, international trade conditions that were favorable to Korea during the brisk growth period in advanced economies are a thing of the past. There is no more high-quality labor that helped fuel the strategic growth of labor-intensive industries.

More important, there have been structural changes in Korea's industry. Consumers are showing a preference for high-quality goods. Therefore, Korean exporters can no longer gain ground in advanced nations' markets with the mass-produced goods that helped build the nation's economy. Thus, the mass-production method has had to change to leaner production methods. The weight of traditional production factors—labor, land, and resources—has been greatly reduced thanks to technological advances. In reality, when compared with twenty years ago, the resource input ratio per unit of output, in advanced nations, has been cut to one third of what it was. This change should be evaluated when Korea's policy makers plan economic development strategies.

A New Development Strategy

Changes in economic development conditions are requiring the nation to set up a new development strategy. Needless to say, Korea needs new "weaponry" to win economic warfare in the twenty-first century.

If that is the case, what kinds of strategies should Korea come up with to continue to grow into the next century? First, there should be a thorough review of existing growth strategies. The government's effort should be focused consistently on improving the industrial structure to favor short-term betterment of development conditions. Additionally, Korea's democratization efforts should not hamper economic growth within the larger political context. Instead, Koreans should make democratization a solid foundation on which they can build further economic growth. To that end, political leaders and corporate managers should strive to reestablish social discipline. From an economic point of view, the way to install economic discipline is to stabilize the industrial structure. "Getting prices right" is not an attempt to achieve economic discipline; rather, it is structural stabilization of productivity and capacity. It should be reviewed with an eye toward reestablishing the way the economy is run.

I would like to stress that Koreans as a group, whether they be industrialists, government officials, or citizens, should adjust to the idea of a global village. In the globalized era, no success can be expected from a xenophobic or nationalistic way of thinking. All economic growth strategies should be established considering domestic and export markets in the same context. Institutions and ideals to guarantee economic justice should be firmly rooted. No nation has survived for long without them. The Korean government should no longer show favoritism to export sectors and apathy to domestic sectors.

Without balanced income redistribution, a stable economy is out of the question. Tumultuous social conflicts will occur if there is imbalanced redistribution of wealth. Korea should flex its economic muscle and create conditions conducive to achieving self-generated economic growth. Korea's remarkable economic growth up to now has been achieved largely by the introduction of various incentives, the government's efforts to foster economic growth, and a sharp increase in overseas demand. However, in the next century, the government will find it tough to bolster growth by providing only policy loans and tax breaks. Therefore, the government should try to create the preconditions for further independent technology development, effective competition, increased corporate efficiency, and innovation.

Facilitating technology development is mandatory for Korea. In the next century, Korean firms' survival in the endless battle of competition lies in the success or failure of technology development (see figure 5.1). To that end, Korea's industrialists should abandon their penchant for going after quick money in real estate. With technological development, Korea's industry can produce more and its international competitiveness can be strengthened. This will guarantee higher profits for firms and new and better products for consumers.

Figure 5.1.
The Korean Response to External and Internal Change
of Economic Conditions

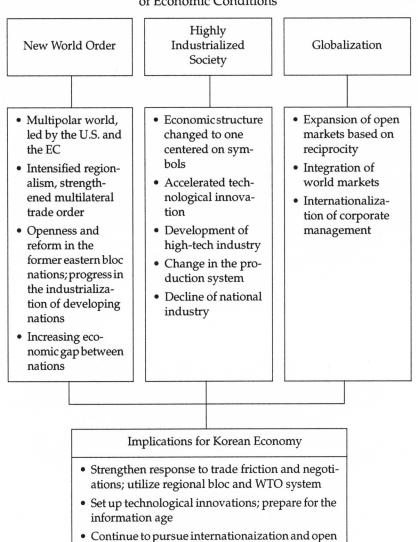

New World Order	Highly Industrialized Society	Globalization
• Multipolar world, led by the U.S. and the EC	• Economic structure changed to one centered on symbols	• Expansion of open markets based on reciprocity
• Intensified regionalism, strengthened multilateral trade order	• Accelerated technological innovation	• Integration of world markets
• Openness and reform in the former eastern bloc nations; progress in the industrialization of developing nations	• Development of high-tech industry	• Internationalization of corporate management
• Increasing economic gap between nations	• Change in the production system	
	• Decline of national industry	

Implications for Korean Economy

• Strengthen response to trade friction and negotiations; utilize regional bloc and WTO system
• Set up technological innovations; prepare for the information age
• Continue to pursue internationaization and open markets; globalize corporate management

ATTITUDES IN AN ERA OF UNLIMITED COMPETITION

Competition and the Borderless Society

Open markets and internationalization are irreversible trends in the world economy. In the twenty-first century, they are certain to pick up speed as information and communication technologies will undergo magnificent metamorphoses. Therefore, the world will become borderless.

From a positive point of view, in a borderless society all production factors travel among countries freely. It looks more or less like utopia. In the future, a business person who has a job in New York could have dinner in Paris, listening to *chanson* after calling it a day. Prestigious Seoul National University graduates will seek high-paying jobs in leading Japanese firms. For example, Hyundai Motors company could try to maximize efficiency while minimizing constraining factors by designing autos in Italy, producing engines in Japan, assembling autos in Ulsan, Korea, and developing an auto-cruise system in Detroit.

However, the reality of the globalized world will be found in unlimited competition on a broader scope. To a firm, globalization could mean expanded competition from local firms to international firms. For an individual, one's competitors could be the people of the world. Even the administrative services of a government will be objects of competition. In the past, intergovernmental competition for better services hardly existed. However, in a borderless world, a company will no longer be of one nation; it will be multinational. Therefore, such firms will roam around the world to find factories and offices with the best conditions. Hence, the Korean government should strive to offer better administrative services at reasonable prices. It should also try to secure infrastructure, communications facilities, transportation, and ports. By so doing, the government could attract more investment to Korea.

The Internationalization of Firms

Generally speaking, the internationalization of industry is found in the production and sales activities of firms. A nation undergoing internationalization at first has a major domestic market with occasional overseas sales. And then overseas sales begin to outpace domestic sales and the firm develops into an export-oriented one. At that stage, most sales and production are done domestically. Export activities are conducted through agents in and out of the nation. However, as globalization progresses, the firm will establish subsidiaries in other countries. Further, it will try to build local sales and production networks. Along with such efforts, the firm will aggressively study ways to work all areas—production, finance, and management—to its advantage, thereby moving itself into full-fledged globalization stage.

The final stage of globalization of a business would be globalized management of firms. Firms will no longer be of a particular nation. They would include all peoples around the globe. To survive in a world of endless competition, Korean firms should think more globally. A capable individual should be employed regardless of nationality. Korean firms should create an environment where they can naturally learn foreign cultures by becoming proficient in foreign languages.

Korea's industrialists should strive for innovation. A firm with executives clinging to the past will soon disappear. In a nutshell, "corporate Korea" should globalize itself and develop products aimed at all people.

Stimulating Investment Overseas

The concept of international trade in a highly competitive world will change to localized production, producing goods in the nation where they are consumed, in contrast to the earlier concept of movement of products and capital as a means of settlement. Trade in services expands more than trade in goods. Capital will move independently, in response to interest rates and foreign exchange rates, not merely as a means of settlement. Accordingly, the international trade arena will be where investments accrete by providing goods in the nation where the demand occurs rather than exporting goods from the manufacturer nation to consumer nation.

Understanding such trends, advanced nations, including the United States, have actively invested in overseas markets. U.S. investments overseas rose from US$230 billion in 1985 to US$474 billion in 1992. In the same year, Japanese investments overseas reached US$251 billion—more than five times the US$44 billion figure for 1985. The figures represent a tendency of nations throughout the world to invest heavily overseas. This explains why Korea's product competitiveness lags behind that of Japan in Southeast Asian markets.

Korea's foreign investment at the end of 1993 stood at a meager US$5.4 billion. Such sluggish investment by Korean firms is due mainly to a lack of capital and government support. However, considering the shortage of workers in labor-intensive industries and the ensuing loss of competitiveness of such industries, Korean firms need to invest more overseas to break out of the current domestic production and export pattern.

To galvanize foreign investment requires a national effort to upgrade technological level in the domestic industries. In addition, the government ought to set up a backup system for foreign investment. Korean foreign investment should be raised from the current restrictive and defensive type of investment to a policy level just to protect the balance of payments. To that end, the government should ease requirements on such investment, raise the investment ceiling, and promote domestic firms' strategic alliances with advanced nations' firms for technology acquisition, design, development, and production of new products.

For effective overseas investment, the government, firms, and allied organizations ought to cooperate fully. The government needs to organize a consultative forum so the private sector can coordinate target nations and sectors. Along with that, the government should revise and strengthen support of foreign investment by providing financial and tax incentives. In the early stages of evaluating target nations, the government should supply domestic firms with needed systemic information. Firms intending to invest overseas should be prudent enough to review and analyze all information and assess the management soundness of the target firms before deciding on the investment (Figure 5.2).

Along with the aforementioned strategies the government ought to use foreign loans because of Korea's limited foreign investment resources and its trade deficit. In other words, the government should consider various ways to direct funds for overseas development by processing foreign loans through Korean banking institutions. This option could prove very useful because it could be one way to galvanize foreign investment without draining domestic capital.

Changing Concepts of Imports and Exports

If Korea is to succeed in an era of unlimited competition, Koreans must reform their ways of thinking. Above all, Koreans should change their opinions about imports and exports. Koreans have been taught from youth that exports are good and imports are bad for the economy. That is why exporters have been treated well and importers have not.

The primary reason for international trade or import and export activities is to make Korea a richer and stronger country.

If the nation only imports, Korean capital will flow out of the country. Conversely, Korean firms can learn advanced technologies from studying imported goods. Using what they have learned from the imports, they can improve production methods and make higher quality goods to sell in overseas markets. Thus, imports can be viewed as instructional aids rather than just drains on the economy.

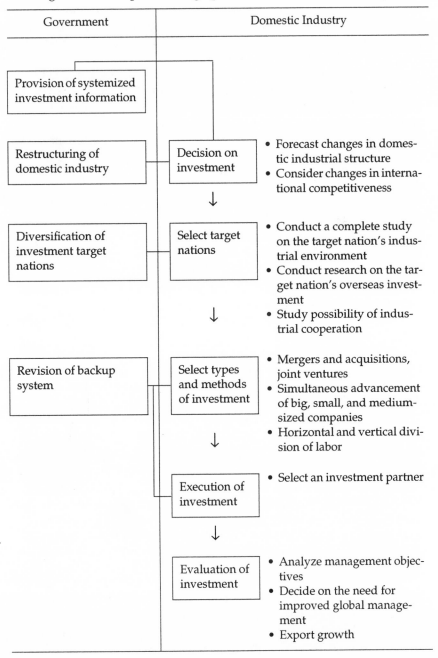

Figure 5.2.
Organization Map for Setting up Overseas Investment Strategies

Korea instituted the "Buy Korean Products" movement, because the nation needed to reduce imports by a large margin. However, this does not mean that Koreans should buy only Korean products, even when they are more expensive than imported goods. It means Koreans should buy Korean goods when they are as good and as reasonably priced as foreign products.

The "Buy Korean Products" slogan was effective when products came from only Korea, America, and a few other nations. However, in a globalized world, the importance of the headquarters location of a firm is minor. Harvard University professor Robert B. Reich, in *The Work of Nations* (1991), mentioned that in the future the importance of a firm will be judged on the basis of where it makes a profit and to which nation it provides more benefits. In that sense, Koreans need to mull over the meaning of the slogan, "Buy Korean Products."

Carrying out Aggressive Open Market Policies

Korea has been making steady progress in opening its markets and globalizing. Domestically, the government has been increasing the import liberalization ratio, and externally it has been globalizing domestic industry by investing overseas.

The Uruguay Round multilateral trade negotiations brought trade frictions with advanced nations to the fore. However, the Korean government and the people have been reacting to the trade friction emotionally rather than strategically. Therefore, currently, the nation's trade conflicts with advanced nations have intensified. If such a trend is left unchecked, Korea will find it difficult to protect its economic interests in the multilateral trade negotiations. It will also be on the defensive against accusations leveled by the United States, Japan, and the EC member nations. Therefore, rather than resorting to stopgap measures, the Korean government should come up with long-term solutions. On the trade front, the Korean government should not consider the domestic and international economies as independent of each other.

For Korea to be firmly entrenched in the international arena, the government and private sector will have to make concerted efforts to fit the mold. Additionally, from now on, Korea's trade policies should be carried out to respond to and encourage participation in the formation of a new world trade order. Concurrently, Korea must strictly observe GATT rules and work hard to open its markets and restructure its industry. By setting such policy directions, Korea will be able to move beyond its current mediocre participation and passive accommodation of what has been decided in international forums.

Regional blocs are challenging Korea. To cope with the trend, the government should cooperate more with nations involved in regional blocs. Reinforcing ties with the Pacific Basin nations would strengthen Korea's position in the global economy. To do this, the government should carefully design and carry out plans.

REVISION OF POLICIES FOR ECONOMIC JUSTICE

Institutional Approach and Stopgap Measures

One definition of economic justice could be the establishment of an economic system in which market order is grounded on the basis of autonomy and competition, with balanced sectoral growth, balanced sharing of the burden among income brackets, and justification for accumulation of wealth. Economic justice has been a goal of nations in the past and now. For Korea, whose objective is to join the ranks of advanced nations in the next century, securing economic justice is a serious undertaking because it determines whether an economy is truly advanced. Accordingly, the government launched programs to achieve economic justice in 1980. These included the provision of health care coverage to all Koreans and the promulgation of laws to curb land speculation. Despite those efforts, more and more people have demanded a fairer distribution of national income and wealth. From blue collar workers to white collar workers, all Korean people are competing to secure their fair shares.

Competition for that fair share by Koreans can be seen as the correction function of capitalism. However, in effect, it undermines national efforts for economic development. Recently, some have frequently demanded certain things that go directly against principles of capitalism. They have claimed ownership of things that were not theirs. They have even asked for more than fair compensation by using the power of numbers.

To correct such, the government should make institutional efforts to realize economic justice. With an institutional approach, Koreans could create a society that has balanced sectoral growth, fair burden sharing among different income brackets, and justified wealth accumulation. The case-by-case approach to economic justice could bring about complaints rather than self-examination because nebulous rules would be applied. Instead, fair rules should be applied to all players of the game so that an individual who breaks a rule may be ashamed. The framework of economic justice, in other words, is removing sources of windfall profits to guarantee fair compensation for hard work. Therefore, the government needs to realize that only when it works consistently to achieve economic justice can economic growth and the easing of social conflict be possible. When the government's efforts are translated into laws, Korea's economic structure will be stabilized, putting Korea one step closer to joining the ranks of advanced nations.

Radical Reform and "Gradual" Reforms

Institutional reform is opposed because it is an attempt to change the existing order. In particular, measures for institutional reforms are often unrealistic. The argument for economic justice has an upper hand over the argument against it. No one can come up with persuasive arguments against reform measures. However, people with vested interests would oppose implementation of economic justice measures, for they would have to give up some of their privileges.

When the government pushed for the enactment of the real-name financial transaction system in 1982, most Koreans supported it. However, during the process of developing the real-name system, many Koreans came up with opposing views. Those who spoke against the system presented the following major arguments. First, because Korea has a vulnerable trade balance, if the system were enacted, capital would be sent out of the country. Second, computerization of all financial transactions—a prerequisite for implementing the system—would be difficult. Therefore, the government decided to enforce the system on a date it would select after January 1986. That was a recognition of the opponents' views. National consensus was gathered in 1986 for the introduction of public land ownership. The concept was debated because most Koreans felt harm had come from heated land speculation. However, when it was actually implemented, it was enacted with many exceptions.

What we can learn from reviewing such cases is that putting in place valid reform measures was delayed under the pretext of "gradual" reform. When toothless reform measures go into effect, more side effects could occur, which would provide fodder for reform opponents' mills. They could then cite those side effects as reasons why reform measures should not be enacted. The nation's policy makers should do their homework if they want successful reform.

First, institutional reforms should be carried out only after intense consensus-building efforts have been made. That is because, no matter how noble the purpose of a reform effort may be, when it goes into effect without thorough discussion and consensus building, it can open up the possibility of opposition and repercussions from the privileged classes. Consequently, policy makers should go the extra mile in their consensus building programs.

Second, if possible, policy makers should avoid "gradual" implementation of reforms. Under the pretext of gradual reform, many reform measures end up lost. Therefore, the policy makers should carry out comprehensive reform.

Third, only when a national leader is determined to carry out reform can it be effective. Therefore, policy makers should convince the leader of a nation of the necessity of that reform. Even during the consensus-building process, the leader of a nation should have unwavering confidence in the reform program.

Fourth, during the process of building national consensus for reform, the uncommitted majority is always inferior to a specified few. To resolve such a dilemma, policy makers should secure the continued support of those who have no stake in the reform, such as professionals on the particular issues and the press.

Concentration of Economic Strength and the Fair Trade System

When a market is monopolistic or oligopolistic due to market failure, the government's market management capacity reaches its limit. With the ensuing weakening of the international competitiveness of firms, steady economic growth is impossible. To revitalize the economy and continue economic growth, the sectoral efficiency should be upgraded.

The introduction of the competitive principle presupposes a galvanized market. When economic strength is concentrated and the degree of concentration in individual products is intensified, a few producers can control the market and the market no longer functions well. To prevent that, an antitrust law is implemented to curb monopoly and get rid of restrictive or unfair trade practices in order to establish free competition in the market.

In Korea, the Law on Price Stabilization and Fair Trade was enacted in 1976. However, the major focus of the law was management of the prices of goods on the monopoly list of items. A fair trade law, in its true sense, went into effect in April 1981, the Law on Monopoly and Fair Trade. First, the law prohibited the abuse of the rights of producers to dominate the market. Second, the law put the reins on forming associations of firms, regulations, or administrative acts designed to limit competition. In terms of transactions, the law restricted unfair trade practices such as illegal collusion to influence the price of goods, formation of associations and unions to block new entrants, limitation on sales activities, false or exaggerated advertisements, and unfair international transactions.

The reason Korea sought promotion of competition by introducing a fair trade system is that it went through a unique economic development process. Since the inception of economic development, the government has implemented policies to support strategic industries and has allocated many of its usable resources to those industries to maximize the effective use of limited resources.

Consequently, in Korea, the vertically integrated conglomerates or chaebols that have enormous economic power came into being. Chaebols had positive effects on the economy's quantitative growth. However, they also had negative effects, which are viewed as stumbling blocks to further economic development. The chaebols' major corporate activities—management, personnel management, and finance (see Table 5.1)—are in the hands of the planning department or secretariat of the president of a group. When recruiting, they have centralized hiring and allocate workers to different areas of business, such as service and heavy industry jobs. Chaebols supply loans by mutually guaranteeing payments between their affiliated firms. Therefore, insolvent affiliates of chaebols are not effectively weeded out. This is a stumbling block to the restructuring of the domestic economy. Transactions between affiliates of chaebols are frequent. When they do business with

Table. 5.1.
Management Structures in Big Corporations in Korea, the United States and Japan

	Korea	U.S.A.	Japan
Forms	Chaebols	Individual big corporation	Business groups
Ownership	Family	Citizens	Mutually owned
Management	Family members are in important corporate positions	CEO and board of directors	Hired president and executives
Characteristics	Individual capitalism	Management capitalism	Corporate capitalism
Background	Capacity to mobilize funds that one-generation development cannot	Huge stock market	Postwar grouping of chaebols

Source: Yun, Sungcheon. "Ownership and Management Structure of Chaebol and Policy Responses in Korea." Spring edition: KDI Press.

nonaffiliates, unfair practices, discriminatory treatment in price, tie-in sales, disruption of transactions, and so forth occur often.

Concentration of economic power leads to a deterioration of the income distribution structure, giving rise to estrangement between members of a society. It hinders the establishment of a sturdy foundation for continued economic development. Accordingly, the question of economic concentration in Korea has been raised not only as an industrial problem linked to lower productivity but also as a social problem that leads to unfair distribution of wealth.

The fair trade regime that our government introduced to solve irregularities has achieved some success. However, to maximize its effect, the government must still implement follow-up measures.

First, instead of resorting to direct measures such as tax audits, the government would be well advised to enact indirect measures such as improving, correcting, and further developing the current fair trade regime, to establish fair trade practices among enterprises. Investigative functions should be strengthened to prevent and rectify collaboration among domestic companies. The antidumping mechanism should be reinforced to prevent dumping in the domestic market by foreign companies. Moreover, a monitoring system should be developed to prevent large conglomerates from abusing their huge power.

Second, for the fair trade regime to stimulate competition, the amendment of regulations should be aimed not only at punishing those involved in unfair trade practices but also at eradicating the root of such practices. In addition, the status of the agencies responsible for administrating the fair trade regime should be upgraded to that of a central government agency so that they can have a greater say in the establishment of various government policies.

Third, we must look at the concentration of economic power from the perspective of how best to respond to the changing world economic environment. It is true that Korean conglomerates are too large in comparison to other domestic companies. However, they are small compared to the large companies of such advanced countries as the United States and Japan. Therefore, for Korean enterprises to survive the fierce international competition, the government should reconsider the current corporate policy on the concentration of economic power, which has too much stick and no carrot. In fact, though the United States has been enforcing the toughest regulations after realizing the side effects of relaxing concentrated economic power, it is now trying to approach the problem from a different angle, by relaxing the antitrust laws (Table 5.2). In the same way, their financial industry is also relaxing its rigid rules on the division of labor between securities and banking industries to win the war against Japan's mammoth financial institutions.

Table 5.2.
Comparison of Fair Trade Regimes in Korea and Major Advanced Countries

	Korea	U.S.A.	Germany	Japan
Relevant agency	Fair Trade Commission	Federal Trade Commission	Federal Cartel Commission	Fair Trade Commission
Assigned to	Minister of the EPB (Economic Planning Board)	Independent (under the Justice Department)	Federal Financial Minister (independent handling of matters)	Cabinet minister (independent exercise of authority)
Powers	Revision of the Fair Trade Act	Punishment of violations of relevant laws	Nullification of violations of relevant law	Ruling on violations of the Fair Trade Act
	Designation of monopolistic enterprises	Investigation into compliance with its decisions	Banning the abuse of power	Designation of international guidelines and determination of unfair trade practices
	Determination of the scope and criteria for maintaining resale prices	Dissemination of information		Designation of products allowed for resale
		Congressional report and proposals for additional legislation		

Enlarging the Concept of Public Land Ownership

Since the early 1960s, land prices have continued to rise. This has emerged as a serious social problem. The increase in land prices was fanned by land speculation. Land speculation not only aggravated the inefficient allocation of resources in national economic development but also caused such serious problems as distortion in income distribution, aggravation of the conflict among classes, and erosion of industrial competitiveness.

Thus, it distorted sound consumption patterns and the economic activities of the private sector. Statistics shows that, in 1988, the unearned income derived from land amounted to 1.7 times the GNP, 4.2 times greater than the average pay of employees, and 5.3 times greater than the GDP of the manufacturing industries. When discretionary surplus funds put into land speculation can produce profits 10 or 100 times the original amount, how can we expect money to flow into manufacturing industries or the real interest rate to go down? Moreover, the conspicuous spending by a minority of the people who had enjoyed unearned income paralyzed the value system of the whole nation, boosted the growth of service sectors at the expense of the manufacturing sector, and pushed up the deficit in the balance of payment.

Recognizing the seriousness of the problem, since 1990, Korea has implemented three laws, including a regulation on the ceiling for land ownership, regulation of profits from development, and regulations on excessive profits from real estate holding—all in the name of the public land concept. The purpose of these regulations is to ensure the equitable ownership of houses by putting a limit on land ownership, to help the people lead comfortable lives by facilitating the supply of housing, and to prevent land speculation and promote efficient use of land by collecting development profits or excess profits derived from land—all intended to contribute to the sound development of the economy.

However, in the process of implementation, these regulations have had various practical problems: too restricted a scope of application, uniform imposition of taxes regardless of the purpose of land use, and the possibility of considerable friction in taxation matters. This makes it difficult for these regulations to serve as comprehensive and effective land policy.

In this increasingly harsh global economic environment, it is difficult to be internationally competitive, have a stable economy, and bear the high cost of land. Therefore, to enhance the competitiveness of domestic companies and inject vitality into their production activities, the government has to come up with effective ways to root out land speculation. While restraining people from owning vast amounts of land, the government should ensure a stable supply of factory sites and change the flow of funds from unproductive purposes, such as land speculation, to productive purposes.

On the other hand, the tax system should be aimed at stabilizing land prices, promoting efficient use of land, and enhancing equity in the distribution of wealth and income. In this connection, the current tax laws should be reviewed and carefully revised to minimize side effects from an imbalance in the supply and demand of land. In particular, to maximize the effectiveness of the public land concept, the government has to improve policies to enlarge the number of people subject to taxation. At the same time, the government should drastically alter or complement existing restrictions on land under the National Development Plan. Thus, while enlarging the concept of public land, the government should loosen up its regulations on land use as much as possible.

Strengthening the Real-Name Financial Transaction System

To maximize the mobilization of domestic capital by getting the most out of domestic savings in the early stage of economic development, Korea allowed financial transactions to be done anonymously or pseudonymously to guarantee the privacy of bank accounts. Admittedly, this policy has contributed to the nation's economic development.

However, as the size of the economy grew and its structure became more complicated, the negative aspects of this policy became evident. Such a practice distorted the financial order and blocked the development of institutional financing. That is, private loans were being used for unsanctioned financial transactions; for example, speculation. That boosted the growth of the underground economy. Furthermore, efforts to eliminate irregularities in the society will be to no avail if those with large financial assets bear a smaller tax burden than the workers, who are subject to comprehensive taxation.

Fortunately, however, boosted by a consensus among the people, the new administration began to discuss the subject again. Even in the financial circles where there had been strong criticism, consent was now expressed. As the electronic processing systems of banks improved and more people were behind it, the environment for implementing the system was ripe.

On August 12, 1993, the real-name financial transaction system was announced, out of the Blue House, by presidential decree. The purpose of the decree was to make financial transactions more transparent and enable fair and reasonable taxation. In addition, the system helped improve the corporate financial structure by legalizing the private, curb market. The real-name system reduced sources of unearned income, rendering legitimacy to honest accumulation of wealth. A sound work ethic was returned. The system also enhanced the efficiency of capital because it stifled the unhealthy underground money market and minimized distorted capital flow.

Impact and Follow-Up Measures of the Real-Name
Financial Transaction System

The implementation of the real-name financial transaction system was imperative because it represented the first step toward moving the Korean economy to a higher level. This is because trying to become a mature economy in a society where the underground economy thrives and unsanctioned economic activities are accepted would be as futile as trying to build a castle in the air.

The RNFTS normalized economic activities, all production activities, and consumption behavior. Accordingly, it will allow future trends in society to be forecast and ensure that all economic activities such as investment, production, consumption, and savings will take place in a predictable, rational manner. Some would try to justify the earlier failure to implement the system by saying that Japan had not fully introduced the system. Look at the many aberrant aspects of the Japanese economy. Analysts say that, since routine activity in each economic unit in Japan, such as in enterprises and households, is conducted in a normal and just manner, implementation of the system would not benefit the general public much except politically. Moreover, it would not be an exaggeration to say that the traditional, rational consumption and savings patterns of the Japanese people have already achieved the goals of the system. Also, the idea that since Japan could not do it, we could not do it was way off the mark. In my view, since capitalism was not as well developed in Korea as it was in Japan, it was high time to implement the system.

The capital flight that was thought to be one of the greatest stumbling blocks to enactment in the early 1980s was as serious a problem as had been feared. Of course, part of the money that people want to stay underground has probably left the country since the introduction of the system. However, this kind of money would inevitably have left the country, with or without the system, because of its inherent nature to seek a safe haven. Therefore, it would not have been right to postpone the introduction of the system for the sole purpose of sheltering such money. Moreover, when Korea is trying its best, as it is now, to bring its economy in line with the global economy in preparation for the twenty-first century, it would have been absurd to worry about capital flight. From this fear arose the anachronistic desire to keep restrictions on foreign exchange. Even if some money left the country, where would it go? It will definitely come back, the Korean economy is not so fragile that the flight of such capital would seriously affect the balance of payments and the procurement of investment resources.

In the post-real-name-system period, we did not have the side effects that its opponents feared. There was no large-scale withdrawal from bank accounts. There was no crash in the stock market. There was no massive bankruptcy of small and medium-sized firms. Nor was there speculation in the real economy. What we have is low interest rates and a recovering economy, quite the opposite to what opponents of the system had predicted. But it is too early to put our minds to rest (see Table 5.3). We do not know what is coming, and the system is yet to take root. I would like to prescribe ways to minimize side effects when full implementation of the system has been completed.

First, when the legislators write the real-name system into law, they must guarantee privacy for financial transactions. Taking concrete measures to guarantee privacy of normal financial transactions would ease people's qualms about revealing their secrets. Exceptions to the protec-

Table 5.3.
History of Implementation of the Real-Name Financial Transaction System in Korea

Date	Related Stories
May 1982	A bill fraud fiasco involving Mrs. Young Cha Chang
July 1982	The Fifth Republic announces that it will introduce the system at once
December 1982	The bill on the system passes the National Assembly after revision
April 1989	A preparatory committee is established to implement the system
April 1990	The committee is disbanded as the introduction of the system is postponed
March 1992	Each party announces during the election campaign that it would introduce the system once elected
July 1992	The Korea Economic Federation discusses gradual implementation of the system
September 1992	The Korea Economic Federation proposes immediate implementation of the system
August 1993	Implementation of RNFTS

tion of privacy in financial transactions should be specified to prevent violation of business secrets by the tax authorities. In Germany, specific items are clearly delineated for the exceptions to privacy order to limit arbitrary application by tax authorities. Even when they investigate people's financial transactions, they are not allowed to simultaneously open the files on names, account numbers, and amounts. Financial institutions are also not obligated to report clients' incomes from their financial assets to the tax authorities. In Korea, there is a safety mechanism to protect transactions under the regulations on the real-name financial transaction system. However, we need to develop more specific and clear safety mechanisms.

Second, policy makers should conduct a complete review of universal taxation, which is the goal of the implementation of the real-name financial transaction system. Once comprehensive taxation goes into effect in 1996, taxpayers will feel the pinch of heavier tax burden. Therefore, stage-by-stage implementation of the universal taxation and acknowledgment of exceptions should be studied.

Third, ways should be found to coax underground funds into banks. To that end, the government needs to ease regulations on the establishment of and credit restrictions for small-scale mutual funds and savings and loans. Thus, the underground economy can easily be absorbed by banks.

Fourth, simultaneous with the real-name system other complementary measures should be carried out. Real-name land transactions and expanded application of the public land ownership concept will check speculation. The fair trade system should be reinforced as well to enhance the economic efficiency, and international competitiveness of "corporate Korea."

Promotion of Competition and the Minimization
of Administrative Regulations

Generally, administrative regulation means government regulation. *Government regulation* here does not mean regulating government activities, but government initiative to regulate the activities of each economic unit. The purpose of the government can be defined as "checking enterprises' and individuals' activities to realize a desirable social and economic order." The primary purpose of the government in checking the activities of economic units is to complement "the failure of the market." Thus, environmental control is used to minimize the negative impact of environmental pollution. Consumer protection is to minimize losses to consumers resulting from misleading information.

The subject, method, and degree of government regulation that is implemented tends to change as society changes. In Korea in the early 1960s, government regulation was focused on guiding the economy and industry in the direction in which they could best develop. However, today, when we have achieved some degree of economic growth and the authoritarian tendencies in Korea are rapidly disappearing, the focus has shifted to protecting the economically underprivileged, ensuring social equity, and minimizing the negative external effects of such problems as environmental pollution. From an economic view point, that is why economic reform policies aimed at achieving social justice are being emphasized.

In the future as well, government regulation should minimize the regulations that directly restrain economic activities and strengthen regulations that lower the negative external effects of business activities. Korea's continued economic development will not be possible with the current government-led strategy. The current government-led economic management method will lose its effectiveness in the twenty-first century when structural transformations and globalization of Korean society will have made remarkable advances. The production system will shift from a mass production system to a lean production system. Future strategies will have to focus on stimulating the autonomous and creative efforts of private-sector companies. To make products that can satisfy the constantly changing demands of customers and effectively respond to the dazzling changes in the international economic environment, the current system of government intervention into each tiny affair will prove fatal.

To respond to this situation, government intervention should be directed at promoting free and fair competition in a market economy. In other words, factors that disrupt the creative activities of enterprises or individuals and restrain the rise in economic efficiency should be radically modified. On the other hand, competition among domestic and foreign enterprises should be further promoted to maximize the efficiency of domestic enterprises.

The government should not limit new businesses or the production of certain products that could cause intense competition or disrupt infant industries. At the same time, it should encourage the establishment of small and medium-sized companies that could lead innovation and technology development. The current government restrictions on the production activities of enterprises, such as various permits, should be abolished.

In managing the economy as well, the government should try to ensure the autonomy of general economic activities by clarifying "what shall be done" and "what shall not be done." Also, in areas where new administrative demand exists and the government needs to expand its role, government should clarify the limits of its function and strictly observe them.

6

A New Paradigm for the Changing Era

INTRODUCTION OF NEW THOUGHT
IN ADMINISTRATION AND BUREAUCRACY

Changes in the Social Environment and New Administrative Demand

In the twenty-first century, the current industrial society will evolve into an information-based society. The industrial sector will shift its focus from manufacturing to information production while technology development will reach new levels never seen before. The world economy will become more globalized and most nations' politics will be influenced primarily by centrifugal factors, events no longer emanating from the center. Alvin Toffler said that, in politics, institutional powers such as the state, president, ministers, and deans will substitute the role of functional powers such as workers, labor unions, students, and farmers. Also, democracy itself will make a shift from representative power to participatory democratic model.

Korea has recently experienced considerable changes. Since 1987, democratization has evolved and had an impact on every social and economic aspect of Korean society. People demand equity and a fairer distribution of the country's wealth. As incomes rise, people demand improvement in the quality of life, including safeguarding the environment. Accordingly, people's core values have shifted from high economic growth only to economic development matched by improvements in the quality of life. People now tend to demand that the government play more the role of an economic manager who will work for realizing a fair distribution of wealth and economic justice and preserving pleasant living conditions.

With education becoming more important as a determinant factor in industrial competitiveness, nurturing talented people who will be able to adjust to the future industrial society emerges as a high-priority task. Just as Lester Thurow said, unskilled labor and those people without skill are becoming liabilities rather than assets. Therefore, the future responsibilities of administrative bureaucrats will revolve around educating capable people who can become assets to the state and society, building facilities for such education, and developing educational programs.

In the twenty-first century, Korea, now the only divided country on earth, is expected to achieve unification. Accordingly, our bureaucrats will be called upon to create an environment where the Korean people can trust each other. That would be a special administrative demand required of bureaucrats only in our country.

Quality improvement in the administrative service and the reduction of administrative costs will be important tasks. In an age of openness with infinite competition, countries with fewer regulations and more efficient administrative organizations will most likely be more internationally competitive than countries with many restrictions and inefficient organizations. Countries with high-quality administrative systems cannot only stimulate the efficient management of private enterprises but also reduce corporate investment costs. This competitiveness gap is evident when you look at countries where a potential investor must go through a lot of arbitrary "red tape" to build a plant versus one where foreign direct investment procedures have been streamlined.

A New Bureaucratic Model

The government's role must be changed in response to current developments in the economy as well as society overall. With this premise in mind, one can safely assert that our bureaucrats, such as governmental administrators, must adopt a totally different model. First and perhaps most important is the fact, some say obsession, that they and the "bureaucracy" can solve all of Korea's social and economic problems. This belief has been central to the traditional Korean bureaucratic model. Korea in the twenty-first century will be complex and diversified, and therefore there will be a natural limit to the bureaucrat's decision making and problem solving. Occasional serious problems have arisen because of this overreliance on the bureaucrats on wide-sweeping economic decisions. For example, in the early 1970s the government implemented an industrial policy that called for excessive promotion of Korea's heavy and chemical industries. This policy proved to be a miserable failure. Since bureaucrats meet a limited circle of people and deal with a limited range of subjects, they lack all the information needed to make this kind of decision safely on their own.

Rather, our bureaucrats should accurately understand potential problematic situations and present high-quality solutions for these problems. Just as Milton Friedman said, there is an inevitable time lag between the point when a problem occurs and that when the policy manager recognizes the problem, comes up with a solution, and then implements it. Accordingly, when a manager tries to solve a problem, it has already disappeared from the market or another one is caused by the first remedy. Therefore, economic managers must try to present timely and high-quality measures to solve potential problems. Moreover, when it comes to reforms like economic justice and the concentration of economic power, the government must present a clear vision for the future, thus instilling confidence in the people as regards their future well-being.

The bureaucrats who will lead Korea in the twenty-first century must be globally minded and future oriented. They will have to master negotiating skills to pursue Korea's national interests in a rapidly changing international arena. As for matters related to coordinating the various interested groups' differences and conflicts in the international setting, they will have to demonstrate their capacities and integrity to win the respect of the citizens. They must be able to compromise to gain the consensus of many. Their operating procedures will have to be transparent and democratic.

New National Development Priorities

People's desire for an improved quality of life rises almost proportionally to the increases in their standard of living. This desire leads people to an interest in taking care of the environment, preserving and even improving it. Currently in Korea, a growing number of citizens work for the environmental movement, sometimes at the expense of economic growth. For example, citizens in a certain area will object to putting a factory from one of the "polluting" industries in their vicinity or will object to construction of a nuclear power plant because of potential environmental problems. They object even though this new factory or plant would mean better jobs, higher incomes, more prosperity for them.

Another changing area is people's complaints regarding distribution of wealth and the related functions from unequal distribution. There are a growing number of cases where people ask the government to support welfare of the growing number of elderly people. Demand for increased investment in the nation's social infrastructure is also increasing.

As the change in people's values inevitably raises the cost of doing business, our economy may face considerable difficulty in maintaining the high growth rates of the past and current decades. Therefore, we must reach a public consensus to live with the delay in the improvement of our quality of life, as well as the decline in economic growth originating from higher welfare and environmental preservation costs.

A BLUEPRINT FOR SHARPENING THE COMPETITIVE EDGE OF KOREAN BUSINESSES

Production Cost Increases and International Competitiveness

Korean industry, in general, and the manufacturing sector, in particular, are currently languishing due to losses in international competitiveness. This is undoubtedly the result of steep increases in production costs stemming from sluggish technological development, high wages, and high interest rates.

Production costs can be divided into three major parts: unit labor costs, unit capital costs, and unit raw material costs (Table 6.1). Since 1985, all three costs increased dramatically and weakened the international position of Korean manufactured goods.

First, let us look at wage-related costs, the greatest burden for Korean industry. Unit labor costs in Korea have climbed sharply compared with those of Japan or Taiwan. This was because nominal wages increased much faster than labor productivity. When the 1985 unit labor cost of each country is put at 100, Korea's unit labor cost in 1993 is 139 while Japan's and Taiwan's stand at 86 and 123, respectively.

The unit cost of capital, which takes financial costs and capital productivity into consideration, has steadily increased in Korea's manufacturing sector since 1988. Huge amounts of capital were rapidly needed as facility investment rocketed up to 1991. But capital productivity did not increase proportionately. In the meantime, Japan, whose goods are the most internationally competitive, has also had increases in unit capital costs since 1988 because of rising interest rates resulting from an increase in the legal interest rates and tight monetary policy. However, in stark contrast to Korea, Japan's unit capital costs fell from 1985 to 1987. The current unit capital cost in Japan is hovering lower than that of 1985.

Another factor contributing to Korea's weakened international competitiveness is the ascent in unit raw material and intermediary material costs. Around the world, the price of raw materials such as crude oil and minerals stabilized; technological development led to a decreased need for raw materials in manufacturing. In Korea, however, skyrocketing prices and higher import prices caused by unfavorable exchange rates led to a rise in unit raw material costs, which in turn increased production costs. In Japan, unit raw materials costs have been stable since 1985.

Table 6.1.
Percent of Increase in Production Costs

		1987	1989	1991	Comparison
Korea	Rate of Increase	2.08 (98.27)	5.37 (109.50)	5.12 (117.47)	
	Contribution:				100.00
	Labor	Δ0.42	3.31	1.45	
	Capital	Δ0.59	3.77	3.18	
	Raw Materials	Δ3.09	Δ1.71	0.49	
Japan	Rate of Increase	Δ2.83 (90.53)	2.04 (92.00)	2.35 (96.28)	
	Contribution:				81.96
	Labor	Δ0.38	Δ0.77	0.28	
	Capital	Δ0.43	3.12	1.46	
	Raw Materials	Δ2.03	Δ0.31	0.61	
Taiwan	Rate of Increase	Δ4.86 (90.24)	1.69 (92.14)	0.26 (93.61)	
	Contribution:				79.69
	Labor	0.31	0.68	0.12	
	Capital	0.25	1.78	Δ1.24	
	Raw Materials	Δ5.42	Δ0.77	1.38	

Note: The figures in the parentheses are indexes based on 1985 = 100.

Assuming that 1991's total production costs—the aggregate of the three costs mentioned earlier—in Korea is 100, Japan and Taiwan's in the same year are 82 and 80, respectively.

Lagging technological development in Korea can be cited as one of the major causes for its weakened international competitiveness. Corporate R&D investment in Korea was below 10 percent that of Japan, represented only 2 percent much less than Japan's 2.7 percent. Also in Korea, more patents, the barometer of technological progress, are registered by foreigners than by Koreans. This indicates that Korea is making little technological headway.

Encouraging Facility Investment

What measures should Korea take to strengthen its undermined international competitiveness and win the trade war? Of course, the answer is to restructure the whole economy by extending facility investment and, thus, increase its growth potential. Japan came to be the strongest competitor because it made investment in economic advances. Even in the late 1980s, when Japan faced overwhelming difficulties due to a rising yen, it continued investing in economic restructuring, forming its export-oriented industries into ones aimed at meeting domestic demand.

In Korea, as unit investment has increased in order to expand the supply of manufactured goods, more facility investment than ever is required to bring such facilities to optimum level. Also, the marginal capital coefficient has been on the rise as more stress is put on capital rather than labor regarding production factors.

As the technological innovations accelerate and diversified consumer demands shorten the cycle of facility investment, the amount of facility investment required has increased rapidly. For instance, information industries in the advanced countries have notably increased their investment to strengthen their competitiveness and adapt to the changing environment, even though it does not automatically enhance productivity.

How much facility investment does Korea have to make to maintain economic growth and stability in the changing industrial environment? If we compare the Korean manufacturing industry's optimal facility investment level with the actual investment made between 1986 and 1993, actual facility investment was less than optimal during those years (Table 6.2).

If Korea is to become an advanced industrialized country and resolve such problems such as unstable prices and perennial trade deficits, the manufacturing sector must increase its growth potential, enhance its competitiveness, and continuously expand its supply capabilities.

More effective distribution of resources and capital is needed to stimulate foreign investment. To this end, the profitability must be enhanced to promote investment, and incentives must be offered to attract inactive capital to business. Also, taxes must be imposed and supervision carried out to curb the flow of capital into nonproductive areas such as land speculation and service industries (Table 6.3), which can trigger too much consumption of luxurious items. To increase "smarter" investment, incentives including tax breaks for facility investment should be offered.

Another important task for Korea is to expand financial institutions' ability to provide business with industrial funds for facility

Table 6.2.
Rate of Increase in Facilities Investment
(annual average increase in real percentage rate)

	1970–75	1975–79	1979–82	1982–85	1985–88	1988–91	1992
Facilities Investment (A)							
Korea	16.6	34.2	Δ6.4	9.7	18.7	15.4	Δ1.1
Japan	0.5	4.1	4.3	8.4	8.5	11.6	Δ13.2
GNP (B)							
Korea	8.2	10.0	3.0	9.6	12.8	8.1	5.0
Japan	4.4	4.9	3.4	4.1	4.4	4.8	0.7
A/B							
Korea	2.02	3.42	Δ2.13	1.01	1.46	1.90	Δ0.2
Japan	0.11	0.84	1.26	2.05	1.93	2.42	Δ18.9

Sources: BOK, National Accounts. BOJ, *Economic Statistics Monthly*.
Note: The rate of increase is calculated on the basis of 1985 constant prices.

Table 6.3.
Growth and Profitability by Industry

	Net Sales Growth Rate		Normal Profit to Net Sales	
	Manufacturing	Service	Manufacturing	Service
1988	15.8	18.7	4.1	6.2
1989	7.0	17.5	2.5	8.0
1990	18.6	26.4	2.3	6.0
1991	17.6	22.9	1.8	4.2
1992	10.1	15.4	1.5	4.2

Source: BOK, financial statement analysis.

investment on more favorable terms. More effort needs to be made to increase funds for facility investments to develop the high-tech industries, quicken technological progress, and nurture small and medium-sized companies, prerequisites for the long-term development of the Korean economy. The government must boost the means for direct financing, such as the stock and corporate bond markets, to diversify the sources of funds. In particular, to facilitate the procurement of funds for facility investment by businesses, tax incentives must be given to those companies issuing corporate bonds aimed at financing facility investment. The government must study ways to help those businesses with good performance to use the overseas financial markets for more facility investment. As a part of these efforts, the government should ease the regulations concerning issuing overseas bonds.

Long-Term Industrial Restructuring

As the life cycle of technology will be shorter in the highly industrialized twenty-first century, all industries will go through fluctuations. Considering the upcoming changes, a high priority must be placed on efficient industrial restructuring. Continuous efforts must be made to expand investment in R&D and production facilities for new goods. Companies that have lost their competitive edge due to structural problems must assimilate automation and other advanced technology to restore competitiveness or else move on to another line of business. The growth potential industries must be nurtured, so they can lead the growth of all Korean industry in the twenty-first century.

The industry that will spearhead economic growth of Korea in the twenty-first century must meet the following requirements concerning production and demand. The industry should be able to easily introduce production automation processes, first. Second, it must actively adapt itself to new technological changes. Third, it must have the ability to enjoy the benefits of the international division of labor.

In terms of demand, the industry must be at the initial stage of supplying its goods and have great potential for future demand. Second, it should be able to create more demand by improving its products. Third, it must have significant technological ripple effects on other industries. Fourth, it must have room to increase demand through supply and management of product components. Fifth, it should be able to penetrate the global market.

Another important task for Korea's long-term development is to improve its weakening consumer goods and components industries, which have been labeled the weakest part of Korea's industrial structure. The Korean economy has a structural problem in that foreign-made machinery and parts must be imported for Korean companies to produce high-quality goods for export. This is due to our inefficient consumer goods and component industries. Therefore, in Korea, export growth has inevitably led to import expansion and subsequently more trade deficits.

People around the world have been paying more and more attention to environmental pollution since the 1992 Rio environmental summit. Businesses will, therefore, have to produce environment-friendly goods and notably expand their investment in the installation of equipment and development of technology to prevent environmental pollution. The government and private sector must make every effort to encourage these industries, whose market size will grow in the twenty-first century. As the development of pollution-free technology and products are expanding around the world, there is much room for Korean businesses to make inroads into the new market.

Also, improvement of production systems is necessary to enhance competitiveness and restructure the Korean economy. The reason is that in the twenty-first century consumer demands will be highly quality oriented and diversified, and thus, with the existing mass production system, it will be impossible to manufacture goods that can meet the expectations of consumers. To strengthen competitiveness, companies must try to streamline their production systems. They must promote the development of related technology, including more efficient inventory adjustment.

Financial Support Based on Industry Performance

The Korean government must change the way it supports industry. In the past, the government selected strategic industries and provided them tax breaks and loans under favorable conditions.

As the economy advanced, this type of government support turned out to be fraught with problems because any business categorized as a strategic industry could be successful thanks to preferential treatment by the government. Too many businesses sought to take part in strategic industries, causing unbalanced and excessive investment. Corporations tended to exaggerate their situations to be designated a strategic company. Some business people even said that their factories were superior to any other production facility in Asia and the machines they purchased were the only ones in the world. Business people scrambled to build facilities and install equipment even though there was little need for them. That is how the current heavy industry sector was created. In some cases, the world's or Asia's largest factories and best machinery were abandoned after being purchased because there was not enough knowhow to operate them.

Another malfunction of past government support is that it delayed the smooth restructuring of declining industries. That is, the government had a tendency to offer support to declining businesses that otherwise would have been closed on the grounds that closure of those companies would have great repercussion on the domestic economy. If these practices are repeated, it will ultimately lead to further reducing the competitive edge for the whole of Korean industry.

Furthermore, if the government continues its practice of supporting specific industries, it will invite trade friction. In other words, tax breaks and low-interest loans to specific industries will raise the chances of antidumping lawsuits against Korean companies by Korea's trading partners. Particularly, following the UR negotiations, any direct, special treatment of industrial policy cannot be adopted by the trade partners. If the selection of a strategic industry is left only in the hands of government officials, it is very likely to end up in failure. Therefore, the government will have to shelve its inefficient support system.

Considering the changing industrial structure, from the middle and long-term perspectives, the government should provide the kind of support that will promote investment in facilities and R&D. Government support must be directed at individual functions such as productivity enhancement, technological development, or energy conservation rather than specific industries. The selection of the industries that receive government support must be put, not in the hands of government officials, but in those of the investors.

Useful Technology Development

Technological progress in the twenty-first century will be rapid and, hence, determine the competitiveness of a country or an industry. Cur-

rently, industrialized countries are increasingly resorting to protectionism, struggling to get a technological advantage over other nations. In
the future, each industrialized country will possess specialized technology, deepening "technological oligarchy," which will lead to "industrial
oligarchy."

In other words, industrialized countries will have a competitive
edge not only in high-tech industries but also in labor-intensive industries by making use of advanced technology. Cooperation between the
advanced and developing countries for transfer of technology will be
improved, especially in advanced technologies. Thus, it will be more
difficult for developing nations to join the ranks of advanced nations. In
this sense, there are fears that the future world economy will be polarized between the developed and developing nations.

To prepare for changes in the world technological arena and narrow
the gap with technologically advanced nations, Korea must more than
double its investment in R&D. Currently the portion of R&D investment to the GNP of developed nations stands at more than 2 to 3 percent, but in Korea it is running lower than 2 percent. Total R&D investment in Korea is far less than in the developed nations. Annual R&D
investment for the entire manufacturing sector is about US$3 billion, an
amount equal to the R&D investment of a single American company,
like IBM.

Korea's economy is quite small in comparison to the industrialized
countries. Therefore, Korea urgently needs to establish cautious mid-
dle- and long-term plans to maximize the efficiency of its limited R&D
investment and personnel. On the basis of these plans, we must make it
easier for the private sector to share "already developed" technology
thus preventing overlapping investments. R&D investments must be
funneled into practical research activities rather than improvement of
the infrastructure, such as construction of laboratories, required for
technological development. Along with this, more attention must be
paid to upgrading the education system to secure top-grade technological experts.

Korea's R&D investment must be centered on practical technology
such as quality control or more efficient production process and com-
mercializing technology that applies to basic science. Korea, with less
capital and labor, cannot directly compete with the economic superpowers in every field. It has been demonstrated that the current economic powers are not countries that developed basic science and technology but those that put it to practical use. For example, the former
Soviet Union had the highest level of basic science and technology in
the world with more than 2,300 research institutes and 1.5 million
researchers. But, its economy is in shambles due to the lack of commer-

cialization of its technology. Japan currently holds the largest share of the U.S. VCR market because the United States, which invented VCRs, did not produce products that satisfied consumer demands. These cases underscore the importance of practical technology.

Upgrading the Industrial Work Force

In the future, traditional production factors including labor and resources will become less important and sound management and efficient production systems will play a more significant role. Weapons in the future trade war will be technology, knowhow and management strategies, not resources as was the case in the 1970s.

A well-educated work force will determine a country's economic development and international competitiveness. In the past, Korea, with abundant low-wage workers, had an export-driven economy that relied on labor-intensive industries. But, Korea's future strategies will be to nurture knowledge-intensive industry, which is highly dependent on an educated, top-quality work force.

Therefore, effective personnel management is closely related to Korea's long-term economic development. In this sense, Korea needs to accurately determine its personnel needs and availability and then provide the necessary training for that work force. In particular, the government must make an effort to cultivate the specialized work force needed for the advance of high-tech industry. To enhance the quality of the specialized work force, Korea desperately needs to improve its college and graduate school education. Systematic measures must be taken such as establishing stricter standards regarding the number of professors and facilities in graduate schools.

Meanwhile, the government must study ways to employ more women. The number of women in the general work force will continue to steadily increase year by year. Efficient use of this work force must be examined as a potential solution for current labor shortages. It must be recognized that more employment and an improvement in the quality of the female work force is closely linked with overall quality enhancement of the entire work force.

The Link Between Productivity and Wages

With economic development and an improved industrial structure, higher wages become inevitable in any society. One of government's ultimate economic objects is to increase national income levels.

In the 1980s, some Korean companies, especially large businesses, offered very high wages to their workers. In Singapore, one of the four tigers of Asia, the government implemented a high-wage policy for several reasons. However, the policy was soon scrapped as the Singaporean economy showed some recessionary signs such as negative economic growth.

The reason the Singaporean government shelved the policy was that wage hikes caused prices to rise too quickly and undermined the international competitiveness of those businesses. In fact, workers tend to be more interested in spending increased wages than enhancing productivity in return for a wage hike. In Korea, there have been up to 20 percent wage increases since 1987, but productivity growth commensurate with the wage hikes did not follow. This can be attributed in significant part to the workers' attitude of putting more focus on consumption than productivity growth.

Therefore, Korea has to hammer out ways to maintain international competitiveness while continually increasing wages to their proper levels. To this end, corporate management must publicize their business performance to clear away workers' suspicions about management. And, business managers themselves should try to improve the treatment of workers, working conditions, and the working environment.

The government must block the channels of unearned income, thus minimizing the workers' desire for wage increases and meeting their expectations for a more equal distribution of wealth. From a long-term point of view, drastic increases in asset values, such as real estate, will deepen the division between the haves and the have-nots. Furthermore, it will aggravate the dissatisfaction of those without real estate in regard to the distribution of wealth, increase pressure for wage hikes, and ultimately undermine the industrial competitiveness.

For wage increases to lead to productivity growth, measures like the introduction of merit pay raise systems must be adopted. Merit systems will enable workers to earn more in real terms and employers to pay as much as they can cover. Thus, it will lead to increased production through more investment.

THE ADVANCEMENT OF THE FINANCIAL SECTOR

Economic Development and the Financial Sector

The improvement of the financial sector and the development of the economy are like two sides of a coin. Therefore, financial sector improvement cannot be achieved without the development of the economy and vice versa. The relationship between the two, however, still reflects the chicken-and-egg argument.

Actually, the relationship between economic and financial development varies depending on the stage of economic development. Regarding the relationship between the two, there are two types of models: demand following and supply leading. The demand-following model suggests that, with an increase in overall demand, the financial sector expands. On the other hand, the supply-leading model assumes that established financial institutions create conditions in which they can offer a variety of services and promote industrial development.

In Korea, where the financial sector tends to be viewed as a helping hand for economic development, the demand-following model is applicable. However, the relationship between economic and financial development has changed little in Korea over the years. In the 1960s, Korean financial institutions played an auxiliary role in promoting exports and investment. Financial institutions put a higher priority on government-chosen strategic industries when they offered funds. It is not an exaggeration to say that all domestic financial institutions were aiming at maximum economic development for Korea.

In the 1970s, this tendency did not change much. Under the guidance of the government, financial institutions had to concentrate their support on government-designated industries. In other words, the government made it obligatory even for commercial financial institutions to provide companies with funds to promote exports. In the late 1970s, when the government tried to further develop the heavy and chemical industries, financial institutions were urged to give preferential financial support to these industries. For its part, the government firmly believed that it had to provide financial support to the heavy and chemical industries because they were essential for advancing the domestic industrial structure. Also, the capital gestation period is long and the risks are enormous for outside investors in those particular industries. Because the government continued selecting those industries eligible for preferential loans for a long time, the domestic financial institutions could not get any opportunity to scrutinize government-selected companies. This delayed the development of the domestic financial institutions.

The freeze on private loans in 1972 was a notable turning point regarding the role of our financial institutions. The measure, taken on August 3, 1972, was aimed mostly at revitalizing the economy, which was suffering from sluggish exports. The main content of the measure was, first, to adjust the maturity and interest rates on loans from the private money lenders; second, to earmark some bank funds for long-term loans with low-interest rates; third, to establish credit guarantee funds; and fourth, to reduce financial institutions' interest rates.

The freeze on private loans proved to be a disaster. As a matter of fact, the freeze was the kind of "emergency measure" rarely taken in a capitalist economic system. The freeze resulted in the collapse of an orderly credit flow in the private sector by distorting normal capital flow. The effects of the measure were short-lived and businesses' financial costs increased soon again, aggravating an already difficult time for the private-corporate sector.

Financial Reforms in the 1980s

Korea's financial sector of the 1980s was much different from that of previous years. In the 1980s many argued that development of the Korean economy had been stymied by our lagging financial sector. Industrialized countries, including the United States, started to put more and more pressure on Korea to open its financial markets.

Amid these changes at home and abroad, Korea in the 1980s stepped up its efforts to develop its financial sector. As a part of these efforts, domestic financial institutions were given limited autonomy (Table 6.4). Starting with the Hanil Bank, which had been privatized in June 1981, Korea's five largest banks were all privatized by September 1982.

It became easier to establish new financial institutions. Thus, two new commercial banks were established: the Shinhan Bank in 1982 and the KorAm Bank in 1983. Financial institutions dealing with short-term savings and loans such as short-term loan companies and mutual trust funds were authorized to commence business. Preferential or discrimi-

Table 6.4.
Characteristics of Financial Development in the 1970s and 1980s

1970s	*1980s*
• Dramatic increase in demand for funds and foreign loans	• Privatization of commercial banks
• Sluggish development of the direct financing market	• Institutional improvement for the promotion of healthy competition among financial institutions
• Growth of nonmonetary financial institutions	
• Expansion of private loan markets	• Financial institutions' activities expanded
• Rapid growth of specialized banks	• Rapid growth of short- and long-term capital markets
	• Partial interest liberalization

Source: Yu Chong Kwon. Financial Development in Korea (July 1991).

natory treatment of Korean branches of foreign banks was abolished, creating an environment in which domestic and foreign financial institutions could compete on an equal basis.

The scope of activities of the existing commercial banks was expanded. They were now authorized to issue credit cards and certificates of deposit, manage trust accounts, engage in factoring, and sell public bonds. Interest rates were partially liberalized. As a result, ailing primary financial institutions including banks were invigorated with an expansion of their business activities.

Considering the current status of the domestic financial sector, it is safe to say that the various measures taken in the 1980s to develop the financial sector failed to meet the government's expectations. Despite a series of financial reforms, small and medium-sized companies are still suffering fund shortages and high interest rates. Domestic financial institutions are still heavily dependent upon inefficient practices. Amid the changes in the overall financial environment, interest rates are not responding to capital demand and supply. Since the partial liberalization of the financial markets, foreign banks have remarkably increased their market share, even though they have only a small number of branches here.

Korea's Financial Sector and the Financial Crunch

Despite the financial reforms enacted in the 1980s, Korea's financial sector is thought to be far behind that of the advanced nations. Korea's financial interrelation ratio (a country's total financial assets to the real GNP) is lower than those of the United States, Japan, and even Taiwan.

Another indicator, the mediating technique of finance, has not improved much. The ratio of national savings and financial assets of the nonfinancial sector (households, businesses, and the government), which demonstrates the ability of financial institutions to induce savings, was 1.12 in 1989 but decreased to 0.87 in 1993 (Table 6.5). The percentage of loans from financial institutions for real investment has diminished since 1989, indicating financial institutions' contribution to fund procurement has recently declined. Due to Korea's sagging financial sector, businesses continue to suffer fund shortages even though the annual monetary growth rates in Korea have grown to 18–19 percent. The central bank is having a hard time supplying current money levels.

Unsound financial practices still exist. Companies are making investments mainly for expansion, thus failing to maintain a healthy financial structure. Financial institutions are still sticking to mortgage loans and compensatory deposits, taking advantage of business's need for funds. Financial institutions seem to be trying to maximize profits at

Table 6.5.
Efficiency in Financial Intermediary Function

	Financial Asset Increase of Nonfinancial Sector/Gross Saving	Loans by Financial Institutions/Gross Fixed Capital Formation	Fund Supply/ Fund Finance
1985	0.85	0.49	0.59
1987	0.94	0.45	0.51
1989	1.12	0.59	0.48
1991	0.96	0.57	0.59
1992	0.87	0.44	0.52
1993	0.87	0.39	0.45

Sources: BOK, Flow of funds accounts and national accounts.

the customers' expense rather than by innovative measures. The government for the most part controls financial institutions' operations by maintaining window guidance and regulating interest rates and the amount of currency in circulation.

Diversified Financial Demands

Which steps must Korea's financial sector take to become competitive and take the initiative in Korea's economic development? To stimulate the financial sector, I suggest the following areas for review.

First, potential changes in demand and the overall economic environment must be accurately forecast. Then, a flexible financial support system should be established in response to these conditions. Second, the structural problems in the domestic financial sector must be detected and measures taken to correct the problems.

With this in mind, it is helpful to take a look at the possible changes in financial demand as we move toward the twenty-first century. Industries, the major recipient of funds, will undergo rapid changes due to accelerated technological progress and the shaping of a new world order. In other words, technological innovation will create a new industry and turn traditional industries into high-tech ones by combining traditional and advanced technology. As the number of the elderly increases and people put more emphasis on individual pursuit of happiness, demand for funds for fields such as leisure is expected to rise enormously all around the world.

Korea has maintained high growth rates, and demand for funds is likely to rise with economic development. Demand for funds will increase steadily in traditional fields such as construction of new facto-ries and enhancement of production capability of existing goods. There will be a growing demand for funds for technological development, creation of a competitive industrial structure through restructuring of the declining industries, and nurturing the high-tech industries (Table 6.6). Investment for pollution-preventing facilities to enhance the qual-ity of life will be needed.

It is almost certain Korean financial institutions will have to pro-vide loans for the reconstruction of the North Korean economy. Thus, a tremendous amount of money will be required to bring the collapsed North Korean economy up to a functioning level. Considering this, pro-viding "national unification funds" will be an important task for finan-cial institutions in the coming decades.

Financial Liberalization and Financial Sector Restructuring

The following trends will emerge in the world's financial markets. Along with the progress in liberalization and globalization of the activ-ities of financial instutions, these institutions will expand and in the process, mega banks will be created through merger and acquisition. An increasing number of specialized banks will target specific classes of borrowers and deal with specific financial services. In other words, existing financial institutions will see historical expansion and growth at the same time more specialized banks will be created.

To cope with the fierce competition, Korean banks also will have to set up their business positioning considering their differenciated busi-ness scope and the operating size (Figure 6.1). Retail banks, for exam-ple, should decide whether they will be large-scale universal banks or small-size specialized banks. According to the strategy, banks will have to decide whether to increase their capital, to expand their operating networks, and to change their business and customers or not.

In the twenty-first century, securitization—capital flow from indi-rect financing to direct financing—will gain momentum. Along with the

Figure 6.1.
Business Position of Banks

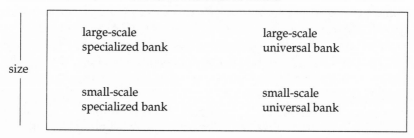

Table 6.6.
Progress Toward a Highly Industrialized Society in the Twenty-First
Century and Demands for Industrial Financing

Industrial Restructuring and Productivity Enhancements	Constant support for industrial restructuring
	Support for development of high technology and its commercialization
	Basic science, microelectronics, new materials, bionics, space and aeronautics, development of marine resources, etc.
	Enhancement of competitiveness through automation
	Application of high technology to traditional industries
	Facility investment for improvement of outdated facilities
Financial Demands of New Industries	Demand for investment in the postindustrial society
	Data processing, service industry, new media, etc.
	Financial demands to counter problems related to population, energy, and the environment
	New industries created by enhanced living standards (silver industry, etc.)
	Development of alternative energy sources
	Nurturing of environment—friendly industries, investment in antipollution facilities
	Advancement of the service sector
	Improvement of distribution and investment for banking and the information industry
Provision of Policy Loans	Areas in which the market mechanism cannot function effectively
	Improvement of national information networks, infrastructure, health care, housing, and the environment
	Balanced development of land and enhancement of living standards
	High-risk technological development
	Small and medium industries with high credit risks and insufficient collateral
Financial Demand Stemming from Reunification	Expansion of infrastructure

progress in financial liberalization and globalization, improved management techniques in the financial institutions due to computerization will give more choices to businesses in obtaining and using funds. The bond and futures markets will be improved with capital liberalization. In particular, transactions in negotiable securities among households, businesses, and financial institutions will be invigorated.

Banks must expand their investment activities so they can offer higher yeilding products. Financial institutions can take the lead in such areas as issuing new securities, buying and selling private securities, off-balancesheet transactions, and financial advisory service.

Conditions must be created that will allow financial institutions to enter these new business arenas. To this end, measures must be taken now by the government to enhance the financial institutions' spirit of enterprise. First, free competition must be promoted in the financial market by allowing entry of new financial institutions. Due to government restraints on establishing new financial institutions, the existing ones have enjoyed a marked advantage. In addition to high interest rates, the established financial institutions were inclined to be passive and easygoing with regard to their management policies. There was no motivation to improve management. This has proven to be a serious impediment to developing Korea's financial sector. To encourage healthy competition, the government must relax entry requirements, not only for short-term loan companies and mutual trust funds, but also for banks.

Second, the current strict division regarding their business activities must be eased to stimulate competition. These restrictions should be gradually lifted, but the Korean financial sector must be restructured toward a universal banking system, in which all financial institutions engage freely in diverse financial activities. If the government continues its current policy of dictating areas of operations for the financial institutions, it will not be possible to improve the management of the financial institutions. If not, domestic financial institutions will inevitably fall even more behind in terms of their operations and developing financial products, which are increasingly diversified due to securitization.

Third, a variety of financial regulations such as loan restrictions must be removed. The financial authorities should suspend their interference in the day-to-day operations of financial institutions. They should also dismantle any remaining barriers between the financial markets.

Deregulation of Interest Rates

Since the initial stages of Korea's economic development, the government has totally controlled interest rates under its administrative guidance and regulations. The government's purpose at the time was to channel limited capital to government-designated strategic loans at low rates, thus lessening those industries' costs. However, with the beginning of free market liberalization and economic restructuring, interest rate control by the government was inefficient and unwarranted. The government then introduced a plan to ease control on interest rates in the late 1980s. In September 1988, controls on most interest rates were eased except for special and public finance funds. However, the 1988 deregulation was scrapped in 1989 when interest rates skyrocketed.

Since then interest rates have begun to stabilize and the developed countries have raised their voices for less regulation of the Korean financial markets. In August 1991, Korea established a plan for a phased deregulation of interest rates. Under this plan, the first-phase of interest rate deregulation was implemented in November 1991 and the second-phase interest rate deregulation in November 1993. Currently, interest rates are deregulated for 75 percent of bank loans and 40 percent of deposits.

The current policy for partial interest rate deregulation has advantages, such as buffering the impact of interest-rate deregulation on the economy. But accelerated-phased interest rate deregulation will have to be carried out because market interest rates have been stable since the implementation of the second-phase of interest rate deregulation.

Considering this, Korean financial authorities seem to be too cautious about interest rate deregulation. Interest rates are like the price of goods in the market. Just as the market cannot function effectively unless prices are controlled by the demand for and supply of goods, the mechanism for controlling capital demand and supply will not work if interest rates are not determined by the market. Therefore, sweeping interest rate deregulation must be implemented in Korea to remove disguised demand for funds and to make interest rates function as a factor controlling the activities of each economic player.

Financial Globalization

With the development of information and telecommunication technology in the twenty-first century, financial regulations will be eased and capital will flow more freely around the globe. Financial markets around the world will become interdependent as cross-border financial transactions gain impetus and financial institutions advance abroad. The types of financial transactions and qualifications of participants in the financial markets will be determined by common standards.

The factors driving financial globalization are the global spreading of the financial markets, international standardization of transaction and settlement systems, and the increase of exchangeability among the financial assets of different nations. As it becomes easier to gain access to the international financial markets, banks and nonbanking institutions will engage in more financial assets transactions in the Eurocurrency and off-shore markets. Worldwide information networks such as transaction-related information collecting and dealing systems will be developed as a means to easy and rapid access to the international financial markets. Also, international settlement systems, such as SWIFT, will play a more significant role. By establishing worldwide settlement networks, financial institutions will be able to distribute capital worldwide and maintain around-the-clock operating systems. The forthcoming integration of financial markets around the globe will stir competition for the development of new financial products and increase exchangeability among financial assets.

The international business activities of financial institutions will expand as they have more access to the Euroexchange and off-shore markets and have more opportunities to profit from international transactions. Therefore, financial institutions will build service systems targeting the whole world. To survive the international competition of the twenty-first century, financial institutions will have to be equipped with far-reaching branch and computer networks, client-oriented information networks aimed at servicing customers better, abundant capital, and advanced financing techniques.

The ongoing financial globalization puts a significant burden on Korea, whose financial sector is weak. Recently, Citibank embarked on retail financing business in Korea and quickly increased its market share, causing fear among some of the domestic financial institutions. By contrast, the overseas business of Korean banks is still confined mostly to trade financing, foreign exchange, and supply of short-term loans for the foreign divisions of Korean companies and Koreans living abroad. Overseas branches of Korean banks are also vulnerable in terms of fund procurement. They rely mostly on call money, loans from other Korean banks, and accounts in their head office and branches.

It is hardly likely that Korean financial institutions will sharpen their competitive edge overnight. Therefore, carefully devised strategies are required for the globalization of Korean financial institutions. Their globalization must be vigorously pursued to enhance their international competitiveness. The Korean government should not restrict the number of banks seeking to advance into foreign countries. Instead, the government should encourage a handful of banks, which have issued foreign currency bonds, introduced loan syndicates, and operated foreign capital, to take the lead in financial globalization. Domestic financial institutions must make more investment in personnel trained in international finance. They must be committed to enhancing their business capabilities by cooperating with prominent foreign financial institutions and launching mergers and acquisition of foreign banks.

Effective Industrial Financing

The total amount of a nation's funds can be divided into financial, household, and industrial funds, depending on their use. In Korea, demand for industrial funds accounts for 70 percent of total fund demand. Therefore, financial institutions are under pressure to provide increasingly more loans for facility investment as the economy grows. In other words, to maintain a 7 percent GNP growth rate, 30 percent of the GNP must be appropriated for fixed capital investment. In this sense, the funds for facility investment provided by financial institutions must be increased year by year as the GNP grows. Demand for funds for expanding production capability, restructuring industries, and enhancing productivity and competitiveness will most likely multiply considerably. Regarding the ways in which the funds are obtained, Korean businesses generally rely on external financing for 60 percent. The other 40 percent generally is obtained from internal capital sources such as business profits and depreciation. Of external financing, 55 percent comes from indirect financing including loans from banks, direct financing accounts for 35 percent, and foreign capital supplies 10 percent.

We can see then that Korean businesses are dependent mostly upon external funds, especially indirect financing, in securing facility investment funds. Korean businesses should reduce their dependency on external funds and find ways to utilize internal capital and direct financing. This would improve the current situation, which puts too much emphasis on indirect financing. This, however, may prove difficult because of the low profitability and weak financial structures of many of our businesses.

There was a time when direct financing exceeded indirect financing in the total corporate capital procurement, thanks to a bullish stock market. But, there exist many roadblocks to totally replacing indirect financing for raising facility investment funding. Funds for facility investment should be long-term capital due to the long-term nature of the investment. Therefore, raising funds by issuing bonds is not the best way since the availability of this money is subject to market sensitivities. This kind of capital is generally utilized for operations. The government has been trying to encourage companies to use industrial bonds to raise money for facility construction, but without much success. Meanwhile, corporate bonds are very useful for facility investment in that the terms of the bonds can be adjusted by each company. According to their long-term plan for facility investment and the funds required, interest payments and redemption can be covered by profits derived from the facility investments. In Japan, corporate bonds are the chief source of facility investment funds, accounting for as much as 30 percent of total facility investment. In Korea, however, the corporate bond maturities are mostly less than three years, and most of them are issued to secure working capital.

As a result, Korean companies are expected to continue the current practice of depending on indirect financing for the foreseeable future. With indirect financing, businesses can secure funds under their own plans and repay the funds and interest with profits from facility investments, since the funds are mostly long term. Furthermore, indirect financing is favorable for businesses in terms of cost. Companies have easy access to indirect financing in most cases once they open an account with a financial institution. Indirect financing through banks will continue to play an important role when Korean companies look to raise funds for facility investment.

As of the end of 1993, 55 percent of Korean companies' facility investment funds were provided by commercial banks, 35 to 40 percent by the Korea Development Bank, and 5 percent by other financial institutions. The funds provided by commercial banks are mostly public finance and policy funds drawn from the central bank of Korea; less than 20 percent of the funds consists of the financial resources of those commercial banks. This could contribute to rising inflation rates. It is contradictory to help businesses grow with funds that can trigger inflation. As banks naturally want to expand, we cannot blame commercial banks for providing the facility investment funds.

Facility investment generally requires huge amounts of long-term funds and entails greater risk. Therefore the banks must enhance their credit investigation abilities. However, this is not being done. The Korea Development Bank thoroughly examines the worthiness of companies seeking loans, since it has experts and organizations that can carry out specialized tasks such as industrial and technological inquiries and profitability tests. However, most Korean commercial banks lack these capabilities. As more and more autonomy is being given to the commercial banking sector, such banks will refrain from giving preferential loans to government-designated companies at the cost of their profits. They will inevitably have to reduce loans available for facility investments. Therefore, financial institutions specializing in providing equipment funds will play a more important role in the Korean banking sector.

In Japan, financial institutions dealing with long-term funds play an essential role in providing equipment and thus contribute a lot to Japan's economic growth. During rapid Japanese economic growth, the equipment funds provided by the long-term loan institutions accounted for

50–80 percent of the total equipment funds provided by all Japanese banks. That percentage has dropped to approximately 12 percent since the early 1970s, when facility investments decreased markedly after the first oil shock. However, this did not pose much of a problem for the long-term institutions. As more attention was paid to the service sector during the economic restructuring of Japan, the service sector, including real estate, required more long-term funds, and city banks tried to meet these demands. Thus the percentage of funds provided by the long-term loan banks was reduced. However, long-term loan banks still play a pivotal role by focusing on providing funds for manufacturing sector and infrastructure expansion.

Considering the general characteristics of industrial financing, I believe the following things should happen. From a long-term perspective, the Korean government should offer tax breaks for businesses to increase their reserves. It should then encourage the companies to appropriate these reserves for facility investments. The government must try to lessen corporate dependency on indirect financing by nurturing capital markets, extending the maturity of corporate bonds and promoting new stock offerings.

As businesses are expected to resort to indirect financing for the time being, the government should enhance the capability of financial institutions dealing with long-term funds to provide equipment funds. Meanwhile, the commercial banks must be encouraged to focus on their primary business—short-term financing—and thus enhance their efficiency.

To increase availability of long term funds, measures must be implemented to facilitate the issuing of bank debentures, such as less regulation of bank debenture interest rates.

Stricter Regulation and Supervision of Financial Institutions

As management is given more autonomy and business activities expand, competition among Korea's financial institutions will intensify as each attempts to attract more customers. During this period of intensified competition, financial institutions would be expected to introduce products paying higher interest rates as well as making loans at higher rates; thus increasing their potential profits.

It will be additionally important for governments to monitor these conditions and introduce necessary regulations. International cooperation will have to increase with standardized worldwide regulation systems introduced to oversee international settlement systems.

As a means to reduce the additional risk stemming from drastic fluctuations in interest and exchange rates, new activities such as futures transactions, swaps and options will be promoted in Korea. This will be further accelerated by entry of more foreign firms into the domestic market. For Korean financial institutions to deal with the changes at home and abroad that could hamper their stability and sound operation, they must enhance their risk control abilities. In the domestic market, they must compete to provide high-quality financial services rather than settle for increased profits only. The risks stemming from introducing new financial products such as options should be reduced by better research, more qualified staffing and clear management strategies. Each financial institution should double its effort to maintain sound capital operation through more efficient asset-liability management. Recently, the Bank for International Settlements has made it obligatory for financial institutions to maintain healthy asset-liability management by introducing specific rules (see Figure 6.2).

The government should continue reducing its level of intervention in the procurement and distribution of funds. However, it should also issue strict regulations for the sound operation of financial institutions, to prevent them from taking excessive risks and thus undermining their stability. The government should introduce deposit insurance systems to protect customers against possible financial institution failure.

Integrated Information Service for Financial Institutions

The Korean financial sector will develop into an industry providing integrated information services by the end of the decade. This will include not only financial transactions but information transmission by linking businesses, households, and banks. International information systems include collecting data on overseas branch activities, international markets, and support systems for international transactions (Figure 6.3). These systems will be increasingly important as financial globalization advance.

With the progress in information technology, banks will be able to provide a variety of information to effectively meet customer demands. They should also be more profitable and internationally competitive. Korea's leading banks of the future will be those that can provide rapid information services to meet customers' extensive and diverse demands. The financial sector of the twenty-first century will become a high-tech industry for communication through huge investments.

Currently, Korean institutions are making strenuous efforts to fully computerize. However, they lag far behind those of developed nations both in amounts invested in their information systems and levels of computerization. Furthermore, their computerization activities are confined mostly to internal business activities in contrast to the advanced

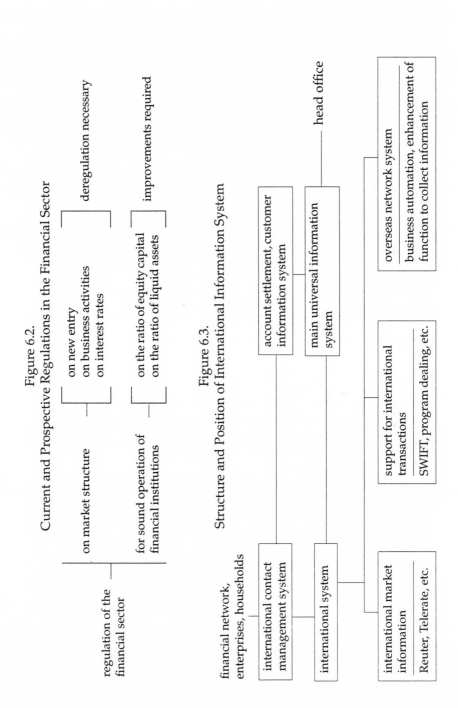

Figure 6.2.
Current and Prospective Regulations in the Financial Sector

regulation of the
financial sector

on market structure
— on new entry
  on business activities
  on interest rates
} deregulation necessary

for sound operation of
financial institutions
— on the ratio of equity capital
  on the ratio of liquid assets
} improvements required

Figure 6.3.
Structure and Position of International Information System

financial network,
enterprises, households

international contact
management system

international system

account settlement, customer
information system

main universal information
system

— head office

support for international
transactions

SWIFT, program dealing, etc.

overseas network system

business automation, enhancement of
function to collect information

international market
information

Reuter, Telerate, etc.

financial institutions, which are very quickly becoming integrated information businesses. For Korea's financial institutions to adjust to globalization trends and engage in independent business activities, they must double their current efforts to develop information systems. Since Korea's financial institutions are very small compared to those in the developed nations, it will be very difficult for individual banks to bear the tremendous costs involved in developing these systems. Hence, domestic financial institutions must hammer out ways to jointly finance information systems by pursuing integration and standardization of their business activities.

REDEFINING THE ROLES OF THE GOVERNMENT AND FINANCE

Night Watch State and Government Interference

The roles of government and finance have been defined differently depending on time and circumstances. Arguments concerning the roles of the government and finance were started in earnest by Adam Smith in the eighteenth century. He claimed that the economy has a self-controlling function, which is often called *the invisible hand*. That is, he maintained that the optimal distribution of resources and maximum efficiency of the economy can be achieved by the self-controlling function of the market with the help of the parametric function of price. He also said that the role of the government must be confined to national defense and maintenance of public order. And he even contended that only the so-called cheap government or "night watch state" could make the mechanism of the market work and thus promote the development of the overall economy.

But because economic policies based upon the cheap government theory by Adam Smith were contradicted by the failure of the market, a change in the policies was inevitable. Thus, extensive government interference in the economy began to be accepted gradually. In a night watch state, where government intervention in the economy was curbed as much as possible, the haves dominated the have-nots. The haves became richer and the have-nots poorer. The Great Depression that swept the United States and other parts of the world revealed the limits of economic policies relying upon the market mechanism. This triggered intense criticism of the cheap government theory and led to "the Keynesian revolution," which stressed the role of the government in setting up and implementing various economic policies. Among the economists who called for strong government intervention in the economy are not only J. M. Keynes but J. S. Mill, A. C. Pigou, and so on.

"The Small Government" and "The Neo-Big Government Theory"

Views calling for aggressive government interference in economic activities had to be reexamined in the late twentieth century. Excessive government intervention in the economy resulted in increased administrative expenses. As the economic structure advanced and the industrial structure centered on the manufacturing sector became knowledge and information intensive, there was an increasing possibility of "the government failure." The government's financial burden increased due to extensive social security costs. The deficit increased and became a major economic problem. Steps to stimulate the economy and countermeasures against inflation and stagflation based on Keynesian theories proved to have minimal effects.

In the meantime, negative external economic conditions emerged as a serious problem. Under these circumstances, "the little government theory" and deregulation were proposed. Currently, the little government theory is being advocated by the United States, Japan, and other major industrialized countries. Among the economists championing the theory is Milton Friedman. There still exists strong objection to the little government theory. Some argue that the role of government must be changed in the age of transnational business activities. In the past, when economies were separated by borders, the more the government spent, the less resources remained for the private sector to spend. Therefore, for a country to develop its economy, especially in its private sector, government spending had to be reduced to a minimum level.

But in the twenty-first century, the role of the government will have to be redefined because a country's resources are not finite. The lack of production factors such as capital, labor, and natural resources will no longer hamper economic activities. Multinational companies are expected to move to those countries that have better administrative services and public infrastructure. Therefore, countries hoping to promote economic growth will have no alternative but to create the conditions needed to attract multinational companies. These countries will have to multiply public investment to expand their infrastructure. In this respect, many argue that the role of the government must be enlarged to expand and enhance the quality of the infrastructure. This means the emergence of the neo-big government theory.

The Change in the Function of Finance

With changes in the government's role, finance's role has also undergone changes. At the beginning of economic development, finance was recognized as the vault of the government; that is, public finance. In the early twentieth century finance started to be accepted as a means for carrying out government policies. The idea that finance was an instrument to promote economic policies gained significance as an economic recession gripped the world. Capitalism's self-stabilizing function weakened. Finance as a means to stabilize the economy was emphasized more at this time because of Korea's effective demand creation theory. In 1933, the United States launched the famous New Deal policies. The same year, the Japanese government increased spending to achieve social and political objectives; it issued government bonds to cover its deficits. The two countries' policies had different aims but both are considered as examples of finance's changing role.

The modern role of finance was established after the second World War, when government financing was utilized primarily as a way to curb inflation, revitalize and stabilize the economy, and redistribute income. This modern concept is well demonstrated in Musgrav's book *Finance*. Musgrav said that finance has three functions in the management of a national economy: first, an allocation function to support the growth of the national economy; second, a redistribution function to promote equality in people's lives; and third, a stabilization function as a mechanism to stabilize the national economy.

The Role of the Government in a Highly Industrialized Society

"The nine most terrifying words in the English language are, 'I'm from the government and I'm here to help.'"

(Ronald Reagan 1986)

Attention has been paid to changes in both the functions of finance and the role of government with the approaching advent of a highly industrialized society. In regard to government's future role, Robert Reich, a Harvard professor, makes an interesting prediction. He says that the future capitalist societies will be linked together in a weblike organization. He also claims that a company's competitive profit margin will be determined by how it meets the demands of specific classes and produces inimitable goods for specific uses. According to Reich, "It won't matter in the future to which nation a competitive company belongs; rather it will be more important where the high profits generated in a company are from."

In this type of society, government's development strategies must be different from those of the traditional industrial society. Future governments must try to restrict the unnecessary and excessive expansion of government. They must commit to creating an economic environment with fair competition and promoting individuals' creativity to come up with solutions for countries' problems. It must provide training for a creative and competent people. In the twenty-first century, only countries with creative and imaginative people will succeed.

To promote creativity, the government should reduce interference and regulations and invigorate the self-controlling function of the market. The government has to restrain direct intervention in the manufacturing industry, in particular. To galvanize the market, the government must make improvement in market-related systems and hammering out basic rules.

The government's role must be strengthened in other fields to meet fresh administrative demands: improved administrative service and defense, protection of public order, prevention of environmental pollution, and the establishment of a comprehensive social security system.

More infrastructure investment, the traditional function of finance, will be required not merely to reduce businesses distribution cost but to strengthen their competitiveness in a time of fierce international competition.

It will be undesirable for the government to take a laissez-faire approach even though it seeks to promote autonomy in the economy and increase competition. A good lesson for Korea can be drawn from the case of the United States and Japan. The U.S. government has been placing more emphasis on industrial development. And, concerted efforts by Japan's Ministry of International Trade and Industry and its corporate sector have led to the economic prosperity of Japan.

The competitive edge of Korea's businesses must be sharpened, and the government must promote industrial restructuring and encourage new businesses that have growth potential. In addition, the Korean government must increase cooperation with other trading partners, lest domestic businesses suffer from trade friction.

The Korean government must seek to enhance public trust. It needs to set up a variety of policies under transparent, objective, and fair rules. It must publicize more government-related information and monitor the government activities to enhance efficiency and minimize "the possibility of failure."

Restructuring Public Finance

Korean public finance can be summarized as follows. First, despite continuing economic growth, the ratio of public finance expenditures to the

GNP has been less than 20 percent, lower than that of developed nations and other nations on a par with Korea in terms of income level (Table 6.7). Second, fixed expenditures account for a high percentage of total public expenditures. Third, not enough money has been appropriated for social security except for education. Fourth, the government's lack of public financing has not been regarded as a serious problem. Considering these characteristics, Korea is thought to have been efficiently pursuing economic growth at low public cost.

However, there is a need for change in public finance. Some argue that the national budget must be increased to expand infrastructure, improve public servants' salaries, establish a social security system for the elderly, strengthen national defense, and guarantee equal opportunity for all people. But others say that the government must take austerity measures while controlling aggregate demand to maintain a healthy public finance structure because dramatic increases in government expenditures may cause inflation.

Both arguments hold true. Infrastructure expansion and establishing a social security system are needed to advance the Korean economy, while reduced public finance is also essential for the stability of the national economy. For Korea to pursue these two policies, financial restructuring must come first. Excessive fixed expenditures must be curbed as much as possible, and the defense budget must be adjusted to effectively respond to changing domestic and international, political, economic, and security conditions. The tax system must be upgraded and develop accurate revenue sources and if necessary increase taxes with fair policies.

Changes are needed in the distribution of resources to stimulate economic growth. So far, public finance in Korea has been used mainly to expand industrial infrastructure aimed at supporting production. However, that role needs to be extended toward demand and supply control. In other words, a supply expansion policy must be pursued along with demand control through management of aggregate demand. With changes in the industrial environment, the government needs to actively embark on new activities such as supporting investment for pollution control. Recently the World Bank and the Asian Development Bank have been encouraging civilians to make investments in the construction of public infrastructure. Korea needs to review this method in operating its public finance.

New Views on the Social Security System

The redistribution of wealth is linked closely to economic growth. Albert Hershman of Harvard University said that a more equal distri-

Table 6.7.
Percent of Fiscal Expenditure Structure by 1986 Income Level

	GNP per Capita	Gross Expenditure/ GNP	National Defence	Education	Health	Housing, Social Security	Debt Service
Low-Income Country	200	20.8	17.7	9.8	3.6	6.2	23.8
Low-Middle-Income Country	750	24.9	15.8	14.5	4.0	9.1	21.5
High-Middle-Income Country	1,890	28.3	10.3	10.2	5.1	17.3	19.6
Advanced Country	12,960	28.6	16.4	4.5	12.9	39.0	9.5
Korea	2,370	17.8	29.2	18.1	1.5	7.2	16.2

Source: *World Development Report*, 1988.

bution of wealth is more important in a homogeneous nation like Korea. Hershman says that a homogeneous people tends to be more patient regarding a higher standard of living for everyone, but once out of patience, their reaction is very strong. Considering this situation from an economic point of view, efforts must be made to facilitate equal distribution of wealth, once the optimum level for doing so is reached.

However, an unrestricted increase in transfer expenditures for income redistribution must be controlled as much as possible. Friedman's analysis presents the intriguing view that welfare policies depending on an unlimited increase of transfer expenditures cannot be successful (Table 6.8). His assumptions are these: in one case, a person tries to be frugal but wants high-quality when making personal expenditures. In another case, a person is frugal but does not have as strong a motive as the first person as most of the money is spent on others. A third person spends others' money on himself or herself, say, having lunch paid for by the company. In this case the person has no interest in the price but a strong motive to make the best use of the money spent. Still a fourth person spends others' money on others, and even less attention is paid to price and quality.

All modern welfare policies correspond to the third and fourth cases. Therefore, the overall welfare of the citizens is likely to weaken, since how the money is spent is not determined by the recipients. As for the recipients, they make little effort to save or maximize the funds through rational consumption because the funds are not their own.

Some recipients of welfare make no effort to better themselves and become totally dependent on welfare spending. When this happens, even a strong national leader cannot drive away poverty, as an old Korean saying goes. When individuals themselves will not try to improve their standard of living, government support is nothing but a make-shift measure whose effects are short-lived. Therefore, policies for the redistribution of wealth and improvement of welfare through public financing must focus on developing people and, at the same

Table 6.8.
Money Ownership and Consumption Behavior

Money Ownership	Consumption Object	
	Oneself	Others
One's Own	I	II
Others'	III	IV

Source: Milton Friedman, *Free to Choose* (1980).

time, efforts must be made to improve education, health care, social security, and so forth. Sweden, Norway, and other northern European nations that pursued very generous welfare policies under the motto of "from the cradle to the grave" are now hampered economically because of these welfare policies. This provides a good lesson for Korea in setting the direction of its social welfare policies.

In the late 1980s, the four political parties in the National Assembly approved a policy aimed at relieving farmers' debts. Policies that truly help farmers in the long-term are not those like debt relief, rather the government should try to encourage farmers to work harder and to produce high-quality goods by developing advanced techniques.

The Public's Changing Attitude Toward the Government

The government must substantively change its economic policies and its role in management of the economy, but first the public must change its expectations of the government. Most of all, people must realize that the government cannot solve their individual problems. The past practice of putting all the blame on the government for everything gone wrong must end. The government cannot be blamed entirely for things like the falling price of cabbages and radishes and the sluggish stock market. Of course, it is not out of the question that the government be held responsible for these problems in significant part. However, there are limits to the function and the role of the government under the market system.

As for Korean's way of thinking, all people should develop smarter consumption habits and work ethics to maximize the effects of any belt-tightening economic policies. Only when people stop shifting the blame to others and take responsibility, will it be possible to create a truly advanced government and nation.

7

The Economic Policy of a Reunified Korea

"There was a time in this business when they had the eyes of the whole world. But that wasn't enough for them. Oh, no! They had to have the ears of the world too. So they opened their big mouths, and out came talk! Talk! Talk! . . ."

(from *Sunset Boulevard*, by Charles Brackett and Billy Wilder)

Many futurists predict the upcoming twenty-first century will be the century of the Pacific just as the twentieth century was the century of the Atlantic. The center of gravity of the world economy, they contend, will be shifted to Northeast Asia. Their prediction is backed up by (Wharton Econometric Forecast Association) economic growth forecast (Table 7.1). It estimates Asian economies will grow 5.5 percent, higher than the world's average growth rate of 3.3 percent during 1993–1998. The estimate says Northeast Asian countries will show stronger economic growth, with annual average growth of 9.6 percent for China and 7.0 percent for Korea.

Although it could play an active role as a bridge between the Asian continent and the Pacific, South Korea has yet to fully explore its geopolitical advantages. With North Korea's recent refusal to allow IAEA nuclear inspections (International Atomic Energy Agency), the relationships between South and North Korea and the United States and North Korea have taken a turn for the worse. Even in late 1993, there was rumoured to be a kind of "crisis situation"; that is, war could break out on the peninsula at any moment. However, considering the dynamics of the international politics, North Korea's economic difficulties, and Korean government's strenuous efforts to achieve peaceful reunification, it is unlikely that a full-scale war will ever develop on the Korean peninsula. In the long run, the relations between the two rivals are likely to get better as South Koreans pin high hopes on the reunification of their divided land.

But the lesson derived from the reunification of East and West Germany and as was seen in recent armed clashes in the unified Yemen indi-

Table 7.1.

Prospects for Economic Growth in Northeast Asia and the World

	Year	Real GDP ($ billions)	Per Capita GNP ($)	Export ($ billions)	Import ($ billions)
Korea	1993	2,925.8	7,432	853.0	870.4
	1998	4,097.9	12,438	1,471.0	1,458.6
	Average Growth Rate	7.0%	6.0%	11.5%	10.9%
China	1993	4,972.3	391	1,009.4	895.3
	1998	7,855.5	609	2,001.4	2,064
	Average Growth Rate	9.6%	8.2%	14.7%	18.2%
Japan	1993	31,502.5	30,950	3,566.2	2,137.4
	1998	38,785.4	44,896	5,496.4	3,542.0
	Average Growth Rate	4.2%	3.9%	9.0%	10.6%
Asia	Average Growth Rate	5.5%	3.4%	11.9%	12.5%
World	Average Growth Rate	3.3%	1.2%	5.8%	5.6%

Source: WEFA, *Asia Economic Outlook* (April 1993).

cate that Korean unification will not automatically usher in an era of hope and prosperity. South Koreans must recognize the harsh truth. For a reunified Korea to meet the high expectations of the people, the following preparations must be made.

First, reunification must be achieved in a peaceful and mutually acceptable way. Only in this way will the people of South and North Korea be able to build mutual trust, paving the way for prosperity. Unlike the peoples of other nations that have been divided, the Korean people underwent the fratricidal Korean War. Therefore, confidence building for the two Koreas is of particular importance.

Second, South Korea will have to increase its economic and political strength to secure the huge amount of funds required for reunification and resolve the inevitable political and economic difficulties following reunification. Even though the former West Germany exceeded South Korea in terms of national strength at the time of German reunification, enormous reunification costs, rising unemployment rates, and raging inflation are now troubling the united Germany. This underscores the significance of building up national strength in preparation for possible reunification.

Third, institutions and systems must be established for a reunified Korea. More effort has to be made to restore the single identity of the people from the two Koreas. To ease tension between the people of South and North Korea and therefore facilitate reconciliation and harmony, both peoples have to be educated about the unique characteristics of each of the countries' marketplaces and economies.

Fourth, the existing sources of conflict among regions and classes must be swept away in South Korea to make it a place where North Koreans aspire to live after reunification. South Korea must get rid of internal sources of conflict and improve its systems to resolve tensions between the people of the two Koreas after reunification.

Finally, economic cooperation with North Korea must proceed gradually. If economic exchanges with North Korea should become overheated due to excessive competition among domestic companies, the aim of economic exchange, a means for ultimate reunification, can hardly be accomplished.

LESSONS FROM THE GERMAN REUNIFICATION

The German reunification was realized in 1990, setting a good precedent for Korean reunification. Therefore, it will be very helpful for Korea to closely review the German unification process to achieve reunification of the two Koreas without a hitch.

Preparatory work for German reunification dates back to the 1950s, but it did not start in earnest until the Social Democratic Party led by Willy Brandt came to power in West Germany in 1969 (Table 7.2). Brandt, who was inaugurated as chancellor twenty years after the creation of West Germany, pressed ahead with Ostpolitik—the policy of rapprochement with the the Communist bloc. He scrapped the Halstein principles that had been pursued since the birth of West Germany and signed an agreement with the Soviet Union. He revised the policy of not recognizing East Germany, which had been in effect since the Adenauer government. He sought cooperation with East Germany by recognizing it and pursuing contacts and reconciliation. East and West Germany simultaneously joined the United Nations and exchanged standing representatives.

West Germany, with its superior economy, then strove to develop economic cooperation with East Germany to boost the latter's economy. The West German government allowed its citizens to freely watch East German TV programs and subscribe to East German periodicals to further mutual understanding.

However, one of the most decisive factors contributing to German reunification was the inauguration of Gorbachev as president of the Soviet Union and the subsequent end to the Cold War. President Gorbachev pushed reforms of the Communist regime under the banner of Perestroika. He helped turn the confrontation between the East and West into reconciliation. Under these circumstances, East Germany and West Germany eventually fulfilled their long-awaited reunification.

What lessons can be drawn from the German experience? First, people in East and West Germany were well aware of each other's societies before reunification because of TV program exchanges and mutual contacts over a long period of time. Understanding of each other by East and West German people paved the way for mutual trust. Second, West Germany's economic support to East Germany served as a catalyst for reunification.

The population of West Germany was three times larger than that of East Germany at the point of reunification. West Germany had a far more advanced economy and higher per capita income level than East Germany, in other words, the higher stage of economic development, and became the cornerstone for the German reunification.

ECONOMIC COOPERATION BETWEEN THE TWO KOREAS

Economic Cooperation For Industrial Restructuring

What steps must be taken for South Korea, which is stepping up its efforts for reunification, to minimize the inevitable troubles after reunification and to bring about a more prosperous future?

Table 7.2.
German Reunification Process

Date	Developments
1949–1963	The Adenauer government started to pursue reunification based on national strength
1963–1966	The Erhard government took the peace offensive against Eastern European nations and East Germany and sought the isolation of East Germany
1966–1969	The Kiesinger government sought improved relations with Eastern bloc nations including East Germany and scrapped the Halstein principle
1969–1974	The Brandt government pursued Ostpolitik
1969	The West German government allowed subscription to East German publications
August 1970	A West German–Soviet Union treaty was signed
May 1972	The inter-German transportation agreement was signed
December 1972	The inter-German basic agreement was signed
September 1973	The two Germanies joined the UN simultaneously
March 1974	Bonn and Berlin exchanged permanent representatives
March 1976	An inter-German postal treaty was signed
October 1979	An inter-German free-passage agreement was signed
September 1981	The Third Inter-German Summit was held
1983–1984	Bonn provided loans to Berlin on two occasions
May 1986	An inter-German cultural agreement was signed
October 1989	The Soviet Union shelved the Brezhnev doctrine
November 1989	The Berlin Wall was dismantled
December 1989	The joint declaration of East and West Germany on treaty union; the opening of the Brandenbourg Gate
February 1990	Chancellor Helmut Kohl visited Gorbachev and got his backing for German reunification
July 1990	Monetary, economic, and social integration of the two Germanies
July 1990	Unification treaty went into effect
October 1990	The two Germanies were reunited

First of all, economic cooperation between the two Koreas must be pursued as preliminary for ultimate industrial restructuring. The German experience demonstrates that economic cooperation is imperative for the required industrial restructuring following reunification. In terms of economic development, East Germany was at the top of the Eastern European nations. Its per capita GNP was more than US $15,000. It was widely accepted that East Germany surpassed other Communist nations in terms of infrastructure, technology, education, personnel, and economic management (Table 7.3). As with other Communist countries, however, East Germany had been virtually cut off from the international community. Therefore, it lacked the capability to survive the intense economic competition of the free, capitalist world. It could not efficiently compete with Western countries, including West Germany, in terms of quality, price, and technology.

We must then examine North Korean economic realities. North Korea is even more reclusive than the former East Germany. Its level of economic development is most certainly behind that of the former East Germany. To maintain the isolation needed for the survival of its Communist system and the personality cult of Kim Il Sung, North Korea blocks any information from the free world. This means North Koreans have no experience with a market economy, and may have a hard time in getting accustomed to it. However, there is also a possibility that North Korea will assimilate the industrial technology and management system of South Korea with ease, because North Korean industry is ailing due to insufficient facility investment.

With this in mind, South Korea must now consider and examine the presumed future industrial structure. This system will maximize the international competitiveness of a reunified Korea and avoid a waste of resources stemming from overlapping investment. Therefore, more attention must be paid to implementing horizontal specialization in light industry when South Korea increases its investment in North Korea. With this approach, South and North Korean companies can avoid unnecessary competition after reunification. North Korean businesses will have to be streamlined and their competitiveness enhanced to compete with their South Korean counterparts after reunification.

A thorough analysis of the industrial structures of South and North Korea will have to be made prior to official reunification in order to maximize industrial growth. For example, joint technological development, rather than competition, should be recommended for those industries, including machine tool manufacturing, in which South and North Korea have compatible levels of development and technology. As for the auto, electric, and electronic industries, in which South Korea

Table 7.3.

Size of Economies: South and North Korea versus East and West Germany

	Population (10,000)	GNP ($100 millions)	Per capita GNP ($)	Exports ($100 millions)	Imports ($100 millions)
South Korea (A)	4,445	3,287	7,466	822	838
North Korea (B)	2,234	211	943	10.2	16.4
A/B (times)	2.0	15.6	7.9	25.8	51.1
West Germany (C)	6,208	9,430	15,190	3,411	2,695
East Germany (D)	1,634	9,430	15,190	3,411	2,695
C/D (times)	3.8	6.0	1.6	25.1	18.8

Sources: Korea Foreign Trade Association, *Major North Korean Economic Indicators*, 1993; Korea Development Institute, *Market Exploration Strategies in the Unified Germany*, 1991.

Notes: Data are as of 1992 for South and North Korea and 1989 for East and West Germany; East and West German GNPs are based on buying power.

excels, construction of assembly lines and component production facilities must be undertaken in North Korea.

With regard to North Korea's abundant natural resources, one of the promising areas will be to jointly develop them and then manufacture highly value-added products from them.

South Korea will have to maximize the opportunities presented by reunification to help shore up the competitive edge of some industries. For now, South Korean light industries like textiles, footwear, leather manufacturing, and wood processing have suffered because of high labor costs. These industries will be able to utilize North Korea's large, well-disciplined work force. The reprocessing of North Korean goods by South Korea and their subsequent export to a third country will be one of the additional benefits of Korean unification.

Enhancement of Economic Cooperation and Improvement of the Two Economic Systems

Korea has been divided for almost half a century and thus has two completely different economic systems. Consolidation of the two economic systems will be the first task to restore a single identity and achieve economic development. The integration of the divergent economic systems is necessary to step up inter-Korean economic cooperation before official reunification and to operate the economic system smoothly after reunification.

First, to step up inter-Korean economic cooperation, the agreements signed by the two Koreas must be fully implemented. For example, specific measures must be taken to put the settlement system for inter-Korean trade into effect. The South Korean government must then examine ways to simplify the government authorization procedures for private trade with North Korea. Comprehensive planning to integrate the two economic systems is necessary prior to official reunification. The South Korean government must seek ways to provide technological and administrative support to North Korea to harmonize economy-related laws and regulations, such as private ownership. Plans to improve economy-related laws must be carefully devised in case of sudden reunification. South Korea, with a longer term view, should try to maintain technological cooperation with North Korea to help North Korea get accustomed to the mechanism of the market economy.

Obtaining Funds for Reunification

When two countries with different economic systems are reunified after half a century's division, costs will vary depending on the method of reunification, the different stages of economic development, and the gap between the two economies. Whatever formula Korean reunification will take, the cost is expected to be huge, amounting to hundreds of billions of dollars.

Therefore, it will be almost impossible to secure the necessary funds from the national budget alone. Germany provides a very good example. It has earmarked 10 percent of its budget for the reconstruction of the former East Germany and other reunification-related projects. South Korea has to seek ways to minimize reunification costs and find the means to secure funds for reunification.

To obtain domestic capital, a fund for inter-Korean exchange and cooperation must be expanded. Not only the government, but also private South Korean businesses, will have to take part in securing these funds.

The South Korean government has to study ways to finance reunification, such as imposing a "reunification tax" and issuing "reunification bonds." The government must consider appropriating "the peace dividend" for reunification since military spending cuts should be substantial.

Ways must also be devised to secure foreign capital. It is very likely that South Korea will have to rely on foreign capital for a significant part of the reunification costs. In the past, cash-strapped South Korea secured foreign capital for the development of its struggling economy, and this experience will be helpful for South Korea when it promotes the economic development of North Korea after reunification.

Financial institutions in South Korea must be assigned to specific tasks for securing and management of the reunification funds. For instance, financial institutions experienced in international financing must assume responsibility for securing the foreign funds. The cost of obtaining this can be controlled and the timing to secure these funds can be preplanned. Specialized management systems must be established to most effectively carry out financing the expected massive development of the North. Experienced banks like the Korea Development Bank could be assigned responsibility for managing funds for big, long-term projects, requiring a thorough profitability review, such as the development of natural resources, the tourism industry, and the infrastructure.

Finally, South Korea has to carefully examine ways of supporting North Korea's entry into international financial organizations such as IMF, IBRD, and ADB to help North Korea resolve its economic problems. If North Korea secures funds and gains the necessary knowhow from these organizations, the burden on South Korea after reunification will be significantly diminished.

Gradual Economic Exchanges Between South Korea and North Korea

When the preceding conditions are met, inter-Korean economic exchanges will gain impetus. The current indirect trade by way of Hong Kong will be upgraded in stages to direct trade and eventually joint venture projects.

South Korea is not likely to enjoy any gains from economic exchanges with North Korea in the near future. But, South Korea must pursue economic exchanges with North Korea from a long-term perspective, therefore risking some economic loss.

As mentioned before, the former West Germany proceeded with economic exchanges with the former East Germany as a means to give the country economic support. Just as these economic exchanges accelerated the German reunification process, gradual expansion of inter-Korean trade will lay the groundwork for opening North Korea and minimizing the burden on South Korea after reunification.

8

A Vision for the Korean Economy and the Attitude of Koreans in the Twenty-First Century

Koreans must accomplish two special tasks in the twenty-first century to join the ranks of advanced nations: use its current level of economic development as a stepping-stone and achieve the long-sought reunification of the Korean peninsula. Concerted efforts by all Koreans are desperately needed to accomplish these two goals. However, only when there is a change in the "Korean mindset" will Korea be able to emerge as an economic power on a par with the so-called G-7 countries.

THE HISTORICAL MEANING OF THE TWENTY-FIRST CENTURY FOR KOREA

"You cannot fight against the future. Time is on our side."
(William Gladstone)

The twenty-first century is around the corner and we are at a historic crossroads. Futurists predict that what is in store for the coming ten years will serve as a catalyst to the new economic prosperity that humans aspire to in an advanced industrial society.

The global economy is opening a new world order following the end of the confrontational power game between the United States and the former Soviet Union. With regard to the global economic order, it is expected that the United States, Japan, and the European Community will continue as the dominant players for some years to come, and new regional powers will emerge, especially in the Pacific rim economies, that will maintain remarkable growth rates and take the lead in the global economy.

All nations are trying to maximize the benefits provided by the ongoing profound changes in the global economy. Governments, academic circles, and the industries of both developed and underdeveloped nations are working hard, preparing themselves for the twenty-first century.

The twenty-first century has very special meaning for Korea in that we hope to join the ranks of industrialized nations as well as achieve our long-awaited goal of reunification. What then will the twenty-first century hold for Korea?

POSSIBLE SCENARIOS FOR THE KOREAN ECONOMY

"Even children learn in growing up that 'both' is not an admissible answer to a choice of 'Which one?'"

(Paul A. Samuelson)

In the changing world economic environment, what course will be taken by the Korean economy, which is currently beset with many structural problems? From a long-term perspective, two scenarios can be presented for the future of the Korean economy.

Pessimistic Scenario

This scenario is centered on ungrounded optimism that high economic growth and stability will be achieved and the trade imbalance will be redressed as time goes by. Thus, it opts for the economic policies favored by majority rather than urging people to bear the burden.

Under this scenario, economic growth can be maintained for a time, but the government will have to intervene in the market to control the factors triggering price increases and reduce imports. The government will fail to galvanize the economy, and ultimately, prices will go up and economic growth will be hampered. Then, the general public will have no confidence in the future, feel frustrated over the economic performance, and in turn, become hesitant to make investments. Thus, there will be a vicious circle of stagnant investment, sluggish exports, low income, and a reduced share of the global market.

The division between large and small and medium-sized companies will deepen, and more and more problems of capitalism will unfold. To resolve the heap of problems, protectionist measures and stricter regulations will be sought, inviting trade friction.

Scenario for Economic Reforms

The gist of the scenario is that Korea will pursue institutional reforms to resolve the structural problems of its economy under the basic principle that it should actively participate in the free market systems of the twenty-first century. Under this scenario, economic growth and income gains can be slowed for a while. However, heated competition in the liberalized system will maximize economic efficiency. And institutional reforms based upon economic justice will give the general public confidence in economic development and thus eventually boost the economy. In the long run, economic growth will be accelerated and the trade imbalance will be redressed by restoring economic stability, international competitiveness and increasing exports.

Economic structures will be improved to enhance the international competitiveness of Korean industries to a level commensurate with the liberalized and democratized Korean society. Exchange and interest rates, wages and other factors that have a great influence on policy-making will be stabilized. And specific measures for institutional reforms will be proposed, and a variety of regulations will be abolished. Special steps will be taken for the industries that do not survive the cut-throat competition.

MIDDLE- AND LONG-TERM PROSPECTS FOR THE KOREAN ECONOMY

"To succeed it is necessary to accept the world as it is and rise above it."
(Michael Korda 1977)

A Remarkable Increase in Growth Potential

Among the two scenarios, the latter one must be realized if Korea is to join the ranks of advanced nations. If this happens, Korea will become the first country to develop into an advanced nation from an underdeveloped nation after the Second World War.

Korea's growth potential can be extended enormously, because national reunification will expand the economy and combine the human and material resources of two Koreas. The combination of low-cost labor from North Korea and technology from South Korea will boost the South Korean industries troubled by recent wage hikes. With reunification the Korean people will be able to restore pride in the nation. And this will become a locomotive for the Korean economy's leap into the circle of the world's economic powers.

Political and economic democratization will play a pivotal role in enhancing the quality of the overall Korean economy. In the past, when mass production was pursued in Korea, an authoritarian economic management was effectively operated. But in the twenty-first century, an era of change, only democratic management of the economy will bear fruit.

In this respect, the current ongoing political and economic democratization will become a driving force to increase Korea's growth potential. Undoubtedly, technological innovation will propel economic development also. Although most Korean technology still lags behind that of industrialized nations such as Japan, in some areas Korean technology excels that of some advanced nations. The outstanding technological progress made by Korea during the past thirty years promises another technological breakthrough in the years ahead. Japan had sufficient technological knowhow to produce aircraft carriers and fighter planes even before the Second World War. But Korea, during the early 1960s when it started economic development in earnest, had a very low level of technology. However, Korea's technology levels have been heightened so greatly that developed nations are now curbing their technology transfers to Korea. Considering its rapid technological advances, it can be assumed that technology will soon become the driving force for the economic development in Korea.

Another factor that demonstrates Korea's immense growth potential is the high proportion of the young to the whole population. Even though the percentage of aged people in the total population is increasing in Korea, the country will maintain a much more vibrant work force compared with Japan and other developed nations. That is, the baby boomers who were born in the 1950s and 1960s will play a central role in production in the twenty-first century.

Joining the Ranks of Industrialized Nations

Korea's economic power should increase as its growth potential expands (Table 8.1). The following are forecasts of the Korean economy based on the model made by the Korea Development Bank. Korea is expected to maintain annual economic growth rates of 5–7 percent until 2001. The Korean per capita GNP is likely to exceed $10,000 by 1996 and $17,000 by 2001.

Table 8.1.
Per Capita GNPs of Korea and Japan

	Korea				Japan	
	1991	*1996*	*1997*	*2001*	*1986*	*1991*
GNP ($10 billions)	280.8	470.0	522.6	818.3	1,992.9	3,386.2
Per Capita GNP ($)	6,498	10,383	11,449	17,377	16,379	27,299

Source: Korea Development Bank, Middle- and Long-Term Prospects for the Korean Economy, *Monthly Economic Review* (October, 1992).

Korean exports are expected to triple from US$69.6 billion in 1991 to US$181.7 billion by 2001. The heavy industry and chemical products share of total Korean exports will steadily increase. High-tech products, such as microelectronic and genetic engineering products to total exports will dramatically increase, and those products will emerge as Korea's principal export items.

Imports, which skyrocketed in recent years, will decline with the restoration of economic stability and development of import substitute industries, including capital goods and component manufacturing, which had been heavily dependent upon imports. Therefore, Korea's trade deficit, which stood at US$7 billion in 1991, will be reduced gradually, and Korea is expected to register trade surpluses in 1996 and afterward.

The quality of Korea's overall economic structure will improve. With institutional economic reforms, the GNP will rise and Korea will become a genuinely advanced nation, established upon economic justice.

Improvement of the Industrial Structure and Development of High-Tech Industries

Given Korea's current technological progress, the industrial structure is very likely to change (Table 8.3). First, technology-intensive industry will be expanded and electronic technology-applied high-tech industries will count for much as society becomes increasingly information intensive. Second, the service sector will carry more significance. That is, finance, insurance, and transportation will play more important roles. Third, the production share of intangible goods such as information, knowhow, and service will rise much faster than that of tangible goods, including raw materials. Fourth, with the development of industrial robotic and factory automation, the number of workers in production facilities will be gradually reduced. Therefore, the importance of manual labor will decline by degrees and demand for workers with technological knowhow will notably increase.

In line with a worldwide improvement in industrial structure, more emphasis will be put on the durables and technology-intensive industries in Korea. In the case of the manufacturing sector, production of high-quality durable goods including machinery, electric and electronic goods, and automobiles will increase. By contrast, light industries such as textiles, timber, and toys will decrease because of the loss of price competitiveness due to the wage hikes and the emergence of newly developing nations as powerful competitors.

The industrial structure will become notably technology intensive. Active technological development and facility investment will be pursued centering on high-tech industry. The growth rate of Korean high-

Table 8.2.
Prospects for the Major Economic Indicators in the Twenty-First Century

	1991	1993	1996	2001	1992–1996	1997–2001	1992–2001
Economic Growth Rate (%)	8.4	6.8	7.1	6.8	6.9	6.8	6.8
Trade Balance (%)	Δ70	Δ14	8	37	—	—	—
Exports (%)	696	847	1,139	1,817	—	—	—
(Change)	(10.2)	(10.7)	(10.3)	(9.5)	(10.4)	(9.8)	(10.1)
Imports (%)	766	861	1,131	1,780	—	—	—
(Change)	(17.6)	(8.5)	(9.4)	(9.4)	(8.1)	(9.5)	(8.8)
GNP Deflator	10.9	5.4	4.3	4.0	5.3	4.5	4.9
WPI	5.4	2.4	0.8	1.1	1.6	1.1	1.4
CPI	9.7	6.0	5.0	4.2	5.7	4.7	5.2
GNP ($100 millions)	2,808	3,359	4,700	8.183	—	—	—
Per Capita GNP ($)	6,498	7,621	10,383	17,377	—	—	—

Source: Korea Development Bank, "The Mid- and Long-Term Prospects for the Korean Economy," *Monthly Economic Review* (October 1992).

Table 8.3.
Causes and Effects of Industrial Restructuring

Demand	Incomes rise: progress from primary to secondary and tertiary industry
	Increase in elderly population: expansion in related equipment and medical services
	Increase in leisure time
	Growth of leisure and sports industry
Supply	Scarce natural resources: decline in industries' heavy reliance on energy consumption
	Prices drop thanks to process innovation: supply increases
	New product development: creation of new demand, replacement of existing products
	Facilities investment: capacity expansion and realization of economies of scale
Economic Units	Corporate strategies: deceleration or acceleration of structural changes
	National policy: proper allocation of natural resources, fostering industries with a competitive edge
	International competition: determination of the structure of the international division of labor

Source: Korea Development Bank, Direction for Korean Industrial Development and Industrial Financial Policy for the Twenty-First Century (March, 1991).

tech industries will be dramatically higher than the average growth rate of the global high-tech industries. By the year 2000, high-tech industries will play a leading role in Korean exports and account for a greater part of the national economy.

The light industries will have to be restructured. Some industries will sharpen their competitive edge by introducing high technology. Also, the assimilation of high technology by traditional industries will create vast new markets.

*An Information-Intensive Society and Service-Oriented
Economic Development*

Korean society will become highly information intensive in the twenty-first century. Thus, the welfare of the Korean people will be remarkably enhanced, and the freedom and creativity of individuals maximized. The characteristics of an information-intensive society can be summarized as follows. First, a huge amount of information will be accumulated in the form of searchable databases. Second, communication networks will be installed to give people full access to the information. Third, information processing systems will be established to process the information to meet users' needs.

In Korea, national digital networks based on ISDN will be established, linking various information resources with information networks. This will make information services available all around the nation. Also, information networks in Korea will be connected with overseas networks, forming international networks with overseas offices, research institutes, and information service agencies.

Diverse computer terminals will be integrated into a network inside every organization, and a larger network linking organizations will be built. Public service and information service centers, connected with individuals' terminals, will provide the general public with various services. Ultimately, information resources scattered all around the nation will be shared by people through a network. This will bring about the so-called integration effects of information resources, which, in turn, will result in enhanced international competitiveness.

Development of information networks will lay the groundwork for a highly advanced industrial society, by making industry overall more information intensive and service oriented. Information itself will emerge as a product and subsequently the information industry that produces, transmits, and processes this information will grow. Eventually, the whole industry will be restructured.

Leading a New World Order

Amid a wave of economic globalization, Korea has been pursuing liberalization and internationalization. The world's top-notch multinational companies and domestic businesses are engaged even now in fierce competition to gain a share of the limited Korean market.

Continuous economic growth will bring new prestige to Korea in the world economy. In other words, Korea's trade volume will be extended enormously, making Korea the tenth largest trading country in the world. As such, Korea will have to take a leading role in promoting the growth of the global economy and creating a new economic order.

With this in mind, Korea will join a number of international organizations and widen the scope of its activities in those organizations. Korea is expected to become a member of the OECD, a group of industrialized countries, in the near future. Thus, the remaining restraints on Korea's international trade, including restrictions on foreign exchange and capital transactions, are very likely to be cleared away.

Domestic companies will increasingly become multinational businesses. Koreans' attitudes will mature, and they will actually promote more exchanges with other nations.

Many leading authorities say that world economic leadership in the twenty-first century will probably shift to the Asia-Pacific region, in spite of the recent formation of trading blocks like the EU and NAFTA. Korea and Japan will lead economic development in this region, and currently they are making every effort to pursue development in the region, especially in Southeast Asia. At present, however, Korea is unable to assume a full leadership role in the area. Therefore, Japan, backed by its huge economy, still plays the larger role in Southeast Asian economic development. This has, from time to time, caused a negative reaction from the local populations because of Japan's past role during wartime in the region. Therefore, Korea and Japan should consider strengthening their cooperative relationship and together leading development in the Asia-Pacific region. With this newly gained prestige, Korea will take the initiative in establishing a freer and fairer world order.

The Era of Richness and Reunification

As Korea's national income level rises toward those of the developed nations, the traditional Korean way of life will undergo dramatic changes. People will demand that their basic needs, such as housing and health care, be met more fully. They will pay more attention to culture, art, leisure, and other sources of mental satisfaction, rather than material things.

Koreans' way of thinking will mature. Law and order will be more fully honored as people's consciousness will be raised. People will improve their standard of living by adopting more rational consumption patterns. With a rise in income, consumers will seek higher quality goods and services. During changes in consumer patterns, industries aimed at enhancing consumers' quality of life will expand.

With an enriched daily life, the people of South Korea will push forward exchanges with their counterparts in North Korea. Reunification will most certainly be achieved in the twenty-first century, and provide an opportunity for another economic takeoff. It will give the Korean people a chance to regain its liberal and pioneering spirit, long lost since Japanese colonial rule and the division of the Korean peninsula.

Table 8.4.
Prospects for Economic Power of Korea, the United States, Japan
(in $billion)

	1990	2000	2010
Korea	260	510	918
U.S.A.	5,463 (21)	7,027 (14)	8,736 (9.5)
Japan	2,881 (11)	4,418 (8.6)	6,404 (7.0)

Source: Institute for International Affairs, *Journal of International Affairs* (December 1991).

Notes: Korean estimates are under an assumption of reunification between South and North Korea; numbers in parentheses are each country's estimates divided by that of Korea.

Reunification is not only the integration of the two Koreas but the reunion of the Korean people. Thus, reunification will remove all the hatred and conflict between South and North Korean people, those between Kyongsang province and Junla province, the haves and have-nots, the intelligent and the ignorant. It will pave the way for the creation of a one-people community.

A reunified Korea will gain high status in the global economy. For instance, the U.S. and Japanese economies will be only 14 and 8.6 times larger, respectively, than that of a reunified Korea in the year 2000 (Table 8.4). And the gap will decrease further. The figures will go down to 9.5 and 7.0, respectively, in 2010. Furthermore, the population of a unified Korea will increase to 100 million, and thus Korea will have a self-supporting economy. Reunification will dismantle the remaining political barriers for both Koreas and stimulate exchanges with neighboring countries, including China. On the foundation of extended economic power, Korea will lead the Asia and Pacific region in the new wave of regionalism.

THE ATTITUDE OF KEY ECONOMIC PLAYERS
TOWARD THE TWENTY-FIRST CENTURY

"We can't always cross a bridge until we come to it; but I always like to lay down a pontoon ahead of time."

(Bernard M. Baruch)

As Alvin Toffler said, in his excellent book *Power Shift*, the world will be split between the fast and slow economies. The old division of developed, developing, and underdeveloped countries will fade in significance.

What steps should Korea take to be the forerunner among the fast economies in the twenty-first century? Most of all, all Koreans must have a mature consciousness commensurate with the expansion of the Korean economy and changes in its structure. All must make concerted efforts to create a fair society that fully respects law and order. In preparation for changes in the economic environment at home and abroad, all Koreans must make the strongest effort to restructure industry and strengthen the country's economic power.

Korean leaders must take the initiative in these efforts, putting aside their own interests. They must take action rather than play with political rhetoric when they face problems. Also they must try to maximize economic efficiency and improve the market economy. To this end, "market failures," such as unequal distribution of wealth, must be minimized and economic justice must be achieved.

Businesses must consistently press ahead with technological innovation. They should not seek government protection or simple expansion. Rather, they should adopt management styles that will help them develop in the heated competition of the international market. Above all, technological development must be encouraged. The time has gone when the government can block entry of new companies into the market and provide government subsidies under the guise of prevention of excessive competition and protection of infant industries.

The public, including workers, must be willing to share the burden of national economic development rather than put forward their own interests. They must exercise restraint and frugal consumption and create an atmosphere honoring law and order to improve their society.

Like the current society, the future one will have problems. However, no matter how difficult the problems are, the Korean people will meet the new challenges that are inevitable during the process of change. They must make concerted efforts to solve existing problems, and then they will be able to enjoy the honor of being citizens of a truly advanced nation. I strongly believe that what we do now determines our future.

APPENDIX 1
PRINCIPAL ECONOMIC
INDICATORS

Gross National Product

Year	Gross National Product At Current Prices In Billion Won	In Billion Dollars	Constant Prices (billion Won)	Per Capita GNP in Current Prices In Thousand Won	In Dollars	Growth Rate (%)
1953	47.9	1.4	2,205.2	2.4	67	—
1954	66.2	1.5	2,318.5	3.2	70	5.1
1955	114.5	1.4	2,422.6	5.3	65	4.5
1956	151.5	1.5	2,389.8	6.9	66	−1.4
1957	197.1	1.7	2,570.5	8.7	74	7.6
1958	204.7	1.9	2,711.1	8.8	80	5.5
1959	217.5	1.9	2,814.9	9.1	81	3.8
1960	244.9	1.9	2,845.6	9.9	79	1.1
1961	294.2	2.1	3,004.6	11.4	82	5.6
1962	355.5	2.3	3,071.1	13.4	87	2.2
1963	502.9	2.7	3,350.7	18.4	100	9.1
1964	716.3	2.9	3,671.5	25.6	103	9.6
1965	805.7	3.0	3,885.0	28.1	105	5.8
1966	1,037.0	3.7	4,378.5	35.2	1,285	12.7
1967	1,281.2	4.3	4,669.4	42.5	142	6.6
1968	1,652.9	5.2	5,195.6	53.6	169	11.3
1969	2,155.3	6.6	5,911.4	68.3	210	13.8
1970	2,785.0	8.1	24,973.0	86	252	7.6

Principal Economic Indicators *(continued)*

| | Gross National Product | | | Per Capita GNP in Current Prices | | |
Year	In Billion Won	In Billion Dollars	Constant Prices (billion Won)	In Thousand Won	In Dollars	Growth Rate (%)
	At Current Prices					
1971	3,416.7	9.5	27,128.0	104	289	8.6
1972	4,191.2	10.7	28,504.7	125	319	5.1
1973	5,376.3	13.5	32,273.8	158	396	13.2
1974	7,597.4	18.8	34,903.6	219	542	8.1
1975	10,135.8	20.9	37,143.3	288	594	6.4
1976	13,912.7	28.7	42,001.6	389	803	13.1
1977	17,806.6	36.8	46,135.4	490	1,012	9.8
1978	24,001.6	51.5	50,645.6	651	1,396	9.8
1979	30,801.8	61.5	54,289.5	823	1,644	7.2
1980	36,749.7	60.5	52,260.8	968	1,592	–3.7
1981	45,528.1	66.8	55,354.3	1,181	1,734	5.9
1982	52,182.3	71.3	59,322.2	1,334	1,824	7.2
1983	61,722.3	79.5	66,803.0	1,554	2,002	12.6
1984	70,083.9	87.0	73,004.0	1,739	2,158	9.3
1985	78,088.4	89.7	78,088.4	1,910	2,194	7.0
1986	90,598.7	102.8	88,173.5	2,207	2,505	12.9
1987	106,024.4	128.9	99,611.6	2,557	3,110	13.0
1988	126,230.5	172.8	111,979.9	3,015	4,127	12.4
1989	141,794.4	211.2	119,576.7	3,353	4,994	6.8
1990	171,488.1	242.2	130,685.1	4,007	5,659	9.3
1991	206,681.2	281.7	142,623.2	4,782	6,518	8.4
1992	229,938.5	294.5	148,251.0	5,270	6,749	4.7

Source: Bank of Korea.

Notes: Figures up to 1969 are compiled at 1975 prices. Figures from 1970 to 1992 are compiled at 1985 prices. Figures in 1992 are preliminarily estimated.

Industry Breakdown, Percent at Current Prices

Year	Growth Rate				Structure					
	Agriculture, Forestry, and Fishing	Mining and Manufacturing	Manufacturing Alone	Others	Agriculture, Forestry, and Fishing	Mining and Manufacturing	Manufacturing Alone	Light Industry	Heavy and Chemical Industry	Others
1953	—	—	—	—	46.7	10.0	8.9	78.9	21.1	43.3
1954	8.0	11.5	18.1	1.2	39.4	12.6	11.6	78.4	21.6	48.0
1955	1.5	19.9	21.3	5.8	43.9	12.5	11.4	79.9	20.1	40.9
1956	-6.9	13.6	15.2	2.4	46.5	12.6	11.4	80.2	19.8	42.6
1957	9.4	9.9	7.1	5.2	44.8	12.6	11.1	80.5	19.5	46.3
1958	7.3	9.1	10.3	2.9	40.4	14.3	12.7	78.6	21.4	15.3
1959	-0.3	10.0	9.2	7.1	33.6	15.8	14.0	78.4	21.6	50.6
1960	-2.1	10.9	8.2	2.3	26.5	15.8	13.7	76.6	23.4	47.7
1961	12.2	4.4	4.0	-0.5	38.7	14.4	13.5	73.7	26.3	45.9
1962	-6.0	13.4	11.7	8.6	36.6	16.3	14.3	71.4	28.6	47.1
1963	9.5	14.2	16.1	7.5	43.1	16.2	14.5	70.3	29.7	40.7
1964	15.6	10.5	9.9	3.5	46.5	17.2	15.5	69.6	30.4	36.3
1965	-1.0	18.3	20.5	9.7	37.6	19.9	17.9	68.9	31.4	42.5

Industry Breakdown, Percent at Current Prices (continued)

Year	Growth Rate				Structure					
	Agriculture, Forestry, and Fishing	Mining and Manufacturing	Manufacturing Alone	Others	Agriculture, Forestry, and Fishing	Mining and Manufacturing	Manufacturing Alone	Light Industry	Heavy and Chemical Industry	Others
1966	11.6	15.3	17.3	13.0	34.4	20.2	18.4	65.9	34.1	45.4
1967	-5.9	20.2	21.6	14.6	30.1	20.6	18.8	65.3	34.7	49.3
1968	1.3	23.4	27.2	15.3	28.3	21.3	19.8	62.0	38.0	50.4
1969	10.5	19.2	23.2	14.2	27.6	21.5	20.1	62.4	37.6	50.9
1970	-1.4	19.6	19.9	9.5	26.7	22.5	21.3	61.9	38.1	50.8
1971	3.0	15.9	17.8	9.9	27.2	22.5	21.3	60.7	39.3	50.3
1972	2.4	11.6	13.3	4.7	26.8	23.5	22.4	63.9	26.1	49.7
1973	7.3	27.7	28.7	12.3	25.0	26.2	25.1	60.1	39.9	48.8
1974	6.5	15.3	16.2	6.4	24.8	27.1	26.0	51.9	48.1	48.1
1975	3.9	12.2	12.0	5.5	25.0	27.5	26.1	54.1	45.9	47.5
1976	9.8	21.6	23.6	10.6	23.6	28.7	27.6	53.0	47.0	47.7
1977	2.8	14.9	15.1	12.0	22.4	28.9	27.5	50.8	49.2	48.7
1978	-9.8	19.9	21.0	15.0	20.6	29.4	28.1	49.5	50.5	50.0

Year										
1979	7.0	9.5	10.4	5.4	19.2	29.9	28.8	47.9	52.1	50.9
1980	-19.1	-1.0	-0.7	-1.5	14.9	31.0	29.7	48.8	51.2	54.1
1981	14.3	9.4	9.9	1.2	15.6	31.3	29.9	47.9	52.1	53.1
1982	7.4	5.9	6.7	7.1	14.7	30.4	29.2	47.2	52.8	54.9
1983	7.7	15.0	15.4	13.5	13.6	31.0	29.9	44.9	55.1	55.4
1984	-1.5	16.8	17.3	7.2	12.9	31.8	30.8	43.9	56.1	55.3
1985	3.8	7.0	7.1	10.2	12.8	31.3	30.3	43.3	56.7	55.9
1986	4.6	18.0	18.3	12.3	11.5	32.6	31.7	42.6	57.4	55.8
1987	-6.8	18.2	18.8	13.7	10.5	33.0	32.2	43.0	57.0	56.5
1988	8.0	13.1	13.4	12.1	10.5	33.2	32.5	39.5	60.5	56.3
1989	-1.1	3.5	3.7	6.6	10.1	31.8	31.2	38.8	61.2	58.1
1990	-5.1	8.7	9.1	13.1	9.0	29.4	38.9	37.6	62.4	61.6
1991	-1.0	8.7	8.9	10.6	8.0	28.6	28.2	34.9	65.1	63.4
1992	5.4	4.6	4.8	6.3	7.6	27.7	27.3	34.2	65.8	64.7

Source: Bank of Korea.

Growth Rate by Kind of Expenditure, Percent, at Current Prices

Year	Final Consumption Expenditure			Gross Fixed Capital Formation	Exports		Imports	
	Total	Private	Government		Goods and Services	Goods Alone	Goods and Services	Goods Alone
1953	—	—	—	—	—	—	—	—
1954	4.1	5.7	-2.6	27.3	-39.4	-36.8	-28.9	-19.2
1955	7.7	8.8	2.8	17.1	22.1	-29.5	34.3	34.6
1956	3.8	3.8	3.9	10.7	-9.0	43.0	16.6	16.0
1957	2.2	2.7	-0.4	14.4	33.9	-23.0	17.6	2.7
1958	5.0	5.6	1.6	-5.6	24.6	-11.1	-13.9	-12.0
1959	4.1	5.0	-0.6	3.3	15.9	14.3	-18.6	-20.5
1960	3.5	4.0	1.1	7.0	20.8	66.1	14.1	11.7
1961	0.7	0.9	-0.6	3.5	38.7	24.4	-9.2	-7.3
1962	5.8	6.4	2.1	28.7	13.0	34.1	34.0	37.8
1963	3.1	2.9	4.2	27.3	9.0	53.6	26.8	33.2
1964	6.5	7.7	-0.9	-9.3	23.5	35.2	-24.2	-25.8
1965	6.3	6.5	4.9	27.1	35.9	41.0	12.6	13.1
1966	6.8	6.3	9.6	59.5	42.4	30.6	56.2	59.5

1967	8.3	8.3	8.3	22.6	32.7	27.8	30.8	29.0
1968	9.6	9.7	9.6	34.7	39.5	41.0	43.6	343.2
1969	9.4	9.4	9.5	24.8	36.1	42.6	26.6	27.0
1970	9.5	9.9	6.6	1.0	19.6	28.3	8.0	7.5
1971	8.9	9.0	8.1	3.7	21.8	29.6	19.6	21.3
1972	4.8	4.8	5.2	1.5	36.2	45.7	1.2	1.0
1973	7.3	8.8	-0.3	27.2	53.4	55.5	35.3	36.9
1974	8.2	7.2	13.4	15.5	-0.1	9.7	17.7	17.0
1975	5.9	5.1	9.7	7.9	19.8	20.8	2.4	-0.7
1976	7.5	8.4	3.4	20.9	38.8	38.2	24.6	25.1
1977	6.0	5.8	7.1	29.0	22.0	18.6	20.6	19.7
1978	9.5	9.2	11.3	35.4	13.6	13.4	28.0	27.4
1979	7.6	8.8	1.3	10.0	2.0	-0.6	11.5	11.0
1980	0.3	-1.0	7.4	-11.4	8.9	10.9	-5.1	-7.5
1981	4.9	4.8	5.7	-4.1	15.1	14.9	5.9	3.9
1982	5.6	6.5	1.0	10.4	4.5	2.6	3.0	3.9
1983	8.2	9.1	3.4	17.8	19.2	19.2	12.0	13.9

Growth Rate by Kind of Expenditure, Percent, at Current Prices (continued)

Year	Final Consumption Expenditure			Gross Fixed Capital Formation	Exports		Imports	
	Total	Private	Government		Goods and Services	Goods Alone	Goods and Services	Goods Alone
1984	6.6	7.6	1.5	10.9	7.9	9.8	7.4	8.8
1985	6.3	6.4	5.6	4.7	4.5	4.4	-0.6	0.3
1986	8.4	8.0	10.8	12.0	26.1	25.8	17.8	19.3
1987	8.1	8.3	6.9	16.5	21.6	23.7	19.4	20.1
1988	9.7	9.8	9.4	13.4	12.5	14.0	12.8	12.3
1989	10.7	10.9	9.8	26.9	-3.8	-5.0	16.3	14.2
1990	10.1	10.3	8.9	24.0	4.2	3.4	14.4	14.0
1991	9.3	9.3	9.4	11.8	9.8	9.5	17.5	17.5
1992	6.8	6.4	8.8	-1.8	9.8	9.7	2.9	1.9

Source: Bank of Korea.

Notes: Figures up to 1969 are compiled at 1975 prices. Figures from 1970 to 1992 are compiled at 1985 prices. Figures in 1992 are preliminarily estimated.

Percent of Expenditures, at Constant Prices

Year	Final Consumption Expenditure			Gross Fixed Capital Formation	Exports		Imports	
	Total	Private	Government		Goods and Services	Goods Alone	Goods and Services	Goods Alone
1953	91.2	83.3	7.9	7.2	3.2	2.0	9.6	9.6
1954	93.4	83.2	10.2	9.2	2.1	0.8	7.2	7.2
1955	94.8	86.0	8.8	10.2	2.9	0.7	9.8	9.8
1956	101.9	92.8	9.2	10.3	2.3	1.0	12.7	12.7
1957	94.5	83.7	10.8	10.6	2.2	0.6	10.1	10.1
1958	05.1	82.3	12.8	10.2	2.8	0.6	9.3	9.3
1959	95.8	81.6	14.2	11.0	3.4	0.7	8.8	8.8
1960	99.2	84.7	14.5	10.8	4.1	1.4	10.7	10.7
1961	97.1	83.5	13.6	11.7	6.3	1.8	12.3	12.3
1962	96.8	82.8	14.0	13.7	6.0	2.0	14.3	14.3
1963	91.3	80.4	10.9	13.5	5.4	2.9	13.7	13.7
1964	91.3	82.8	8.5	11.3	6.7	3.9	11.5	11.5
1965	92.6	83.3	9.3	14.8	9.5	5.8	13.7	13.7

Percent of Expenditures, at Constant Prices (continued)

	Final Consumption Expenditure			Gross Fixed Capital Formation	Exports		Imports	
Year	Total	Private	Government		Goods and Services	Goods Alone	Goods and Services	Goods Alone
1966	88.2	78.2	10.0	20.2	11.9	6.6	17.8	17.8
1967	88.6	78.4	10.2	21.4	13.6	7.1	19.2	19.2
1968	84.9	74.5	10.4	25.0	14.7	8.1	22.1	22.1
1969	81.2	70.9	10.3	25.8	15.4	8.8	22.1	22.1
1970	84.2	74.7	9.5	25.4	15.0	9.8	24.0	20.0
1971	85.3	75.6	9.7	22.5	16.1	11.5	26.5	22.1
1972	83.8	73.7	10.1	20.7	20.5	15.7	25.6	21.0
1973	78.0	69.6	8.4	23.9	29.7	24.0	33.5	28.2
1974	79.9	70.3	9.6	26.9	28.1	24.0	40.1	34.2
1975	81.5	70.5	11.0	26.6	28.0	24.2	38.2	31.7
1976	76.3	65.4	10.9	25.5	31.2	27.2	34.3	28.9
1977	73.0	62.2	10.7	28.2	31.7	26.9	33.8	28.1
1978	71.2	60.8	10.4	33.5	29.9	25.1	34.8	28.6
1979	71.8	61.8	9.9	33.8	28.1	22.9	36.5	29.8

1980	76.2	64.6	11.5	32.1	34.7	28.4	45.9	35.5
1981	76.1	64.5	11.6	28.0	37.7	30.5	47.2	35.8
1982	75.0	63.5	11.5	28.4	35.7	28.3	42.7	32.0
1983	71.4	60.7	10.7	29.2	36.5	29.2	40.4	31.4
1984	69.5	59.5	10.0	28.9	37.0	30.3	40.5	31.5
1985	69.3	59.2	10.1	28.2	35.8	29.5	38.0	29.5
1986	66.0	55.9	10.1	27.8	40.0	33.0	36.9	28.9
1987	63.4	53.5	9.9	28.7	42.5	35.8	36.6	29.8
1988	61.7	51.9	9.8	29.2	40.5	34.4	33.5	27.9
1989	64.4	53.9	10.5	31.6	34.7	29.1	32.7	26.9
1990	63.8	53.2	10.6	36.5	31.6	26.1	32.9	26.9
1991	63.3	52.6	10.7	37.8	29.8	24.7	33.1	27.2
1992	64.8	53.5	11.3	35.6	30.6	25.5	32.4	26.3

Source: Bank of Korea.

Notes: Figures up to 1969 are compiled at 1975 prices. Figures from 1970 to 1992 are compiled at 1985 prices. Figures in 1992 are preliminarily estimated.

Employment, Prices, and Wages

| | Population and Employment | | | | | Prices and Wages (% increased) | | | |
Year	Population	Population Increase (%)	Employed (1,000s)	Increase in Employed (%)	Unemployment (%)	Product Prices	Consumer Price	GMP Def.	Manufacturing Wages
1953	20,239	—	—	—	—	25.3	—	—	—
1954	20,823	2.89	—	—	—	28.2	—	31.8	—
1955	21,424	2.89	—	—	—	81.1	—	62.1	—
1956	22,042	2.88	—	—	—	31.6	—	34.0	—
1957	22,677	2.88	—	—	—	16.2	—	22.2	—
1958	23,331	2.88	—	—	—	-6.2	—	-1.3	-6.9
1959	24,003	2.88	—	—	—	2.6	—	1.3	-8.3
1960	24,695	2.88	—	—	—	10.8	—	11.7	-0.9
1961	25,766	4.34	—	—	—	13.3	—	14.0	-12.0
1962	26,513	2.90	—	—	—	9.3	—	18.4	6.5
1963	27,262	2.83	7,662	—	8.2	20.5	—	29.3	14.4
1964	27,984	2.65	7,799	1.8	7.7	34.8	—	30.0	-22.0
1965	28,705	2.58	8,206	5.2	7.4	10.0	—	6.2	18.6

1966	29,436	2.55	8,423	2.6	7.1	8.8	12.1	14.5	17.8
1967	30,131	2.36	8,717	3.5	6.2	6.4	10.1	15.6	22.5
1968	30,838	2.35	9,155	5.0	5.1	8.1	11.1	16.1	26.5
1969	31,544	2.29	9,414	2.8	4.8	6.7	12.4	14.8	34.2
1970	32,241	2.21	9,745	3.5	4.5	9.2	16.2	15.6	25.6
1971	32,663	1.89	10,066	3.3	4.4	8.6	13.5	12.9	16.2
1972	33.505	1.89	10,559	4.9	4.5	13.8	11.7	16.3	13.9
1973	34,103	1.78	11,139	5.5	4.0	6.9	3.1	12.1	18.0
1974	34,692	1.73	11,586	4.0	4.1	42.1	24.3	30.4	35.3
1975	35,281	1.70	11,830	2.1	4.12	6.5	25.3	24.6	27.0
1976	35,849	1.61	12,556	6.1	3.9	12.2	15.3	21.0	34.7
1977	36,412	1.57	12,929	3.0	3.8	9.1	10.2	15.9	33.8
1978	36,969	1.53	13,490	4.3	3.2	11.7	14.4	21.6	34.3
1979	37,534	1.53	13,664	1.3	3.8	18.6	18.2	20.0	28.6
1980	38,124	1.57	13,683	0.3	5.2	38.9	28.8	25.3	22.7
1981	38,723	1.57	14,023	2.5	4.5	20.4	21.5	15.4	20.1
1982	39,326	1.56	14,379	2.5	4.4	4.7	7.1	6.7	-14.7

Employment, Prices, and Wages (continued)

Year	Population and Employment				Prices and Wages (% increased)			
	Population	Population Increase (%)	Employed (1,000s)	Increase in Employed (%)	Unemployment (%)	Product Prices	Consumer Price	GMP Def.	Manufacturing Wages
1983	39,910	1.49	13,505	0.9	4.1	0.1	3.4	3.9	12.2
1984	40,406	1.24	14,429	-0.5	3.8	0.8	2.3	3.8	8.1
1985	41,806	0.99	14,970	3.7	4.0	0.9	2.4	4.2	9.9
1986	41,214	1.00	15,505	3.6	3.8	-1.4	2.7	2.8	9.2
1987	41,622	0.99	16,354	5.5	3.1	0.4	3.0	3.5	11.6
1988	42,031	0.98	16,708	2.2	2.5	2.7	7.1	5.9	19.6
1989	42,449	1.99	17,511	4.8	2.6	1.5	5.7	5.2	25.1
1990	42,869	0.99	18,036	3.0	2.4	4.2	8.6	10.6	20.2
1991	43,268	0.93	18,576	3.0	2.3	4.7	9.3	11.2	16.9
1992	43,663	0.91	18,921	1.9	2.4	2.2	6.2	6.3	15.7

Source: National Statistical Office and Bank of Korea.
Note: Product price and consumer price are annual average basis.

Imports, Exports, and Foreign Exchange

Year	External Transactions				Foreign Exchange Holdings ($ millions)	Exchange Rates (Won to $, %)	Money Supply, M2 (% change)	Marginal Fixed Capital Coefficient	Marginal Propensity of Savings
	Exports ($ million)	Export Increases (%)	Imports ($ million)	Import Increases (%)					
1953	39.6	42.7	345.4	61.3	108.7	6.6	—	—	—
1954	24.2	-38.7	243.3	-29.6	107.8	18.0	—	1.3	21.3
1955	18.0	-25.9	341.4	40.3	96.1	30.2	—	1.8	-65.9
1956	24.6	36.9	386.1	98.6	50.2	—	-6.5	0.0	
1957	22.2	-9.7	442.2	14.5	115.6	50.0	—	1.3	69.9
1958	16.5	25.9	378.2	-14.5	146.5	50.0	—	1.6	9.7
1959	19.8	20.4	303.8	-19.7	147.3	50.0	—	2.2	-6.2
1960	32.8	65.7	343.5	13.1	157.0	62.8	—	7.5	0.0
1961	40.9	24.5	316.1	-8.0	207.0	127.4	60.5	1.5	86.9
1962	54.8	34.1	421.8	33.4	166.8	130.0	24.9	5.1	0.0
1963	86.8	58.4	560.3	32.8	131.5	130.0	7.4	1.5	65.6
1964	119.1	37.2	404.4	-27.8	136.4	214.2	14.8	1.2	35.5
1965	175.1	47.0	463.4	14.6	146.3	266.3	52.7	2.3	0.3

Imports, Exports, and Foreign Exchange (continued)

	External Transactions					Exchange Rates (Won to $, %)	Money Supply, M₂ (% change)	Marginal Fixed Capital Coefficient	Marginal Propensity of Savings
Year	Exports ($ million)	Export Increases (%)	Imports ($ million)	Import Increases (%)	Foreign Exchange Holdings ($ millions)	Exchange Rates (Won to $, %)	Money Supply, M$_2$ (% change)	Marginal Fixed Capital Coefficient	Marginal Propensity of Savings
1966	250.3	42.9	716.4	54.6	245.2	271.3	61.7	1.6	50.7
1967	320.2	27.9	996.2	39.1	356.6	270.5	61.7	3.7	-10.0
1968	455.4	42.2	1,462.9	46.8	391.0	276.6	72.0	2.5	23.9
1969	622.5	36.7	1,823.6	24.7	562.9	288.3	61.4	2.3	40.1
1970	835.2	34.2	1,984.0	8.8	609.7	3310.6	27.4	3.2	-4.7
1971	1,067.6	27.8	2,394.3	20.7	568.1	347.2	20.8	2.3	10.8
1972	1,624.1	52.1	2,522.0	5.3	739.7	392.9	33.8	3.8	15.7
1973	3,225.0	98.6	4,240.3	68.1	1,094.4	398.3	36.4	1.7	52.0
1974	4,460.4	38.3	6,851.8	61.6	1,055.7	404.5	24.0	2.9	15.9
1975	5,081.0	13.9	7,274.4	6.2	1,550.2	484.0	28.2	3.3	21.3
1976	7,715.3	51.8	8,733.6	20.6	2,960.6	484.0	33.5	2.1	52.5
1977	10,046.5	30.2	10,810.5	23.2	4,306.4	484.0	39.7	2.8	50.0
1978	12,710.6	26.5	14,971.9	38.5	4,937.1	484.0	35.0	3.4	31.0

1979	15,055.5	18.4	20,338.6	35.8	5,708.1	484.0	24.6	4.9	17.6
1980	17,504.9	16.3	22,291.7	9.6	6,571.4	607.4	26.9	0.0	0.0
1981	21,253.8	21.4	26,131.4	17.2	6,891.0	681.0	25.0	4.0	56.3
1982	21,853.4	2.8	24,250.8	-7.2	6,983.7	731.1	27.0	5.5	40.8
1983	24,445.1	11.9	26,192.2	8.0	6,909.7	755.8	15.2	3.2	53.9
1984	29,244.9	19.6	30,631.4	16.9	7,649.6	806.0	7.7	4.0	59.1
1985	30,283.1	3.6	31,135.7	1.6	7,748.6	870.0	15.6	4.4	38.4
1986	34,714.5	14.6	31,583.9	1.4	7,955.2	881.5	18.4	2.6	65.3
1987	47,280.9	36.2	41,019.8	29.9	9,192.9	822.6	18.1	2.7	64.3
1988	60,696.4	28.4	51,810.6	26.3	12,378.3	731.5	21.5	2.9	57.4
1989	62,377.2	2.8	61,464.8	18.6	15,245.2	671.5	19.8	6.2	28.1
1990	65,015.7	4.2	69,843.7	13.6	14,822.4	707.8	17.2	4.4	50.1
1991	71,870.1	10.5	81,524.9	16.7	13,733.0	733.4	21.9	4.9	49.2
1992	76,631.5	6.6	81,775.3	0.3	17,153.9	780.7	14.9	7.9	40.0

Source: Bank of Korea.

Note: Export and import are customs clearance basis.

APPENDIX 2
GROSS NATIONAL PRODUCT
BY INDUSTRY

Current Prices (in 10 billion won)

Year	Gross National Product	Agriculture, Forestry, and Fishing	Mining, Quarrying, and Manufacturing	Mining and Quarrying	Manufacturing	SOC and Others	Electricity, Water, Gas, and Construction
1953	47.9	22.4	4.8	0.5	4.3	20.7	1.2
1954	66.2	26.1	8.4	0.7	7.7	31.8	2.1
1955	114.5	50.3	14.3	1.2	13.1	49.9	4.1
1956	151.5	70.5	19.1	1.8	17.3	61.9	4.9
1957	197.1	88.4	24.9	2.9	22.0	83.8	8.2
1958	204.7	82.7	29.4	3.3	26.1	92.6	8.4
1959	217.5	73.0	34.3	3.9	30.5	110.1	9.3
1960	244.9	89.3	38.7	5.2	33.5	116.9	10.1
1961	294.2	113.9	45.3	5.5	39.7	135.1	12.9
1962	355.5	130.3	57.7	7.1	50.6	167.6	16.2
1963	502.9	217.0	81.6	8.4	73.2	204.3	19.6
1964	716.3	333.0	123.3	12.4	110.9	260.0	26.6
1965	805.7	303.3	160.0	16.2	143.8	342.4	37.6
1966	1,037.0	356.9	209.5	19.1	190.3	470.7	52.2

Year							
1967	1,281.2	385.9	264.2	23.8	240.5	631.1	67.1
1968	1,652.9	467.3	352.2	24.9	327.3	833.4	101.6
1969	2,155.3	594.8	462.5	29.4	433.2	1,098.0	153.1
1970	2,785.0	738.5	623.5	35.2	588.3	1,513.0	180.8
1971	3,146.7	930.9	771.1	41.0	730.1	1,714.7	200.4
1972	4,191.2	1,127.8	988.6	44.1	944.5	2,074.8	237.8
1973	5,376.3	1,356.4	1,417.7	57.7	1,362.2	2,600.0	315.0
1974	7,597.4	1,904.8	2,080.8	89.1	1,991.7	3,611.8	421.2
1975	10,135.8	2,571.0	2,831.1	144.1	2,687.0	4,733.7	615.8
1976	13,912.7	3,326.5	4,045.5	160.0	3,885.5	6,540.7	829.4
1977	17,806.6	4,051.1	5,224.2	251.4	4,972.8	8,531.3	1,269.0
1978	24,001.6	5,018.8	7,151.7	320.6	6,831.1	11,831.1	2,190.1
1979	30,801.8	6,013.6	9,379.4	347.3	9,032.1	15,408.8	3,184.4
1980	36,749.7	5,677.4	11,789.8	491.3	11,282.5	19,282.5	3,937.9
1981	45,528.1	7,430.6	14,845.2	646.6	14,198.6	23,252.3	4,459.8
1982	52,182.3	7,989.2	16,544.1	636.5	15,907.6	27,649.0	5,419.4

Current Prices (in 10 billion won) *(continued)*

Year	Gross National Product	Agriculture, Forestry, and Fishing	Mining, Quarrying, and Manufacturing	Mining and Quarrying	Manufacturing	SOC and Others	Electricity, Water, Gas, and Construction
1983	61,722.3	8.678.2	19,974.1	688.6	19,105.5	33,250.0	6,748.1
1984	70,083.9	9,392.1	23,107.9	732.6	22,375.3	37,583.9	7,739.6
1985	78,088.4	10,351.8	25,321.3	790.9	24,530.4	42,415.3	8,517.6
1986	90,598.7	10,728.6	30,482.6	903.2	29,579.4	49,387.5	9,543.6
1987	106,024.4	11,353.3	35,819.5	916.2	34,903.3	58,851.6	11,266.1
1988	126,230.5	13,493.9	42,545.2	927.9	41,617.3	70,191.4	13,693.5
1989	141,794.4	14,457.8	45,463.1	813.1	44,650.0	81,873.5	17,394.6
1990	171,488.1	15,583.5	50,672.8	788.1	49,884.7	105,231.8	26,496.0
1991	206,681.2	16,566.2	59,502.9	875.5	58,627.4	130,612.1	36,559.8
1992	229,938	17,682.4	64,021.1	811.8	63,209.3	148,235.0	40,105.5

Source: Bank of Korea.

Constant Prices (in 10 billion won)

Year	Gross National Product	Agriculture, Forestry, and Fishing	Mining, Quarrying, and Manufacturing	Mining and Quarrying	Manufacturing	SOC and Others	Electricity, Water, Gas, and Construction
1953	2,205.2	1,078.5	129.4	25.0	104.3	997.4	37.10
1954	2,318.5	1,164.7	144.3	21.1	123.2	1,009.6	45.53
1955	2,422.6	1,181.7	173.1	23.7	149.4	1,067.9	45.59
1956	2,389.8	1,100.3	196.5	24.4	172.1	1,093.0	43.71
1957	2,570.5	1,204.2	215.9	31.6	184.4	1,150.3	53.86
1958	2,711.1	1,291.5	235.7	32.4	203.3	1,183.9	56.67
1959	2,814.9	1,287.8	256.4	37.4	221.9	1,267.7	68.96
1960	2,845.6	1,261.1	287.7	47.5	240.2	1,296.8	68.95
1961	3,004.6	1,414.3	300.4	50.6	249.8	1,289.9	75.06
1962	3,071.1	1,329.6	340.6	61.6	279.0	1,401.0	87.18
1963	3,350.7	1,456.4	388.8	64.9	323.9	1,505.5	102.22
1964	3,671.5	1,684.1	429.6	73.6	356.1	1,557.8	111.50
1965	3,885.0	1,667.8	508.3	79.2	429.1	1,708.9	138.51
1966	4378.5	1,861.0	586.1	83.0	503.2	1,931.4	167.07

Constant Prices (in 10 billion won) *(continued)*

Year	Gross National Product	Agriculture, Forestry, and Fishing	Mining, Quarrying, and Manufacturing	Mining and Quarrying	Manufacturing	SOC and Others	Electricity, Water, Gas, and Construction
1967	4,669.4	1,750.9	704.5	92.5	612.0	2,213.9	201.40
1968	5,195.6	1,774.4	869.6	91.1	778.5	2,551.6	274.88
1969	5,911.4	1,960.9	1,036.8	89.8	946.1	2,913.7	375.41
1970	24,973.0	6,943.2	3,920.3	499.1	3,421.2	14,109.5	1,637.1
1971	27,128.0	7,152.5	4,544.6	513.4	4,031.2	15,430.9	1,659.9
1972	28,504.7	7,326.8	5,070.6	503.7	4,566.9	16,107.3	1,693.1
1973	32,273.8	7,862.2	6,474.9	596.8	5,878.1	17,936.7	2,098.9
1974	34,903.6	8,373.7	7,463.6	633.1	6,830.5	19,066.3	2,367.1
1975	37,143.3	8,697.1	8,372.1	723.8	7,648.3	20,074.1	2,596.5
1976	42,001.6	9,545.6	10,176.4	721.8	9,454.6	22,279.6	2,958.8
1977	46,135.4	9,811.3	11,691.1	813.4	10,877.7	24,633.0	3,701.3
1978	50,645.6	8,845.5	14,020.1	854.3	13,165.8	27,780.0	4,789.9
1979	54,289.5	9,460.3	15,351.7	817.0	14,534.7	29,477.5	5,112.1
1980	52,260.8	7,656.8	15,201.3	775.3	14,426.0	29,402.7	5,183.8

1981	55,354.3	8,749.8	16,632.6	781.3	15,851.3	29,971.9	5,128.0
1982	59,322.2	9,401.2	17,613.1	699.5	16,913.6	32,307.9	5,925.8
1983	66,803.0	10,128.5	20,652.3	738.7	19,913.6	36,022.2	7,272.1
1984	73,004.0	9,977.2	20,279.6	762.2	19,517.4	42,747.2	7,985.1
1985	78,088.4	10,351.8	25,321.3	790.9	24,530.4	42,415.3	8,517.6
1986	88,173.5	10,829.6	29,873.5	856.0	29,017.5	47,470.4	9,401.4
1987	99,611.6	10,097.5	35,305.3	845.3	34,460.0	54,208.8	10,584.4
1988	111,979.9	10,902.6	39,926.2	840.1	39,086.1	61,151.1	11,601.4
1989	119,576.7	10,779.9	41,322.6	778.8	40,543.8	67,474.2	13,277.8
1990	130,685.1	10,231.8	44,911.1	694.9	44,216.2	75,542.2	16,139.9
1991	142,623.2	10,133.8	48,838.9	702.3	48,136,6	83,650.5	17,801.0
1992	148,251.0	10,677.6	51,090.8	621.9	50,468.9	86,482.6	17,887.2

Source: Bank of Korea.

APPENDIX 3
EXPENDITURE ON GROSS
DOMESTIC PRODUCT

Current Prices (in 10 billion won)

Year	Expenditure on GDP	Final Consumption Expenditure	Households	Gross Capital Formation	Gross Fixed Capital Formation	Increase in Stocks	Exports of Goods and Services	Imports of Goods and Services
1953	47.9	43.6	39.9	7.4	3.5	3.9	0.9	4.7
1954	66.2	61.8	55.1	7.9	6.1	1.8	0.7	4.9
1955	114.5	108.5	98.4	14.1	11.7	2.4	1.9	11.4
1956	151.5	154.4	140.6	13.5	15.7	-2.1	2.1	20.0
1957	197.1	186.2	164.9	30.2	20.9	9.2	3.0	23.7
1958	204.7	194.8	168.6	26.4	20.8	5.6	4.2	22.1
1959	217.5	208.3	177.4	24.3	24.1	0.2	5.9	22.4
1960	245.0	242.9	207.4	26.6	26.5	0.1	8.2	31.0
1961	294.2	285.2	245.8	38.7	34.3	4.4	15.8	43.8
1962	355.5	343.9	394.3	45.5	48.6	-3.1	18.0	59.1
1963	502.9	459.2	404.5	91.9	68.0	23.1	23.7	79.4
1964	716.4	653.7	592.6	100.7	81.3	19.4	42.1	96.4
1965	805.7	746.3	671.5	120.9	119.0	1.9	68.6	127.8
1966	1,037.0	914.2	810.8	223.9	209.7	14.2	106.8	207.8

279.4	144.6	6.1	274.6	280.7	1,005.2	1,135.5	1,281.2	1967
416.8	209.3	14.0	413.6	425.6	1,231.0	1,403.6	1,652.9	1968
541.8	287.8	65.6	555.7	621.3	1,528.7	1,749.3	2,155.3	1969
658.7	389.7	-3.7	695.6	690.6	2,049.3	2,330.8	2,767.9	1970
879.0	527.6	93.9	768.4	862.3	2,555.4	2,919.4	3,421.1	1971
1,032.8	838.5	22.7	871.1	893.8	3,073.1	3,529.1	4,209.6	1972
1,757.3	1,598.7	79.1	1,297.5	1,376.6	3,736.7	4,226.2	5,420.3	1973
2,972.8	2,131.8	384.5	2,066.6	2,451.2	5,348.1	6,131.2	7,669.4	1974
3,727.5	2,859.1	215.2	2,741.1	2,956.3	7,202.8	8,398.2	10,302.2	1975
4,621.5	4,369.7	183.7	3,588.9	3,772.7	9,141.6	10,752.3	14,101.0	1976
5,812.7	5,706.8	60.2	5,099.8	5,159.9	11,147.0	13,187.4	18,074.1	1977
8,063.3	7227.0	131.6	7,909.3	8,041.0	14,643.5	17,315.1	24,327.1	1978
10,831.4	8,735.5	702.1	10,575.6	11,277.7	19,181.9	22,475.7	31,323.1	1979
15,774.1	12,943.5	-154.3	12,225.6	12,071.3	24,343.0	28,971.3	38,041.1	1980
19,718.7	17,340.6	718.0	13,275.5	13,993.5	30,343.4	6,147.6	47,482.0	1981
20,173.6	18,769.5	17.3	15,445.6	15,562.9	34,210.2	40,808.7	54,442.8	1982
23,048.6	22,748.4	-307.9	18,668.7	18,360.8	38,258.5	45,580.0	63,832.8	1983

Current Prices (in 10 billion won) (continued)

Year	Expenditure on GDP	Final Consumption Expenditure	Households	Gross Capital Formation	Gross Fixed Capital Formation	Increase in Stocks	Exports of Goods and Services	Imports of Goods and Services
1984	72,644.3	50,463.5	42,593.9	21,662.2	20,998.1	668.1	26,125.8	26,038.9
1985	80,846.9	56,010.8	47,131.4	23,673.1	22,836.6	836.5	27,937.2	26,919.4
1986	93,425.8	61,686.6	51,496.5	26,485.8	25,993.4	492.4	36,034.2	30,365.4
1987	108,428.3	68,697.1	57,112.5	31,944.3	31,131.3	813.0	45,050.7	36,356.1
1988	127,962.7	78,954.8	65,409.6	39,211.2	37,354.5	1,856.7	51,101.3	40,566.6
1989	143,001.4	92,081.9	75,814.6	47,693.2	45,259.4	2,433.8	48,812.7	44,784.8
1990	172,723.8	110,205.3	90,459.4	63,816.7	62,992.3	824.4	53,468.1	54,448.8
1991	208,200.6	131,866.6	107,996.8	81,256.7	78,783.4	2,473.4	60,759.7	66,050.0
1992	231,726.5	150,044.5	121,820.5	83,127.9	82,603.8	524.1	69,373.1	71,773.7

Source: Bank of Korea.

Constant Prices (in 10 billion won)

Year	Expenditure on GDP	Final Consumption Expenditure	Households	Gross Capital Formation	Gross Fixed Capital Formation	Increase in Stocks	Exports of Goods and Services	Imports of Goods and Services
1953	2,205.2	2,151.9	1,748.0	301.0	123.4	177.6	49.0	332.9
1954	2,318.5	2,241.0	1,847.6	255.5	157.1	98.4	29.7	236.6
1955	2,422.6	2,413.7	2,009.4	260.8	184.0	76.7	36.3	317.8
1956	2,389.8	2,505.2	2,085.4	193.9	203.8	-9.9	33.0	370.5
1957	2,570.4	2,559.7	2,141.3	373.6	233.0	140.5	3.0	435.9
1958	2,711.0	2,686.7	2,261.7	316.0	220.0	96.0	44.2	375.4
1959	2,814.9	2,797.0	2,374.6	230.3	227.3	3.0	55.1	305.5
1960	2,845.6	2,896.2	2,469.2	237.2	243.4	-6.1	63.9	348.6
1961	3,004.6	2,917.0	2,492.7	295.9	251.9	43.9	77.2	316.5
1962	3,071.1	3,086.1	2,653.0	294.8	324.3	-29.5	107.1	424.2
1963	3,350.6	3,182.2	2,730.8	597.0	413.0	184.0	121.0	537.8
1964	3,671.5	3,389.2	2,942.1	453.2	374.5	78.7	131.9	407.7
1965	3,885.0	3,602.1	3,133.3	473.3	476.2	-2.9	162.9	459.0
1966	4,378.5	3,845.6	3,331.6	824.0	759.8	64.1	221.4	717.0

Constant Prices (in 10 billion won) (continued)

Year	Expenditure on GDP	Final Consumption Expenditure	Households	Gross Capital Formation	Gross Fixed Capital Formation	Increase in Stocks	Exports of Goods and Services	Imports of Goods and Services
1967	4,666.4	4,165.7	3,609.3	941.9	931.8	10.1	315.2	937.7
1968	5,195.6	4,566.3	3,958.0	1,282.4	1,280.3	2.1	418.3	1,346.4
1969	5,911.3	4,944.8	4,328.8	1,819.3	1,597.3	222.0	583.4	1,704.5
1970	24,812.8	21,820.8	18,010.5	5,169.4	4,595.9	573.5	794.2	5,149.2
1971	27,112.5	23,755.2	19,593.6	5,762.4	4,764.4	998.0	2,651.5	6,160.4
1972	28,563.9	24,906.4	20,558.4	5,322.8	4,836.8	486.0	3,229.9	6,231.8
1973	32,432.4	26,714.2	22,369.7	6,868.0	6,151.9	716.1	4,399.5	8,429.7
1974	35,117.1	28,901.4	24,000.8	9,053.9	7,108.4	1,945.5	6,749.7	9,919.1
1975	37,620.8	30,597.8	25,223.6	8,740.1	7,666.8	1,073.3	6,744.1	10,160.6
1976	42,470.6	32,901.3	27,333.3	10,200.3	9,268.2	932.0	8,080.7	12,661.5
1977	46,749.2	34,880.7	28,898.1	11,956.0	980.7	11,216.2	15,267.7	
1978	51,288.7	38,207.4	31,536.9	17,081.8	16,191.7	890.1	13,684.7	19,537.3
1979	55,181.5	41,101.9	34,328.5	19,924.0	17,806.9	2,117.1	15,858.8	21,777.7
1980	53,988.7	41,241.3	33,984.3	15,906.3	15,770.5	135.8	17,227.6	20,661.5

1981	57,615.4	43,267.5	35,636.9	16,208.4	15,126.4	1,082.0	19,889.9	21,870.6
1982	61,810.9	45,675.5	37,955.5	17,467.0	16,693.1	773.9	20,780.0	22,527.9
1983	69,101.0	49,421.3	41,334.6	19,830.9	19,661.6	169.3	24,776.1	25,233.1
1984	75,606.4	52,707.6	44,378.2	22,795.8	21,811.6	984.2	26,744.2	27,090.2
1985	80,846.9	56,010.8	47,131.4	23,673.1	22,836.6	836.5	27,937.2	26,919.4
1986	90,867.8	60,725.7	50,939.7	26,247.3	25,568.5	678.8	35,238.5	31,713.6
1987	101,803.5	65,656.7	55,184.8	30,892.8	29,799.6	1,093.2	42,848.7	37,871.4
1988	113,492.2	72,057.8	60,565.5	35,583.1	33,806.2	1,776.9	48,209.3	42,732.2
1989	120,477.2	79,797.3	67,210.5	43,007.7	39,527.5	3,480.2	46,369.5	49,682.9
1990	131,502.9	87,874.4	74,178.9	50,888.9	49,017.3	1,871.6	48,318.7	56,816.1
1991	142,633.0	96,029.1	81,065.1	59,068.5	54,805.0	4,263.5	53,053.5	66,764.4
1992	149,463.0	102,531.2	86,270.3	55,947.7	53,817.5	2,130.2	58,269.9	68,704.3

Source: Bank of Korea.

Notes: Figures up to 1969 are compiled at 1975 prices. Figures from 1970 to 1992 are compiled at 1985 prices. Figures in 1992 are preliminarily estimated.

APPENDIX 4
POPULATION AND
EMPLOYMENT (1,000s)

Year	Population	Economically Active Population	Employed					Unemployment (%)
			Total	Agriculture, Forestry, Fishing, and Hunting	Mining and Manufacturing	Manufacturing Alone	Others	
1963	27,262	8,343	7,662	4,837	667	610	2,158	8.2
1964	27,984	8,449	7,799	4,825	690	637	2,284	7.7
1965	27,705	8,859	8,206	4,810	849	772	2,547	7.4
1966	29,436	9,071	8,423	4,876	913	833	2,634	7.1
1967	30,131	9,295	8,717	4,811	1,115	1,021	2,791	6.2
1968	30,838	9,647	9,155	1,801	1,282	1,170	6,072	5.1
1969	31,544	9,888	9,414	4,825	1,346	1,232	3,243	4.8
1970	32,241	10,199	9,745	4,916	1,395	1,284	3,434	4.5
1971	32,883	10,542	10,066	4,876	1,428	1,336	3,762	4.5
1972	33,505	11,058	10,559	5,346	1,499	1,445	3,714	4.5
1973	34,103	11,600	11,139	5,569	1,821	1,774	3,749	4.0
1974	34,692	12,080	11,586	5,584	2,062	2,012	3,940	4.1
1975	35,281	12,340	11,830	5,425	2,265	2,205	4,140	4.1

1976	35,849	13,061	12,566	5,601	2,743	2,678	4,222	3.8
1977	36,412	13,440	12,929	5,405	2,901	2,798	4,623	3.8
1978	36,969	13,932	13,490	5,181	3,123	3,016	5,186	3.2
1979	37,534	14,206	13,664	4,887	3,237	3,126	5,540	3.8
1980	38,124	14,431	13,683	4,654	3,079	2,955	5,950	5.2
1981	38,723	14,683	14,023	4,801	2,983	2,859	6,239	4.5
1982	39,326	15,032	14,379	4,612	3,143	3,033	6,624	4.3
1983	39,910	15,118	14,505	4,315	3,375	3,266	6,815	4.1
1984	40,406	14,997	14,429	3,914	3,491	3,348	7,024	3.8
1985	41,806	15,592	14,970	3,733	3,659	3,504	7,578	4.0
1986	41,214	16,116	15,505	3,662	4,013	3,826	7,830	3.8
1987	41,622	16,873	16,354	3,580	4,602	4,416	8,172	3.1
1988	42,031	17,305	16,870	3,484	4,807	4,667	8,579	2.5
1989	42,449	17,971	17,511	3,418	4,933	4,840	9,160	2.6
1990	42,869	18,487	18,036	3,292	4,928	4,847	9,816	2.4
1991	43,268	19,012	18,576	3,103	5,005	4,936	10,468	2.3
1992	43,663	19,384	18,921	3,025	4,828	4,768	11,068	2.4

Source: National Statistical Office.

APPENDIX 5
STRUCTURE OF
MANUFACTURING
INDUSTRY

Constant Prices, in Billion Won

Year	Manufacturing Industry	Food, Beverages, and Tobacco	Textile, Wearing Apparel, and Leather	Wood and Wood Products, Including Furniture	Paper, Paper Products, Printing, and Publishing
1953	13.7	3.7	5.1	0.6	0.7
1954	24.1	6.6	8.9	1.0	1.2
1955	42.4	14.5	13.1	2.1	1.9
1956	58.3	20.5	19.0	2.8	2.1
1957	73.4	25.8	23.5	3.6	2.1
1958	79.1	27.5	24.6	3.2	3.3
1959	91.6	29.4	27.3	4.3	3.8
1960	111.5	34.8	31.7	5.6	5.3
1961	129.7	41.5	35.5	4.3	6.3
1962	172.5	51.7	48.3	7.4	8.8
1963	237.8	70.8	60.8	10.6	12.8
1964	336.5	96.1	83.7	15.1	20.5
1965	459.4	123.3	118.7	20.7	27.5
1966	600.1	154.1	154.2	28.4	35.7
1967	785.7	205.1	201.0	35.0	43.9

1968	1,100.7	272.2	273.8	54.6	56.0
1969	1,397.9	358.0	342.4	61.6	66.8
1970	2,304.2	840.4	419.0	96.6	100.3
1971	2,991.5	1,073.9	565.9	121.3	124.3
1972	3,821.5	1,286.4	836.8	150.7	152.2
1973	5,490.8	1,496.2	1,316.5	242.9	212.2
1974	8,604.2	2,253.0	1,654.9	237.2	372.8
1975	11,236.4	2,896.8	2,204.2	323.7	436.4
1976	15,416.4	3,698.2	3,088.1	428.7	564.0
1977	19,493.6	4,496.3	3,662.1	511.9	674.7
1978	26,283.8	6,087.6	4,759.5	623.0	846.4
1979	35,805.5	8,150.7	599.3	908.5	1,087.4
1980	48,092.3	10,203.5	8,145.7	947.6	1,513.7
1981	60,296.5	11,882.6	10,273.4	1,017.6	1,969.3
1982	66,581.0	13,860.7	10,541.8	1,093.4	2,220.6
1983	76,434.6	14,803.6	11,622.4	1,239.8	2,763.2
1984	88,560.0	16,036.2	13,450.3	1,352.9	3,215.6
1985	95,597.6	17,204.7	14,435.2	1,357.9	3,438.5

Constant Prices, in Billion Won (continued)

Year	Manufacturing Industry	Food, Beverages, and Tobacco	Textile, Wearing Apparel, and Leather	Wood and Wood Products, Including Furniture	Paper, Paper Products, Printing, and Publishing
1986	112,258.0	19,343.1	17,420.8	1,448.5	4,053.9
1987	133,295.9	20,469.7	21,443.2	1,745.3	4,880.9
1988	152,239.9	22,704.3	21,897.2	2,092.9	5,724.5
1989	159,416.5	24,344.9	21,573.5	2,215.3	6,320.4
1990	175,498.2	26,282.7	21,758.7	2,387.2	6,733.4
1991	199,088.1	28,234.6	22,249.3	2,659.7	7,475.4

Year	Chemicals and Chemical, Petroleum, Coal, Rubber, and Plastic Products	Nonmetallic Mineral Products, Except Petroleum and Coal	Basic Metal Industry	Fabricated Metal Products, Machinery, and Equipment	Other Manufacturing Industries
1953	1.6	0.6	0.1	1.2	0.1
1954	2.9	1.0	0.3	2.1	0.3
1955	4.6	1.4	0.4	3.5	0.7
1956	5.2	1.9	0.9	4.9	0.9
1957	7.3	2.2	1.6	6.1	1.1

Year					
1958	7.9	3.0	2.0	6.7	1.0
1959	11.0	3.5	2.7	8.9	1.5
1960	13.8	3.9	4.9	9.7	1.4
1961	15.8	4.8	4.7	14.6	2.2
1962	20.4	6.3	7.2	19.6	2.9
1963	32.7	1.9	11.5	27.0	3.9
1964	54.4	13.1	14.8	34.2	4.6
1965	72.0	16.9	23.4	49.9	7.0
1966	92.4	21.3	28.6	75.5	9.8
1967	119.6	29.6	35.9	102.0	13.6
1968	188.8	42.7	47.5	147.9	17.1
1969	235.4	54.8	61.8	193.8	23.3
1970	373.4	84.8	74.2	264.0	51.4
1971	497.2	107.3	112.2	337.5	51.9
1972	609.2	124.1	158.6	436.0	67.6
1973	856.8	174.3	320.8	762.6	108.6
1974	1,629.1	287.5	657.4	1,353.0	159.4
1975	2,253.4	402.2	695.4	1,719.6	204.9

Constant Prices, in Billion Won (continued)

Year	Chemicals and Chemical, Petroleum, Coal, Rubber, and Plastic Products	Nonmetallic Mineral Products, Except Petroleum and Coal	Basic Metal Industry	Fabricated Metal Products, Machinery, and Equipment	Other Manufacturing Industeries
1976	3,199.7	512.5	1,062.9	2,605.9	301.4
1977	3,997.9	696.4	1,367.7	3,686.4	400.3
1978	4,743.1	871.1	2,039.9	5,851.0	462.1
1979	6,839.9	1,308.2	3,473.2	7,514.4	523.8
1980	11,490.0	1,771.4	5,410.9	7,978.5	631.2
1981	14,507.3	1,944.4	7,007.0	10,765.9	929.0
1982	15,544.6	2,182.4	7,582.2	12,586.3	968.9
1983	17,445.5	2,755.0	8,810.0	15,850.0	1,145.1
1984	19,769.1	3,182.5	10,195.6	19,969.1	1,388.7
1985	21,259.1	3,413.2	10,712.3	22,268.6	1,508.2
1986	22,418.1	3,891.8	10,967.0	30,520.0	2,194.8
1987	24,360.2	4,329.8	13,091.1	40,321.6	2,664.1
1988	28,110.3	5,033.2	15,265.8	48,673.9	2,737.8
1989	28,500.0	5,224.7	17,085.6	51,735.6	2,416.5

| 1990 | 32,094.5 | 6,170.9 | 18,646.0 | 60,089.2 | 2,335.5 |
| 1991 | 37,951.5 | 8,023.3 | 21,382.8 | 68,692.0 | 2,419.6 |

Source: Bank of Korea.

Notes: Figures up to 1969 are compiled at 1975 prices. Figures from 1970 to 1992 are compiled at 1985 prices. Figures in 1992 are preliminarily estimated.

APPENDIX 6
INVESTMENT RESOURCES

Current Prices, in Billion Won

Year	GNP	Gross Investment	Investment Ratio (%)	Gross Savings	Savings Ratio (%)	Private Savings	Government Savings	Net Lending	Ratio to the Rest of the World (%)	Statistical Discrepancy (%)
1953	47.88	7.38	15.4	4.23	8.8	5.38	-1.15	3.15	6.6	0.00
1954	66.20	7.90	11.9	4.38	6.6	6.08	-1.80	3.52	5.3	0.00
1955	114.49	14.12	12.3	5.99	5.2	8.68	-1.69	8.13	7.1	0.00
1956	151.50	13.53	8.9	-2.95	-1.9	1.47	-4.42	16.48	10.9	0.00
1957	197.10	30.21	15.3	10.88	5.51	16.89	-6.01	19.33	9.8	0.00
1958	204.70	26.39	12.9	9.93	4.9	16.36	-6.43	16.46	8.0	0.00
1959	217.49	24.27	11.2	9.21	4.2					
1960	244.93	26.63	10.9	2.00	0.8	7.01	-5.01	20.99	8.6	-3.64
1961	294.18	38.70	13.2	8.36	2.8	13.71	-5.35	25.29	8.6	-5.05
1962	355.54	45.51	12.8	11.59	3.3	17.07	-5.48	37.95	10.7	4.03
1963	502.90	91.14	18.1	43.72	8.7	45.56	-1.84	52.36	10.4	4.94
1964	716.31	100.59	14.0	62.64	8.7	59.31	3.33	49.13	6.9	11.18
1965	805.72	120.88	15.0	59.39	7.4	45.60	13.79	51.53	6.4	-9.96
1966	1,037.04	223.93	21.6	122.83	11.8	94.28	28.55	87.63	8.5	-13.47

1967	1,281.23	280.70	21.9	145.76	11.4	93.21	52.55	112.86	8.8	-22.10
1968	1,652.93	427.66	25.9	249.33	15.1	148.46	100.87	184.33	11.2	6.00
1969	2,155.27	621.33	28.8	405.92	18.8	278.47	127.45	229.02	10.6	13.61
1970	2,766.9	682.5	24.6	449.60	16.2	305.6	144.0	251.5	9.1	-18.60
1971	3,406.9	856.8	25.1	493.00	14.5	340.1	152.9	356.6	10.5	7.20
1972	4,177.5	871.4	20.9	655.20	15.7	575.7	79.5	210.8	5.0	5.40
1973	5,355.5	1,320.9	24.7	1,144.80	21.4	986.7	158.1	196.5	3.7	-20.34
1974	7,564.5	2,408.1	31.8	1,458.00	19.3	1,309.2	148.8	899.4	11.9	50.70
1975	10,064.6	2,767.1	27.5	1,695.60	16.9	1,454.5	241.1	1,032.1	10.3	39.34
1976	13,818.2	2,545.4	25.7	3,062.80	22.2	2,475.4	587.4	353.1	2.6	129.50
1977	17,728.6	4,903.9	27.7	4,503.30	25.4	3,702.6	800.7	219.4	1.2	181.20
1978	23,936.8	7,624.0	31.9	6,533.60	27.3	5,253.5	1,280.1	1,032.2	4.3	58.20
1979	30,741.1	11,074.3	36.0	8,149.70	26.5	6,140.4	2,009.3	2,748.2	8.9	176.40
1980	36,672.3	11,788.9	32.1	7,618.20	20.8	5,630.0	1,988.2	4,206.5	11.5	-35.86
1981	45,126.2	13,679.0	30.3	9,245.20	20.5	6,716.5	2,528.7	4,418.3	9.8	15.50
1982	50,724.6	14,509.6	28.6	10,613.00	20.9	7,497.5	3,115.5	3,539.4	7.0	357.20
1983	58,985.8	17,620.8	29.9	14,950.50	25.3	10,679.6	4,270.9	2,799.3	4.7	-129.00

Current Prices, in Billion Won (continued)

Year	GNP	Gross Investment	Investment Ratio (%)	Gross Savings	Savings Ratio (%)	Private Savings	Government Savings	Net Lending	Ratio to the Rest of the World (%)	Statistical Discrepancy (%)
1984	66,408.2	21,207.3	31.9	18,50.80	27.9	13,863.8	4,687.1	2,666.1	4.0	-9.60
1985	72,849.8	22,644.8	31.1	20,830.60	28.6	15,775.4	5,055.2	2,256.8	3.1	-442.60
1986	83,975.8	25,281.1	30.2	27,474.50	32.8	21,981.9	5,492.6	-2,309.1	-2.8	115.70
1987	106,024.4	39,953.0	37.7	39,045.30	36.8	31,685.1	7,360.2	8,008.7	7.6	-907.70
1988	126,230.5	49,421.2	39.1	48,683.20	38.6	38,236.7	10,446.5	10,210.0	8.1	-738.00
1989	141,794.4	51,035.7	35.9	50,234.20	35.4	38,423.4	11,810.8	3,342.5	2.3	-801.50
1990	171,488.1	62,218.4	36.3	61,900.90	36.1	46,868.1	15,032.8	-1,598.3	-0.9	-317.50
1991	206,681.1	74,847.5	36.2	75,215.40	36.4	58,320.6	16,894.8	-6,409.2	-3.1	367.90
1992	229,938.5	79,577.6	34.6	80,512.20	35.0	62,104.8	18,407.4	-3,570.3	-1.5	954.60

Source: Bank of Korea.

APPENDIX 7
SCALE OF
FINANCIAL SAVINGS
(IN 100 MILLION WON)

Year	Total Net	Savings Deposits	CDs	Nonbank Deposit	Issuance	Short-term Finance	Public Bonds	Stocks	Corporate Bonds
1965	440	306	—	148	48	—	—	—	—
1966	939	701	—	272	74	—	—	—	—
1967	1,732	1,289	—	492	121	—	—	—	—
1968	3,409	2,555	—	819	177	—	64	92	—
1969	5,771	4,515	—	1,136	288	—	269	153	—
1970	7,634	5,763	—	1,449	399	—	451	225	—
1971	9,665	7,087	—	2,089	509	—	516	254	—
1972	13,015	9,115	—	2,885	679	39	1,214	403	99
1973	18,828	12,211	—	4,768	914	672	1,822	913	138
1974	24,069	14,718	—	6,822	1,242	1,622	1,823	1,378	316
1975	32,295	19,437	—	8,905	1,626	2,542	1,816	2,606	613
1976	45,288	26,134	—	13,766	2,110	4,381	1,925	4,366	1,280
1977	65,605	35,882	—	21,114	2,994	6,587	3,113	6,226	2,854
1978	96,565	51,320	—	31,466	4,585	9,407	3,841	9,493	5,888
1979	133,555	65,314	—	46,597	8,029	13,378	5,542	11,161	11,099
1980	186,874	85,770	—	70,616	11,491	20,984	8,882	13,372	18,391

Year								
1981	260,055	114,998	—	106,206	16,461	32,153	15,242	16,432	25,667
1982	330,171	136,597	—	150,925	25,032	42,273	26,739	19,201	33,771
1983	408,153	156,727	—	194,995	36,830	54,971	33,415	23,827	44,132
1984	494,076	173,066	6,842	250,263	52,048	70,118	41,832	28,617	53,339
1985	597,627	202,462	10,809	314,935	69,086	68,845	49,863	21,563	71,971
1986	749,915	245,911	13,076	426,658	92,073	88,816	62,153	39,971	85,483
1987	960,417	297,001	16,552	556,250	127,539	100,670	76,323	58,958	99,173
1988	1,266,486	356,150	17,534	758,543	171,044	131,191	86,158	136,659	116,868
1989	1,781,894	437,782	16,885	1,058,511	226,154	185,845	115,607	278,414	161,198
1990	2,314,894	524,337	68,035	1,395,057	301,568	218,931	146,096	307,592	238,605
1991	2,799,316	608,884	99,400	1,666,184	388,942	176,750	198,034	334,463	311,423
1992	3,353,415	707,273	119,433	2,154,074	459,771	224,915	227,511	354,167	351,450

Source: Ministry of Finance.

Note: Intersector trading is not included in total net.

APPENDIX 8
MAJOR CURRENCY INDEX
(IN BILLION WON)

Year	Reserve Money	Bank Notes and Coins	Money Supply (M_1)	Cash	Deposit	Money Supply (M_2)	Time and Savings Deposits	Liquidity (M_3)
1960	16.8	14.7	22.7	14.3	8.5	25.1	2.4	—
1961	25.4	18.1	35.8	16.7	19.1	40.2	5.4	—
1962	29.8	20.8	39.4	17.6	21.8	51.6	12.2	—
1963	27.9	21.9	41.9	18.3	23.6	54.7	12.8	—
1964	32.7	27.8	48.9	24.9	24.0	63.4	14.5	—
1965	48.4	35.2	65.6	31.6	34.0	97.1	20.6	—
1966	80.2	46.5	85.1	42.9	42.2	157.0	70.1	—
1967	110.9	68.0	123.0	57.6	65.4	253.8	128.9	—
1968	156.2	95.7	177.9	81.9	95.9	436.6	255.5	—
1969	216.0	129.9	252.0	111.3	140.7	704.6	451.5	—
1970	299.7	158.9	307.6	133.7	173.9	897.8	576.3	—
1971	288.2	186.5	358.0	162.1	195.9	1,084.9	708.7	1,278.0
1972	427.5	245.2	519.4	217.7	301.7	1,451.8	911.5	1,683.8
1973	624.1	353.3	730.3	311.4	418.9	1,980.5	1,221.1	2,391.1
1974	775.0	454.6	945.7	410.5	535.2	2,456.5	1,471.8	3,041.1
1975	1,077.0	560.9	1,181.8	507.2	674.2	3,150.0	1,943.7	3,903.3

Year								
1976	1,437.7	736.3	1,544.0	676.8	867.2	4,204.8	2,613.4	5,293.7
1977	2,071.6	1,034.0	2,172.6	953.4	1,219.2	5,874.3	3,588.2	7,515.5
1978	2,802.0	1,491.8	2,713.8	1,364.4	1,349.4	7,928.7	5,132.0	10,210.6
1979	3,468.0	1,817.5	3,274.5	1,604.0	1,670.0	9,877.8	6,531.4	13,379.3
1980	3,243.9	2,038.6	3,807.0	1,856.4	1,950.6	12,534.5	8,577.0	17,810.8
1981	2,801.6	2,205.5	3,982.4	2,025.4	1,957.0	15,671.1	11,499.8	23,243.2
1982	3,825.3	2,792.2	5,799.3	2,573.7	3,225.6	19,904.2	13,659.7	30,964.6
1983	4,095.2	3,099.2	6,783.4	2,874.4	2,909.0	22,938.1	15,672.7	37,647.7
1984	4,248.4	3,392.8	6,820.7	3,109.4	3,711.4	24,705.6	17,306.6	45,204.1
1985	4,319.0	3,569.5	7,557.8	3,285.5	4,272.3	28,565.2	20,246.2	54,763.9
1986	5,016.3	4,001.6	8,808.9	4,001.6	5,130.2	33,833.1	24,591.1	69,117.1
1987	7,469.2	4,843.2	10,107.3	4,442.7	5,664.6	40,279.5	29,700.0	90,474.4
1988	9,728.4	5,629.6	12,151.4	5,133.4	7,018.0	48,938.8	35,615.0	120,358.6
1989	12,818.6	6,793.7	14,329.0	6,139.6	8,189.4	58,638.0	43,778.2	153,831.2
1990	13,811.2	8,228.1	15,905.3	7,011.1	8,894.2	68,707.5	52,433.7	197,847.0
1991	16,321.7	9,102.3	21,752.4	7,913.1	13,839.3	83,745.9	60,888.4	243,955.9
1992	18,107.3	9,807.7	24,586.4	8,580.6	16,005.3	96,258.6	70,727.3	294,843.7

Source: Ministry of Finance.
Note: Outstanding amount at the end of the year.

APPENDIX 9
CONSOLIDATED CENTRAL
GOVERNMENT FINANCING
(IN 100 MILLION WON)

Year	Tax Receipts					Expenditures and Lending			Budget Surplus or Deficit
	Total Revenue	Subtotal	Internal Taxes	Customs Duties	Monopoly Profits	Total	Expenditures	Net Lending	
1966	1,311	960	705	180	75	1,724	1,583	141	-413
1967	2,155	1,392	1,038	254	100	2,507	2,311	196	-352
1968	2,725	2,107	1,564	379	164	2,967	2,809	158	-242
1969	3,946	2,871	2,181	447	243	4,706	4,344	362	-760
1970	4,735	3,648	2,838	509	301	5,220	4,941	279	-485
1971	5,856	4,531	3,555	522	454	6,400	6,004	396	-544
1972	62,94	4,763	3,743	591	429	8,515	8,212	303	-2,221
1973	7,639	5,785	4,391	824	570	8,543	8,308	235	904
1974	11,856	9,137	7,180	1,267	690	13,566	13,321	245	-1,710
1975	16,834	13,910	10,123	1,810	1,355	20,072	19,840	232	-3,238
1976	23,721	20,927	13,705	2,755	1,780	25,601	25,262	339	1,880
1977	32,276	26,227	16,752	3,859	2,200	31,630	31,263	367	646
1978	39,136	36,523	22,525	6,464	2,800	38,186	37,741	445	950
1979	60,742	47,617	30,375	7,323	3,600	54,096	53,368	728	6,646
1980	73,345	58,149	36,758	7,661	5,100	77,580	76,374	1,206	-4,235

1981	88,864	72,681	45,958	8,906	6,800	92,857	91,374	1,483	-3,993
1982	108,583	84,098	52,507	10,126	7,600	113,398	111,250	2,148	-4,815
1983	113,342	100,507	61,884	14,632	8,300	106,823	105,775	1,048	6,519
1984	121,094	108,997	66,974	15,940	8,460	113,449	113,452	-3	7,645
1985	133,103	118,763	74,969	15,661	8,290	124,196	123,650	546	8,907
1986	162,786	136,063	84,640	19,425	9,840	153,200	153,105	95	9,585
1987	191,623	163,437	100,120	26,965	9,043	174,888	174,883	5	16,736
1988	239,483	194,842	125,402	25,736	9,470	212,499	213,233	-734	26,984
1989	288,479	212,341	152,084	21,176	15	284,041	283,671	370	4,438
1990	345,383	268,475	191,302	27,654	—	337,833	338,369	-536	7,549
1991	393,285	303,198	240,891	34,355	—	410,352	409,968	384	-17,067
1992	462,666	352,184	300,800	31,532	—	469,551	469,604	-53	-6,885

Source: Bank of Korea.

APPENDIX 10
TAX RECEIPTS
(IN 100 MILLION WON)

Year	Internal Taxes	Direct Taxes	Income Tax	Corporate Taxes	Indirect Taxes	Value Added Taxes	Customs Duties	Defense Surtaxes	Total (ratio of amount of taxes)
1949	1.3	0.5	0.4	0.04	0.8	—	—	—	—
1950	4.2	2.9	0.5	0.4	1.3	—	—	—	—
1951	39	23	6	2	16	—	—	—	—
1952	96	58	11	3	37	—	—	—	—
1953	215	119	29	8	95	—	—	—	—
1954	514	239	75	21	272	—	—	—	—
1955	1,093	493	160	56	596	—	—	—	—
1956									
1957	1,158	574	139	52	576	—	—	—	—
1958	1,434	739	181	51	685	—	—	—	—
1959	2,159	1,293	219	71	854	—	—	—	—
1960	2,461	1,314	213	91	1,133	—	—	—	—
1961	179	98	25	17	74	—	53	—	284(9.7)
1962	215	195	46	20	109	—	68	—	376(10.6)
1963	247	123	59	29	110	—	67	—	433(8.6)
1964	292	170	86	41	108	—	85	—	507(7.1)

1965	421	233	117	57	175	—	128	—	696(8.6)
1966	700	338	203	109	337	—	180	—	1,122(10.8)
1967	1,038	511	309	159	492	—	254	—	1,535(12.0)
1968	1,564	777	476	246	752	—	379	—	2,301(13.9)
1969	2,181	1,104	696	331	1,029	—	447	—	3,137(14.6)
1970	2,838	1,386	845	424	1,416	—	509	—	3,981(14.8)
1971	3,555	1,785	1,076	567	1,726	—	522	—	4,929(15.0)
1972	3,743	1,754	1,047	548	1,866	—	591	—	5,229(13.0)
1973	4,391	1,985	1,237	498	2,295	—	824	—	6,526(12.5)
1974	7,179	3,131	1,647	1,103	3,837	—	1,267	—	10,217(13.0)
1975	10,123	3,809	1,986	1,305	5,687	—	1,810	622	15,498(15.8)
1976	13,705	5,481	3,190	1,712	7,696	—	2,755	2,687	23,133(17.4)
1977	16,752	7,067	3,527	2,349	10,280	2,416	3,859	3,416	29,593(17.4)
1978	22,525	8,420	4,678	3,587	13,828	8,352	6,464	4,733	40,95(17.9)
1979	30,375	11,249	6,147	4,932	18,734	10,878	7,323	6,319	53,606(18.4)
1980	36,758	11,788	6,614	4,852	24,039	14,708	7,661	8,558	65,754(19.2)
1981	45,958	15,467	8,862	5,941	29,168	18,048	8,906	10,915	81,723(18.8)

Year	Internal Taxes	Direct Taxes	Income Tax	Corporate Taxes	Indirect Taxes	Value Added Taxes	Customs Duties	Defense Surtaxes	Total (ratio of amount of taxes)
1982	52,507	18,799	10,055	7,813	32,602	20,944	10,125	11,753	95,156(18.8)
1983	61,884	20,928	11,361	8.637	39,222	25,593	14,632	13,060	114,479(19.4)
1984	66,974	22,347	12,291	9,235	42,562	27,043	15,940	14,775	124,081(18.7)
1985	74,969	26,714	14,816	11,267	45,570	29,012	15,661	16,632	135,311(18.6)
1986	84,640	30,464	17,846	11,914	51,279	32,012	19,425	18,434	154,161(18.4)
1987	100,120	39,24	21,589	16,824	57,358	36,505	26,965	23,195	185,839(17.5)
1988	125,402	53,535	29,641	22,474	68,522	42,052	25,736	29,111	225,842(17.9)
1989	152,084	68,974	35,569	31,079	80,632	52,602	21,176	34,832	261,949(18.5)
1990	191,302	83,404	47,231	32,261	103,841	69,644	27,654	44,306	332,148(19.4)
1991	240,891	116,273	64,594	45,855	120,851	82,526	34,355	12,631	383,550(18.6)
1992	300,800	145,734	80,084	59,410	150,001		31,532	1,629	436,717(19.0)

Source: Ministry of Finance.

APPENDIX 11
BALANCE OF PAYMENTS
(US$ MILLIONS)

		Trade Balance			Invisible Trade Balance			Long-Term Capital Balance	Basic Balance	Short-Term Capital Balance	Overall Balance
Year	Current Balance	Net	Export	Import	Net	Credit	Debit				
1950	23.1	-54.6	25.3	79.9	17.5	19.8	2.7	0.0	23.1	0.0	21.7
1951	52.8	-113.9	15.6	129.5	55.5	59.2	3.7	0.0	52.8	0.0	56.5
1952	61.2	-186.4	27.8	214.2	83.0	86.6	3.7	0.0	61.2	0.0	61.2
1953	-67.8	-305.7	39.7	345.4	43.7	50.5	6.9	0.0	-67.8	0.0	-67.9
1954	-33.4	-218.2	25.1	243.3	29.2	36.4	8.1	0.0	-33.4	0.0	-32.4
1955	-36.3	-309.9	17.7	327.6	43.3	52.9	9.7	-5.6	-41.9	-0.9	-46.4
1956	-34.1	-354.8	25.3	380.1	25.6	39.4	13.9	0.0	23.1	-3.2	18.7
1957	-2.6	-370.9	19.5	390.4	-16.5	52.9	75.8	0.0	-2.6	-2.9	-4.1
1958	37.7	-326.4	17.3	343.7	15.4	75.1	59.9	0.0	37.7	7.0	45.2
1959	16.4	-253.6	19.8	273.4	26.2	83.8	57.7	-0.8	-15.6	-0.6	15.1
1960	13.4	-272.5	32.9	305.4	10.2	84.0	73.8	7.9	21.3	0.6	19.8
1961	33.1	-242.2	40.9	283.1	43.8	104.7	60.9	16.4	49.5	-2.0	45.9
1962	-55.5	-335.3	54.8	390.1	43.3	108.4	65.1	7.8	-47.7	-6.7	-56.5
1963	-143.3	-410.2	86.8	497.0	7.4	88.7	81.3	69.5	-73.8	18.4	-55.8

1964	-26.1	-244.9	120.0	364.9	23.9	91.0	67.1	29.0	2.9	-4.4	-2.7
1965	9.1	-240.3	175.6	415.9	45.1	114.2	68.1	37.3	46.4	-23.1	16.2
1966	-103.4	-429.5	250.4	679.9	106.5	204.3	97.8	211.8	108.4	6.4	119.2
1967	-191.9	-574.2	334.7	908.9	157.1	308.2	151.1	201.2	9.3	85.9	118.2
1968	-440.3	-835.7	486.3	1,322.0	169.3	394.0	224.7	433.8	-6.5	13.2	-13.5
1969	-548.6	-991.7	658.3	1,650.0	197.3	492.4	295.1	593.5	44.9	56.5	93.7
1970	-622.5	-922.0	882.2	1,804.2	119.3	496.8	377.5	501.0	-121.5	122.4	-4.2
1971	-847.5	-1,045.9	1,132.3	2,178.2	27.8	483.7	455.9	512.0	-335.5	134.6	-187.8
1972	-371.2	-573.9	1,676.5	2,250.4	32.9	550.3	517.4	521.0	149.8	-16.3	163.6
1973	-308.8	-566.0	3,271.3	3,837.3	67.1	849.4	782.3	666.3	357.5	84.0	460.3
1974	-2,022.7	-1,936.8	4,515.1	6,451.9	-308.3	837.8	1,146.1	946.4	-1,076.3	-45.4	-1,093.8
1975	-1,886.9	-1,671.4	5,003.0	6,674.4	-442.2	880.6	1,322.8	1,178.3	-708.6	679.5	-150.6
1976	-313.6	-590.5	7,814.6	8,405.1	-71.8	1,642.7	1,714.5	1,371.2	1,057.6	356.5	1,173.6
1977	12.3	-476.6	10,046.5	10,523.1	266.0	3,027.0	2,761.0	1,312.7	1,325.0	21.4	1,314.7
1978	-1,085.2	-1,780.8	12,710.6	14,491.4	224.0	4,450.1	4,226.1	2,166.3	1,081.1	-1,171.0	401.9
1979	-4,151.1	-4,395.5	14,704.5	19,100.0	-194.6	4,826.2	5,020.8	2,662.9	-1,488.2	843.6	973.3
1980	-5,320.7	-4,384.1	17,214.0	21,598.1	-1,385.9	5,363.3	6,749.2	1,856.5	-3,464.2	1,944.5	-1,889.6

		Trade Balance			Invisible Trade Balance			Long-Term Capital Balance	Basic Balance	Short-Term Capital Balance	Overall Balance
Year	Current Balance	Net	Export	Import	Net	Credit	Debit				
1981	-4,646.0	-3,628.3	20,670.8	24,299.1	-1,518.4	6,598.1	8,116.5	2,841.9	-1,804.1	-82.3	-2,297.0
1982	-2,649.6	-2,594.4	20,879.2	23,473.6	-554.2	7,476.3	8,030.5	1,230.3	-1,419.3	3.6	-2,711.2
1983	-1,606.0	-1,763.5	23,303.9	24,967.4	-434.6	7,178.7	6,613.3	1,270.4	-335.6	893.3	-384.4
1984	-1,372.6	-1,035.9	26,334.6	27,370.5	-877.6	7,316.3	8,193.9	2,067.4	694.8	-757.9	-957.5
1985	-887.4	-19.0	26,441.5	26,460.5	-1,446.1	6,664.4	8,110.5	1,100.8	213.4	-587.5	-1,254.5
1986	4,617.0	4,205.9	33,913.2	29,707.3	-627.5	8,051.7	8,679.2	-1,981.8	2,635.1	-392.1	1,699.5
1987	9,853.9	7,659.0	46,243.8	38,584.8	977.4	10,010.0	9,032.6	-5,835.8	4,018.1	-7.0	5,202.1
1988	14,160.7	11,445.4	59,648.2	48,202.8	1,267.2	11,251.9	9,984.7	-2,732.8	11,427.9	1,336.3	12,175.2
1989	5,054.6	4,597.2	61,408.7	56,811.5	210.8	12,641.6	12,430.8	-3,362.5	1,692.1	60.3	2,453.1
1990	-2,179.4	-2,003.6	63,123,6	65,127.2	-450.6	14,268.6	14,719.2	547.5	-1,631.9	3,333.7	-273.9
1991	-8,727.7	-6,979.8	69,521.5	76,581.3	-1,595.5	15,529.4	17,124.9	4,195.8	-4,514.9	41.2	-3,740.9
1992	-4,528.5	-2,146.4	75,169.4	77,315.8	-2,614.3	16,010.2	18,624.5	7,232.7	2,704.2	1,109.9	4,898.1

Source: Bank of Korea.

APPENDIX 12
STRUCTURE OF
COMMODITY EXPORTS
(US$ MILLIONS)

Year	Total	Food	Crude and Fuels	Light Industry	Textiles	Footwear	Heavy Industry	Chemicals	Iron and Steel
1964	119	27	28	54	33	0.9	11	0.6	8
1965	175	29	31	91	55	4	24	0.4	18
1966	250	47	36	141	81	5	25	0.7	15
1967	320	45	43	204	125	8	27	2	11
1968	455	53	44	317	193	11	40	3	12
1969	623	65	51	422	254	10	84	10	19
1970	835	79	67	582	342	17	107	11	31
1971	1,068	85	62	769	487	37	151	15	41
1972	1,624	121	76	,081	680	55	345	37	121
1973	2,225	269	146	2,043	1,277	106	767	48	259
1974	4,460	347	249	2,414	1,526	179	1,449	92	581
1975	5,081	669	224	2,916	1,844	191	1,271	75	364
1976	7,715	587	326	4,536	2,837	389	2,245	99	610
1977	10,047	1,054	372	5,389	3,229	487	3,231	229	993
1978	12,711	1,045	328	6,931	4,190	686	4,406	347	1,143

Year									
1979	15,056	1,167	357	7,741	4,733	738	5,789	544	1,757
1980	17,505	1,244	349	8,650	5,214	874	7,261	814	2,517
1981	21,254	1,439	457	10,362	6,364	1,024	8,734	699	3,028
1982	21,853	1,201	559	9,730	6,023	1,154	10,126	728	3,113
1983	24,445	1,216	807	9,947	6,166	1,235	12,252	740	3,367
1984	29,245	1,276	1,068	11,542	7,199	1,351	15,358	918	3,582
1985	30,283	1,251	1,166	11,690	7,083	1,534	16,175	1,006	3,422
1986	34,713	1,677	934	15,287	8,763	2,059	16,817	1,158	3,508
1987	47,281	2,191	1,522	19,634	10,997	2,731	23,934	1,321	3,983
1988	60,696	2,621	1,402	23,937	13,461	3,407	32,736	1,879	5,377
1989	62,377	2,466	1,666	24,782	14,427	3,219	33,462	2,050	5,763
1990	65,016	2,290	1,719	25,147	13,938	4,024	35,859	2,511	5,663
1991	71,807	2,409	2,658	25,305	14,722	3,575	41,499	3,191	5,989
1992	76,632	2,347	3,170	24,828	15,007	2,910	46,285	4,455	7,019

Source: Ministry of Finance.

APPENDIX 13
IMPORTS BY TYPE AND
FINANCIAL RESOURCES
(US$ MILLIONS)

Year	Total	K.F.X. Imports	Foreign Loans	Others	Food and Direct Consumer Goods	Resources for Industry	Capital Goods	Consumer Goods
1964	404	185	35	184	69	257	71	5
1965	436	248	31	183	64	317	75	7
1966	716	402	100	213	74	453	170	18
1967	996	673	167	155	9	557	311	27
1968	1,463	964	290	213	170	707	523	61
1969	1,824	1,087	475	140	309	849	577	86
1970	1,983	1,256	400	166	326	1,004	578	75
1971	2,394	1,615	541	131	412	1,212	679	88
1972	2,522	1,702	628	169	366	1,300	754	101
1973	4,240	3,318	644	278	594	2,332	1,132	179
1974	6,851	5,554	638	658	839	3,950	1,847	206
1975	7,274	5,902	886	484	969	4,163	1,929	208
1976	8,773	6,972	898	901	676	5,305	2,413	377
1977	10,811	9,040	1,017	752	772	6,634	2,995	407
1978	14,972	12,251	1,716	1,014	1,014	8,321	5,058	576

1979	20,339	16,832	2,253	1,623	1,623	11,692	6,316	705
1980	22,292	19,535	1,458	2,027	2,027	14,480	5,122	660
1981	26,131	22,132	2,231	2,944	2,944	16,262	6,161	761
1982	24,251	20,783	1,386	1,767	1,767	15,550	6,232	700
1983	26,192	21,919	1,221	1,958	1,958	15,587	7,812	834
1984	30,631	24,938	1,314	1,909	1,909	17,617	10,107	996
1985	31,136	24,633	1,329	1,679	1,679	17,405	11,097	952
1986	31,584	26,968	2,118	1,688	1,688	17,133	11,358	1,402
1987	41,019	36,369	1,563	1,898	1,898	22,539	14,552	2,030
1988	51,811	46,449	1,410	2,637	2,637	27,877	19,033	2,220
1989	61,465	55,809	960	3,486	3,486	32,969	22,370	2,595
1990	69,844	64,138	468	3,585	3,585	37,653	25,451	3,063
1991	81,515	74,121	1,093	4,325	4,325	43,357	30,092	3,751
1992	81,775	73,365	1,146	4,626	4,626	42,620	30,580	3,948

Source: Ministry of Finance

Note: K.F.X. denotes Korean Foreign Exchange.

BIBLIOGRAPHY

Ahn, Dong-Min. 1991. *Korea in the Twenty-First Century*. (In Korean.) Seoul: New Generation Press.

Bank of Korea. 1990. *Post-War Changes in the British Economy*. (In Korean.) Seoul: Bank of Korea.

———. 1991. "Employment Transition of Finance and the Analysis on Economic Policy Effect." *Monthly Bulletin* (June). (In Korean.) Seoul: Bank of Korea.

———. Annual. *Economic Statistics Yearbook*. Seoul: Bank of Korea.

Bell, Daniel. 1991. *The New World Order Toward the 21st Century*. (In Korean.) Seoul: Design House, Inc.

Burnstein, Daniel. 1991. *Euroquake*. New York: Simon and Schuster.

Byun, Hyung-Yun. 1991. *Economy and Humanism*. (In Korean.) Seoul: Dong-A Press.

Chilcote, Ronald H. 1984. *Theories of Development and Under-Development*. Boulder, Colo.: Westview Press.

Cho, Lee-Jay, and Kim, Yoon-Hyung. 1991. *Economic Development in the Republic of Korea*. Honolulu: East-West Center Books, University of Hawaii Press.

Cho, Soon. 1986. *The Present Situation and Way Ahead*. (In Korean.) Seoul: Bee Bong Press.

———. 1991. "The Developing Strategy of Korean Economy." *Economic Articles* 30, no. 3 (September) (In Korean.) [Seoul: Seoul National University, Economic Research Institute].

Choi, Byung-Seon. 1992. *The Theory of Government Regulation—The Political Economy of Regulation and Relaxation of Regulation*. (In Korean.) Seoul: Pub Moon Press.

Choi, Kwang. 1991. *The Major Political Issues of Korean Fiscal Policy*. (In Korean.) Seoul: National Institute for Economic System and Information.

Chun, Hong-Tack, and Chung, Ki-Young. 1989. *The Current Conditions of Financial Development and Issues for the Settlement of Market Financial System*. (In Korean.)

Chung, Un-Chan. 1991. *The Theory of Financial Reform*. (In Korean.) Seoul: Pub Moon Press.

Cole, John. 1987. *The Thatcher Years—A Decade of Revolution in British Politics*. London: BBC Books.

Conners, Leila, and others. 1991. *Millennium*. New York: Random House.

Dertouzos, Michael L., and others. 1989. *Made in America: Regaining the Productive Edge*. Cambridge, Mass.: MIT Press.

Devinney, Timothy M. and others. 1991. *European Markets After 1992*. Lexington, Mass.: Lexington Books.

Drucker, Peter F. 1992. *Managing for the Future*. Stoneham, Mass.: Butterworth Heinemann.

Economic Planning Board. 1988. *Economic Status and Issues in Korea*. (In Korean.) Seoul: EPB Press.

————. 1992. *The Seventh Five-Year Socio-Economic Development Plan*. (In Korean.) Seoul: EPB Press.

————. Annual. *Economic White Paper*. (In Korean.) Seoul: EPB Press.

Edokoro, Hideki. 1991. *The Development Economics*. (In Japanese.) Tokyo, Japan: Hosei University Press.

Fair Trade Commission. 1991. *The Ten-Year History of Fair Competition, Accomplishments and Issues of Competitive Policies*. (In Korean.) Seoul: Fair Trade Commission.

Federation of Korean Industries. 1992. *Industrial Policy—Search for Right Direction*. (In Korean.) Seoul: Federation of Korean Industries.

————. 1992. *The Current International Movement and Strategy on the Environmental Affairs*. (In Korean.) Seoul: Federation of Korean Industries.

Friedman, George, and others. 1991. *Coming War with Japan*. New York: St. Martin's Press.

Friedman, Milton, and Friedman, Rose. 1980. *Free to Choose: A Personal Statement*. New York: Harcourt Brace Jovanovich

Fukuyama, Francis. 1992. *End of History and the Last Man*. New York: The Free Press.

Goldman, Marshall I. 1991. *What Went Wrong with Perestroika*. New York: W. W.Norton and Co.

Goto, Shohachiro. 1974. *The Fundamental Theory of Economic Policy*. (In Japanese.) Tokyo: Sekai Shoin.

Han, Young-Whan. 1989. *National Progress and Administration*. (In Korean.) Seoul: Asia Moon Hwa Press.

Heller, Walter W. 1966. *New Dimensions of Political Economy*. Cambridge, Mass.: Harvard University Press.

Hyundai Research Institute. 1991. *The Change of Financial Environment and Strengthening of Firm's International Competitiveness*. (In Korean.) Seoul: Hyundai Research Institute.

————. 1992. *The Search for New Korean Economic Development Model*. (In Korean.) Seoul: Hyundai Research Institute.

Ito, Motoshige. 1988. *The Economic Analysis on Industrial Policy*. (In Japanese.) Tokyo: Tokyo University Press.

Ito, Takatoshi. 1992. *Japanese Economy*. Cambridge, Mass.: MIT Press.

Iwasaki, Teruyuki, and others. 1992. *Development Strategies for the Twenty-First Century.* (In Japanese.) Tokyo: IDE.

Japan Economic Planning Board. 1987. *Internationalization and Liberalization of Finance.* (In Japanese.) Tokyo: Japan Economic Planning Board.

———. 1990. *Financial System in the Globalization Era.* (In Japanese.) Tokyo: Japan Economic Planning Board.

———. 1991. *New Choice Toward 2010.* (In Japanese.) Tokyo: Japan Economic Planning Board.

Japanese Ministry of Commerce. 1986. *The Basic Conception of the Industrial Society in Twenty-First Century.* (In Japanese.) Tokyo: Japanese Ministry of Commerce.

———. 1987. *The Financing Under the Stabilized Growth.* (In Japanese.) Tokyo: Japanese Ministry of Commerce.

———. 1990. *The Structure of Industry in 2000.* (In Japanese.) Tokyo: Japanese Ministry of Commerce.

Jeong, Jin-Young. 1991. *Large-Scale Company Group and Fair Trade System.* (In Korean.) Seoul: National Institute for Economic System and Information.

Jwa, Sung-Hee. 1991. *The Analysis of Determining Factors of the Mechanism of Financial Industry.* (In Korean.) Seoul: Korea Development Institute.

KIET. 1989. *The Theory and Its Application in Industrial Readjustment.* (In Korean.) Seoul: KIET.

———. 1991. *The Theory and Its Application in Industrial Policy.* (In Korean.) Seoul: KIET.

———. 1992. *Industrial Policies in the Twenty-First Century.* (In Korean.) Seoul: KIET.

Kanemitsu, Hideo. 1991. *International Economic Policy.* (In Japanese.) Tokyo: Toyo Keizai Shinpo Inc.

Kang, Ho-Jin. 1992. *The Concentration of Economic Power in Korea.* (In Korean.) Seoul: National Institute for Economic System and Information.

Kato, Hiroshi. 1988. *Economics of the Government.* (In Japanese.) Tokyo: Yuhikaku.

Kernell, Samuel. 1991. *Parallel Politics.* Washington, D.C.: Brooking Institute.

Kim, Ki-Tae and others. 1992. *International Economy & Korean Economy.* (In Korean.) Seoul: Park Young Press.

Komaki, Toruo. 1991. *The Korean Economy in the Internationalization Era.* (In Japanese.) Tokyo: Asian Economy Research Institute.

Koo, Bon-Ho, and Lee, Kyu-Uck. 1991. *Historical Approach on the Korean Economy.* Seoul: (In Korean.) Korea Development Institute.

Korea Chamber of Commerce and Industry. 1988. *The Improvement of*

Business Activity by Economic Democratization. (In Korean.) Seoul: Korea Chamber of Commerce and Industry.

———. 1990. *The Progress of Economic Liberalization and the Direction of Deregulation in Government Policy.* (In Korean.) Seoul: Korea Chamber of Commerce and Industry.

———. 1990. *The Status and Issues of Korean Capitalism.* (In Korean.) Seoul: Korea Chamber of Commerce and Industry.

———. 1991. *The Direction of Reform in Tax System Connected with Land.* (In Korean.) Seoul: Korea Chamber of Commerce and Industry.

———. 1992. *Korean Industry and Growing Enterprises in the Twenty-First Century.* (In Korean.) Seoul: Korea Chamber of Commerce and Industry.

Korea Development Bank. 1985. *Elevation of Industrial Structure and Policy Direction.* (In Korean.) Seoul: Korea Development Bank.

———. 1986. *Growing Industries in the 90s.* (In Korean.) Seoul: Korea Development Bank.

———. 1988. *The Change of International Competetiveness and the Plan of Industrial Coordination.* (In Korean.) Seoul: Korea Development Bank.

———. 1989. *Prospect of Industrial Structure in 2000.* (In Korean.) Seoul: Korea Development Bank.

———. 1990. *Direct Overseas Investment Strategy Responding to the Internationalization of Industry.* (In Korean.) Seoul: Korea Development Bank.

———. 1990. *Industry in Korea.* (In Korean.) Seoul: Korea Development Bank.

———. 1990. *Long-Term Strategy for the Realization of High Industrial Society.* (In Korean.) Seoul: Korea Development Bank.

———. 1991. "The Analysis of the Variation Factor of Industrial Structure." *Monthly Economic Review* (October). (In Korean.) Seoul: Korea Development Bank.

———. 1992. *Enterprise Business Strategy Preparing for the Twenty-First Century.* (In Korean.) Seoul: Korea Development Bank.

———. 1992. "The Mid and Long-Term Prospect of Korean Industry." *Monthly Economic Review* (October). (In Korean.) Seoul: Korea Development Bank.

———. 1992. *The Current Condition and the Improvement Plans of Korea's Industrial Technology Support Policy.* (In Korean.) Seoul: Korea Development Bank.

Korea Development Institute. 1991. *The Forty-Year History of Korean Finances.* (In Korean.) Seoul: KDI Press.

Korea Economic Research Institute. 1988. *Fundmental Strategy for Economic Democratization.* (In Korean.) Seoul: Korea Development Bank.

————. 1992. *New Government's National Administration Economic Public Desires*. (In Korean.) Seoul: Korea Development Bank.

Korea Export and Import Bank. 1991. *North Korean Economy and Direction of Economic Cooperation*. (In Korean.) Seoul: Korea Export and Import Bank.

Korea Financial Academy. 1992. *Financial Policy Business Workshop*. (In Korean.) Seoul: Korea Financial Academy.

Korea Institute for International Economic Policy. 1991. *Environment and Forecast of Economic Cooperation in Far East*. (In Korean.) Seoul: Korea Institute for International Economic Policy.

Korea Trade Promotion Corporation. 1988. *Impending Issues of International Economy*. (In Korean.) Seoul: Korea Trade Promotion Corporation.

Krause, Lawrence B., and others. 1989. *Liberalization in the Process of Economic Development*. Berkeley: University of California Press.

Kuroda, Tohiko. 1989. *International Finance Under Policy Cooperation in 1992*. (In Japanese.) Tokyo: Kinyu Zaisei.

Kwak, Soo-Il. 1991. *Which Direction Is Korean Economy Going?* (In Korean.) Seoul: Sam Sung Press.

Lee, Man-Woo, and others. 1992. *Economic Revolution and Taxation Reform*. (In Korean.) Seoul: *Korea Economic Research Institute*.

Lee, Han-Koo. 1991. *The Promotion of a Free Market Economy and the Role of Government*. (In Korean.) Seoul: Daewoo Economy Institute.

Lee, Hyun-Jae, and Kim, Soo-Haeng. 1986. *The Theory of Economic Development*. (In Korean.) Seoul: Seoul National University Press.

Lee, Hyun-Jae. 1986. *Fiscal Economics*. (In Korean.) Seoul: Park Young Press.

Lee, Hyung-Koo. 1988. *Korean Economics*. (In Korean.) Seoul: Pub Moon Press. Korea

Lee, Jang-Hee. 1991. "The Process of German Unification and the UN." *Unification Affairs Research* 3, no. 3 (Autumn). (In Korean.) Seoul: Institute for Unification Affairs.

Lee, Sang-Man. 1992. "The Practical Way of Economic Trade Between South and North Korea." *Unification Affairs Research* 4, no. 1 (Spring). (In Korean.) Seoul: Institute for Unification Affairs.

Lee, Yung-Sun. 1990. *A Research into Economic Policy Making Process in Democratic Countries*. (In Korean.) Seoul: National Institute for Economic System and Information.

Liewellyn, John, and others. 1991. *Economic Politics for the 1990s*. Cambridge, Mass.: Basil Blackwell, Ltd.

Lim, Jong-Chul, and others. 1986. *Fiscal and National Economy*. (In Korean.) Seoul: Park Young Press.

Maeil Kyungje. "One Hundred Questions and Answers About World Economic Issues." (In Korean.) Seoul: Maeil Kyunjie.

Makino, Noboru. 1990. *The World in the 1990s*. (In Japanese.) Tokyo: Diamond Inc.

Makridakis, Spyros G. 1990. *Forecasting, Planning and Strategy for the Twenty-First Century*. New York: The Free Press.

Matsuura, Katsumi, and others. 1991. *The Economic Analysis on the Function of Finance*. (In Japanese.) Tokyo: Tokyo Keizai Shinbo, Inc.

McKinnon, Ronald I. 1991. *The Order of Economic Liberalization*. Baltimore: Johns Hopkins University Press.

Meadows, Donella H. 1992. *Beyond the Limits*. Mills, Vt.: Chelsa Green Publishing Co.

Ministry of Foreign Affairs. 1992. *Today's World Environments and Diplomacy*. (In Korean.) Seoul: Ministry of Foreign Affairs.

Moore, John. 1992. "British Privatization—Taking Capitalism to the People." *Harvard Business Research* (January–February). Boston, Mass.: Harvard Business School Press.

Morishima, Michio. 1986. *Why Did Japan Succeed?* (In Korean.) Seoul: Il Cho Kak.

Motomitsu, Keiji. 1990. *The New Economic Policy*. (In Japanese.) Tokyo: Sinholon Press.

National Institute for Economic System and Information. 1991. "Directions and Issues of Institutional Reform for Establishing the Criterion of Value." *Economic Research*, no. 91–01. (In Korean.) Seoul: National Institute for Economic System and Information.

Nelson, Richard R. 1984. *High-Technology Policies-Five Nations Comparison*. Washington, D.C.: American Enterprise Institute for Public Policy.

Nihon Keizai Shimbun, Inc. 1989. *The Book on World Economy*. (In Japanese.) Tokyo: Nihon Keizai Shimbun, Inc.

———. 1990. *The Book on World Economy*. (In Japanese.) Tokyo: Nihon Keizai Shimbun, Inc.

———. 1991. *One Hundred Common Senses in Banking*. (In Japanese.) Tokyo: Nihon Keizai Shimbun, Inc.

———. 1991. *The World and Japan in the 1990s*. (In Japanese.) Tokyo: Nihon Keizai Shimbun, Inc.

Nixon, Richard M. 1992. *Seize the Moment*. New York: Simon and Schuster.

Obuchi, Toshio, and others. 1984. *The Structure of the Current Fiscal Policy*. (In Japanese.) Tokyo: Yachiyo Publishing Co.

Ohmae, Kenichi. 1990. *Borderless World*. New York: Harper Business.

Park, Bong-whan. 1990. *Contemporary Capitalism—Problems and Solutions*. (In Korean.) Seoul: Park Young Press.

Park, Jun-Gyung. 1991. *The Basic Methodologies for Industrial Environments and Policies in 1990s*. (In Korean.) Seoul: Korea Development Institute.

Park, Seung. 1990. *Development Economics*. (In Korean.) Seoul: Park Young Press.

Park, U-Hee. 1986. *Science, Philosophy and New Understanding of Korean Economy*. (In Korean.) Seoul: Korea Economic Daily, Inc.

Park, Yung-Chul. 1986. *Research into the Revolution of Korean Banking Industry*. (In Korean.) Seoul: Korea Development Institute.

Porter, Michael E. 1991. *Competitive Advantage: Creating and Sustaining Superior Performance*. New York: The Free Press.

Pyo, Hak-Kil. 1991. "The System of World Capitalism and Korean Economy." *Economic Articles* 30, no. 3 (September) (In Korean.) [Seoul: Seoul National University, Economic Research Institute].

Raelin, Joseph A. 1991. *Clash of Cultures*. Cambridge, Mass.: Harvard Business School Press.

Ranis, Gustav, and Schultz, Paul T., eds. 1988. *The State of Development Economics—Process and Perspectives*. Cambridge, Mass.: Basil Blackwell, Ltd.

Reich, Robert B. 1991. *The Work of Nations*. New York: Alfred A. Knopf.

Sakong, Il. 1993. *Korea in the World Economy*. (In Korean.) Seoul: Institute for International Economics.

Schwarz, John E., and Volgy, Thomas J. 1988. "Experiments in Employment—A British Cure." *Harvard Business Research* (March–April). Boston, Mass.: Harvard Business School Press.

Sekiguchi, Sueo. 1991. *The World and Japan in 2000*. (In Japanese.) Tokyo: Nihon Keizai Shimbun Inc.

Sekimi, Toshihiko. 1986. *The Fiscal System of the World*. (In Japanese.) Tokyo: Kinyu Zaisei Jijo.

Senou, Yoshihiko. 1986. *The Economic Policy and the Governmental Role*. (In Japanese.) Tokyo: Yuhikaku

Shin, Tae-Gon. *Korean Economic Policies*. (In Korean.) Seoul: Pub Moon Press.

Shinohara, Miyohei, and others. 1989. *Global Adjustment and the Future of Asian-Pacific Economy, APDC*. (In Japanese.) Tokyo: IDE.

Shudo, Megumi, and others. 1986. *The Current Corporate Finance and Financial System*. (In Japanese.) Tokyo: Yuhikaku

Skidelsky, Robert. 1988. *Thatcherism*. London: Chatto and Windus Publication Co.

Son, Sang-Ho. 1992. *UR Subsidies, Financial Deregulation versus New Approach in Industrial Financing and Taxation*. (In Korean.) Seoul: Korea Institute for Economics and Technology.

Stein, Herbert. 1984. Presidential Economics. New York: Simon and Schuster.

Stein, Jerome L. 1991. *International Financial Markets: Integration, Efficiency*. Cambridge, Mass.: Basil Blackwell, Ltd.

Study Group for Nationalism and Internationalism. 1991. *New World Order and Korean Reunification*. (In Korean.)

Sunagawa, Akikazu. 1990. *The Governmental Economics*. (In Japanese.) Tokyo: Yachiyo Publishing Co.

Suzuki, Takashi. 1990. *The Analysis on the Japanese Economy*. (In Japanese.) Tokyo: Tokyo Keizai Shinpo Inc.

Suzuoki, Takabumi. 1992. *What Is the Problem of the Korean Economy?* (In Korean.) Seoul: Korean Productivity Center.

Temporary Research Group for Unification of East-West German Economies and Societies. 1990. *Research into Socio-Economic Trends in Germany*. (In Korean.) Seoul: Temporary Research Group for Unification of East-West German Economies and Societies.

Thurow, Lester. 1992. *Head to Head*. New York: William Morrow.

Toffler, Alvin. 1990. *Powershift*. New York: Bantam Books.

Toma, Takeo. 1992. *North-East Asian Economic Zone Begining to Move*. (In Korean.) Seoul: Dong-A Publishing Co.

Ueda, Kazuo. 1991. *International Finance in the 1990s*. (In Japanese.) Tokyo: Nihon Keizai Shimbun.

United Nations. 1990. *Global Outlook 2000: An Economic, Social, and Environmental Perspective*. New York: United Nations Publications.

———. 1990. *Global Outlook*. New York: United Nations Publications.

———. 1990. *Overall Socio-economics Perspective of the World Economy to the Year 2000*. New York: United Nations Publications.

Volcker, Paul A. 1992. *Changing Fortunes*. New York: Times Books.

Webster, Allan. 1989. *Structural Change in the World Economy*. New York: Routledge.

World Bank. 1991. *The Uruguay Round*.

World Politic and Economic Research Center. 1991. *Realities in Capitalism and Socialism Societies*. (In Korean.) Seoul: Deulnyuck.

Yagi, Hiroshi. 1990. *Strategies for Financial VAN*. (In Japanese.) Tokyo: Kinyu Zaisei Jijo.

———. 1987. *Finance in 2005, Way to the Great Financial Country*. (In Japanese.) Tokyo: Kinyu Zaisei Jijo.

INDEX